2 to 22 DAYS IN GERMANY, AUSTRIA, AND SWITZERLAND

THE ITINERARY PLANNER
1994 Edition

RICK STEVES

22 Days Itinerary Route

John Muir Publications
Santa Fe, New Mexico

Thanks to my hardworking team at *Europe Through the Back Door*, Steve Smith for research assistance, the many readers who shared tips and experiences from their travels, my wife, Anne, and the many Europeans who make travel such good living.

JMP travel guidebooks by Rick Steves
Asia Through the Back Door (with Bob Effertz)
Europe Through the Back Door
Europe 101: History and Art for Travelers (with Gene Openshaw)
Kidding Around Seattle
Mona Winks: Self-Guided Tours of Europe's Top Museums (with Gene Openshaw)
2 to 22 Days in Europe
2 to 22 Days in Norway, Sweden, and Denmark
2 to 22 Days in Spain and Portugal
2 to 22 Days in Great Britain
2 to 22 Days in Germany, Austria, and Switzerland
2 to 22 Days in France (with Steve Smith)
2 to 22 Days in Italy
Europe Through the Back Door Phrasebooks:
  German, French, Italian, Spanish/Portuguese

John Muir Publications, P.O. Box 613, Santa Fe, NM 87504
© 1987, 1988, 1989, 1992, 1993, 1994 by Rick Steves
Cover © 1987, 1988, 1989, 1992, 1993, 1994 by John Muir Publications
All rights reserved.
Printed in the United States of America
First Printing December 1993

ISSN 1058-6059
ISBN 1-56261-131-3

Distributed to the book trade by
W.W. Norton & Company, Inc.,
New York, New York

Design Mary Shapiro
Maps Dave Hoerlein
Typography Ken Wilson
Printer Banta Company
Cover photo Leo de Wys Inc./Jeanetta Baker

Although the author and publisher have made every effort to provide accurate, up-to-date information, they accept no responsibility for loss, injury, loose stools, or inconvenience sustained by any person using this book or eating strudel recommended herein.

CONTENTS

Europe

This book is the tour guide in your pocket. It lets you be the boss by giving you the best 22 days in Germany, Switzerland, and Austria and a suggested way to use that time most efficiently.

The 2 to 22 Days series is for do-it-yourselfers who would like the organization and smoothness of a tour without the straitjacket. It's almost like having your strudel and eating it, too.

This flexible plan offers maximum travel thrills per mile, minute, and dollar. It's designed for travel by rental car or train (as each chapter explains). The pace is fast but not hectic. It's designed for the American with 2 to 22 days who wants to see everything but doesn't want the "if it's Tuesday, this must be Salzburg" craziness. The plan includes the predictable "required" biggies (Rhine castles, Mozart's house, and the Vienna Opera) with a good dose of "Back Door" intimacy mixed in (cozy Danube villages, thrilling mountain luge rides, family wine cellars, a Black Forest mineral spa, and traffic-free Swiss Alp towns).

2 to 22 Days in Germany, Austria, and Switzerland is balanced and streamlined, avoiding typical tourist burnout by including only the most exciting castles and churches. I've been very selective. For example, you won't visit both the Matterhorn and the Jungfrau—just the best of the two. The "best," of course, is only my opinion. But after 12 busy years of travel writing, lecturing, and tour guiding, I've developed a sixth sense of what tickles the traveler's fancy. I love this itinerary. Just thinking about it makes me want to slap-dance and yodel.

Of course, connect-the-dots travel isn't perfect, just as color-by-numbers painting isn't good art. But this guide is your friendly Franconian, your German in a jam, your handbook. It's a well thought out and tested itinerary. I've done it—and refined it—many times on my own and with people who join me on my "Back Door Europe" tours. Take advantage of it, but don't let it rule you.

Read this book before you begin your trip. Use it as a rack to hang more ideas on. As you plan, study, travel, and talk to people, you'll fill the book with notes. It's your tool. It is completely modular and adaptable to any trip. You'll find 22 units, or days, each with the same sections:

1. **Introductory Overview** for the day.

2. A daily hour-by-hour **Suggested Schedule** (using the European 24-hour clock).

3. **Orientation** information (with practical details like tourist information numbers, telephone codes, and so on).

4. **Transportation tips** and instructions for both car and train travel.

5. List of the most important **Sightseeing Highlights** (rated: ▲▲▲Don't miss; ▲▲Try hard to see; ▲Worthwhile if you can make it; no pyramid—worth knowing about).

6. **Food and Lodging**: How and where to find the best budget places, including addresses, phone numbers, and my favorites. For maximum information, learn the hotel price/description code explained below.

7. **Itinerary Options** for those with more or less than the suggested time or with particular interests. This itinerary is rubbery!

8. Practical and easy-to-read **maps** locating recommended places. (Map-maker Dave Hoerlein has traveled this entire itinerary. His maps fit the text intimately and point out the major landmarks, streets, and accommodations mentioned. They're designed to help you follow the text, orient you, and direct you until you pick up something more detailed at the tourist information office.)

At the end of the book are "Practical Extras" such as tips on telephoning, and sample train timetables and itineraries.

Travel Smart

This itinerary works great for well-organized travelers who lay departure groundwork upon arrival in a town, read a day ahead in this book, use the local tourist information offices (abbreviated "TI" and listed with phone numbers for every town in this book), and enjoy the hospitality of

the Germanic people. Ask questions. Most locals are eager
to point you in their idea of the right direction. Use the
telephone, wear a money belt, use a small pocket note-
book to organize your thoughts, and make simplicity a
virtue. If you insist on being confused, your trip will be a
mess. Those who expect to travel smart, do. (My book,
Europe Through the Back Door, 12th edition, 1994, is
packed with the skills and tricks of budget travel.)

Cost

This trip's cost breaks down like this. A basic round-trip
U.S. to Frankfurt flight is $600 to $900, depending on the
season and where you fly from. A three-week car rental
(split between two people and including tax, insurance,
and gas) or a three-week first-class railpass comes to
about $650 per person. For room and board, figure $50 a
day per person, double occupancy: $1,100 each. This is
more than feasible. (Students or older bohemians could
eat and sleep for $40.) Add $400 for admissions and fun
money and you've got a great European adventure for
around $3,000.

When to Go

Summer is peak season—best weather, snow-free Alpine
trails, and the busiest schedule of tourist fun, but crowded
and most expensive. Most of us travel during this period
anyway, so this book tackles the only serious peak-season
problem—finding a room. Arrive early, call ahead (nearly
every place will hold a room until late afternoon if you
call that morning), and utilize local information sources as
explained throughout this book.

"Shoulder season" travel (May, early June, September,
and early October) is ideal. Shoulder-season travelers
enjoy minimal crowds, decent weather, sights and tourist
fun spots still open, and the ability to just grab a room
almost whenever and wherever they like.

Winter travelers find absolutely no crowds, but many
sights and accommodations are closed or run on a limited
schedule. The weather can be cold and dreary, and night-
time will draw the shades on your sightseeing before

dinnertime. The weather is predictably unpredictable, but you may find the climate chart in the back of this book helpful.

Prices in this Book
I haven't cluttered this book with many minor prices (specific admission fees and student discounts and so on). When you keep the large picture in mind, admission fees shouldn't affect your sightseeing plans. But remember to get your discounts if you're a senior or student. Students are recognized as such only with the official ISIC card (from your foreign study office).

Prices as well as hours and telephone numbers are accurate as of mid-1993. Things are always changing, and I've tossed timidity out the window knowing you'll understand that this book, like any guidebook, starts to yellow even before it's printed. These countries are more stable than most European countries, but do what you can to double-check hours and times when you arrive.

This book is best consumed by 1995. If you must use this book past its pull date, prices, details about accommodations, and some times and phone numbers will have changed. Basic sightseeing ideas should be good well into the next millennium—barring unforeseen military or volcanic activity.

Currency Conversion
I've priced things in local currencies throughout the book. Figure about 1.6 deutsche marks (DM) per dollar, 11 Austrian schillings (AS) per dollar, and 1.5 Swiss francs (SF) per dollar. Roughly: 1 DM = $.60, 1 AS = $.10, and 1 SF = $.70 (as of late 1993).

Subtract a third off DM and SF prices (e.g., 60 DM or 60 SF = $40), and divide AS by 10 to get dollars (e.g., 450 AS = about $45). So that 30-DM cuckoo clock is about $20, the 15 SF lunch is about $10, and the 800 AS taxi ride through Vienna is . . . uh-oh.

Telling Time
I've used the 24-hour clock (or "military" time) through- out. Everything's the same until noon. Then, instead of

"p.m." times, you'll see 13:00, 14:00, and so on (to convert, just subtract 12 and add "p.m."). Get comfortable with this standard European time system.

Hours listed are for peak season. Many places close an hour earlier off-season. Some are open only on weekends or are closed entirely in the winter. Confirm your sightseeing plans locally—especially when traveling between October and April. Many sights stop selling tickets 30 to 45 minutes before closing.

Borders, Passports, Visas, Shots, and Culture Shock
Traveling throughout this region requires only a passport—no shots and no visas. Border crossings between Germany, Switzerland, and Austria are extremely easy, often just a wave-through. When you change countries, however, you do change money, telephone cards, postage stamps, and *unterhosen.*

You'll be dealing with a few differences. Work to adapt. While we think shower curtains are logical, many countries just cover the toilet paper and let the rest of the room shower with you. In Europe, what we call the second floor is the "first" and Christmas is 25-12-93. Europeans give their 1's an upswing and cross their 7's. If you don't adapt, your 7 will be mistaken for a sloppy 1 and you'll miss your train.

Keeping in Touch
The *International Herald Tribune* comes out almost daily via satellite from many places in Europe. *USA Today* is available, if you're in the mood for a slice of pie chart. News in English will be sold only where there's enough demand—in big cities and tourist centers. If you're concerned about how some event might affect your safety as an American traveling abroad, call the U.S. consulate or embassy in the nearest big city for advice. The best way to keep in touch with loved ones back home is to periodically call home direct. Most phone booths allow international calls. (See "Telephoning" in Practical Extras.)

Ugly Americanism

We travel all the way to Europe to experience something different—to become temporary locals. Americans have a knack for finding certain truths to be God-given and self-evident—things like cold beer, a bottomless coffee cup, long hot showers, free public toilets, and bigger being better. One of the beauties of travel is the opportunity to see that there are logical, civil, and even better alternatives. You'll be traveling in countries with people who consume less while enjoying a higher standard of living than we do and who have a broader understanding of the world beyond their borders. Most Europeans like Americans, but they don't envy us and wouldn't trade places.

If there is a European image of you and me, it is that we are big, loud, a bit naïve, aggressively friendly, and rich. Still, I find warmth and friendliness throughout the Continent. An eagerness to go local and an ability—when something's not to my liking—to change my liking ensures that I'll enjoy a full dose of this European hospitality. I work to fit in. If the bed's too short, the real problem is that I'm too long.

Scheduling

Your overall itinerary is a fun challenge. To give you a little rootedness, I've minimized one-night stands. Two nights in a row, even with a hectic travel day before and after, is less grueling than changing lodging daily.
Try to alternate intense and relaxed periods. Every trip (and every traveler) needs at least a few slack days. I followed the biblical "one in seven" idea religiously on my last trip. If you can stretch this trip to 28 or 30 days, you won't need a vacation when you get home.

Read through this book and note special days (festivals, colorful market days, days when sights are closed, itinerary options). Sundays have pros and cons as they do for travelers in the U.S.A. (special events, limited hours, shops and banks closed, limited public transportation, no rush hours). Saturdays are virtually weekdays. Popular places are even more popular on weekends. Most sights are closed during one weekday (often Monday). I've listed many more sights than can be seen in the allotted time. Assume you will return!

Driving

This route is ideal by car. Every long stretch is autobahn (super freeway), and nearly every scenic backcountry drive is paved and comfortable. Drivers over 21 need only their U.S. license and the insurance that comes automatically with the rental car. Besides the rare insurance card check, there are no border formalities to worry about. The local rules of the road are much like ours. Learn the universal road signs (charts explain them in most road atlases and at service stations). Seat belts are required, and two beers under those belts is enough to land you in jail.

Use good local maps and study them before each drive. Familiarize yourself with which exits you need to look out for, which major cities you'll travel in the direction of, where the ruined castles lurk, and so on. Pick up the "cardboard clock" (*Parkscheibe*, available free at gas stations, police stations, and Tabak shops) and display your arrival time on the dashboard so parking attendants can see you've been there less than the posted maximum stay (blue lines indicate 90-minute zones on Austrian streets).

To understand the complex but super-efficient autobahn (no speed limit, toll-free) pick up the "Autobahn Service" booklet at any autobahn rest stop (free, listing all intersection signs, stops, services, road symbols, and more). Use a good map, and study the intersection signs: *Dreieck* means three corners, a "Y" in the road; *Autobahnkreuz* is a "cross" or intersection. Gas stations are spaced about every 30 miles, normally with a restaurant, a small shop, and sometimes a tourist information desk. Unleaded (*Bleifrei*) gas is now everywhere. Exits are often 20 miles apart. Know what you're looking for—*nord, süd, ost, west,* or *mittel*—miss it and you're long autobahn-gone. When driving slower than 120 mph, stay out of the left-hand passing lane. Remember, in Europe, the shortest distance between any two points is the autobahn. Signs directing you to the autobahn are green in Austria and Switzerland, blue in Germany.

Get used to metric. A liter is about a quart, four to a gallon; a kilometer is six-tenths of a mile. I figure kilometers to miles by cutting them in half and adding back 10 percent of the original (120 km is 60 + 12 miles, 300 km is 150 + 30 miles).

Try to rent a car with a trunk so you can leave "deep storage" things safely out of sight. I keep a box in the trunk for things I don't need to cart in and out of hotels. My pantry box sits on the back seat, and I equip it for easy and enjoyable, time- and money-saving car picnics (either at the very pleasant autobahn picnic areas or as I drive—if my navigator can play cook). I stock up with plenty of orange juice in liter boxes, paper towels, plastic cups, and so on. Copy the car key as soon as possible for safety and so two people have access to the car.

Car Rental
If you plan to drive, it's cheapest to rent a car through your travel agent well before departure (not in Germany). You'll want a weekly rate with unlimited mileage. For three weeks or longer, it's cheaper to lease the car (a scheme that can save you money on taxes and insurance). Plan to pick up the car at the Frankfurt airport and drop it off there (or in Koblenz) at the end of your trip. Remember, if you drop it early or keep it longer, you'll be credited or charged at a fair, prorated price. Every major car rental agency has a Frankfurt airport office. Comparison shop through your agent. DER (tel. 800-782-2424), a German company, often has the best rates. Expect to pay $500 to $600 for a small car for three weeks with unlimited mileage, plus around $70 a week for the collision-damage waiver full-insurance option.

I normally rent a small inexpensive model (e.g., Ford Fiesta). For a bigger, roomier, and more powerful inexpensive car, move up to the Ford 1.3-liter Escort or VW Polo category. For peace of mind, I splurge for the CDW (collision-damage waiver insurance supplement, ridiculously high because the base rental price doesn't really allow a reasonable profit), which gives a zero deductible rather than the standard deductible—which can be as high as the value of the car. With the luxury of CDW you can enjoy the autobahns knowing you can bring back the car in an unrecognizable shambles and just say, "S-s-s-sorry."

By Train

With a few modifications, this itinerary works as well by train as by car. The trains are punctual and cover all the cities very well, but frustrating schedules make a few out-of-the-way recommendations (such as the concentration camp at Mauthausen) just not worth the time and trouble. This itinerary covers enough ground to make a three-week first-class Eurailpass worthwhile—especially for a single traveler (about $648, available from your travel agent or by mail from *Europe Through the Back Door*—see catalog). You can save $100 by managing with the "any 10 days out of two months" Eurail Flexipass. But this small saving requires some serious streamlining. Each individual country has its own train passes, but patchworking several second-class country passes together usually costs as much as a single first-class Eurailpass for the total traveling time. For example, a $286 ten-days-in-a-month second-class German Railpass, $103 four-days-in-ten Austrian Rabbit pass, and a $186 eight-day Swiss Pass give you 22 days of second-class rail travel for about $575.

Eurailers should know what extras are included on their pass—like any German buses marked "Bahn" (run by the train company); city S-bahn systems; boats on the Rhine, Mosel, and Danube rivers and the Swiss lakes; and the Romantic Road bus tour. While this itinerary justifies a 21-day train pass, if you decide to buy tickets as you go, look into local specials. Seniors (women over 60, men over 65) and youths (under 26, Transalpino or BIGE tickets) can enjoy substantial discounts with the appropriate ID cards. While Eurailers automatically travel first-class, those buying individual tickets should remember that second-class tickets provide the same transportation for 33 percent less. Hundreds of local train stations rent bikes for about $6 a day (less for train-pass holders, ask for a Fahrrad am Bahnhof brochure at any station).

Car or Train?

This tour is a little better by car. But, with a few exceptions, trains cover the entire itinerary just fine. (See chart in Practical Extras for recommended train itinerary and times, frequency, and prices of individual train journeys.) A three-week first-class Eurailpass is best for single travelers, those who'll be spending more time in big cities, and those who don't want to drive in Europe. While a car gives you the ultimate in mobility and freedom, enables you to search for hotels more easily, and carries your bags for you, the train zips you effortlessly from city to city, normally dropping you in the center and near the tourist office. Cars are great in the countryside but a worthless headache in places like Munich, Bern, and Vienna.

Eating

The local cuisine is heavy and hearty. While it's tasty, it can get monotonous if you fall into the schnitzel-or-wurst-and-potatoes rut. To eat well, use a phrase book or menu translator and be adventurous. The *Marling German Menu Master* is the best phrase book for galloping gluttons. Each region has its local specialties which, while not the cheapest, are often the best values on the menu.

There are many kinds of restaurants. Hotels often serve fine food. A *Gaststatte* is a simple, less-expensive restaurant. The various regions' many ethnic restaurants provide a welcome break from the basic Germanic fare. Foreign food is either from the remnants of a crumbled empire (Hungarian and Bohemian—where Austria gets its goulash and dumplings) or a new arrival to serve the many hungry but poor guest workers (Italian, Turkish, and Greek food is commonplace and a good value). The cheapest meals are found in department-store cafeterias, *Schnell-Imbiss* (fast-food) stand-up joints, university cafeterias (*mensas*), and youth hostels. For a quick, cheap bite, have a deli or butcher make you a *Wurstsemmel,* or hearty meat sandwich.

Most restaurants tack a menu onto their door for browsers and will have either an English menu or someone who can translate for you. Even so, sooner or later you'll be rudely surprised—as I was when my *pepperoni* pizza arrived covered with green peppers. Only a rude waiter will rush you. Good service is relaxed (slow to an American). When you want the bill, ask, *Die Rechnung, bitte.* Service is included although it's customary to round the bill up after a good meal. Wish others happy eating with a cheery *Guten Appetit.*

A basic Continental-style breakfast of coffee and rolls almost always comes with your hotel or *Zimmer* (room in a private home). A breakfast roll and a tiny tub of cheese tucked away before you leave your hotel make a handy snack or light lunch later.

For most visitors, the rich pastries, the wine, and the beer provide the fondest memories of Germany's cuisine. The wine (85 percent white) is particularly good from the Mosel, Rhine, Danube, eastern Austria, and southwestern Switzerland areas. Order wine by the *Viertel* (quarter liter) or *Achtel* (8th liter). You can say *ein Viertel suss* (sweet), *halbe trocken* (medium) or *trocken* (dry), *weiss* (white) or *rot* (red) *Wein* (wine) *bitte* (please). *Sekt* is German champagne. Mosel and Saar wines come in a slender green bottle, Rhine wines in a tall brown one, and Franconian in a jug-shaped bottle.

The Germans enjoy a tremendous variety of great beer. The average German, who drinks 40 gallons of beer a year, knows that *dunkles* is dark, *helles* is light, *Flaschenbier* is bottled, and *vom fass* is on tap. *Pils* is barley based, *Weize* is wheat based, and *Malzbier* is the malt beer that children learn on. *Radler* is half beer and half lemonade. When you order beer, ask for *ein Halb* for a half liter or *ein Mass* for a whole liter. Some beer halls only serve it by the liter (about a quart). Menus list drink size by the tenth of a liter (e.g., .2l is a small juice, .5l is a big beer).

Accommodations
While accommodations in Germany, Switzerland, and Austria are fairly expensive, they are normally very comfortable, come with breakfast, and are a good value. Plan on spending $70 per hotel double in big cities, $50 in towns and in private homes.

The more people you put in a hotel room, the cheaper it gets. While hotel singles are most expensive, private accommodations (*Zimmer*) have a flat per-person rate. Hostels and dorms always charge per person. Especially in private homes, where the boss changes the sheets, people staying several nights are most desirable. One-night stays are sometimes charged extra.

In recommending a hotel, I like places that are in convenient, central, quiet, and safe locations; small, family-run places with local character; simple facilities not catering to American "needs"; inexpensive, friendly, English-speaking, clean, and not listed in other guidebooks. Obviously a friendly, clean, quiet, central, cheap room is virtually impossible to find, and all of my recommendations fall short of perfection—sometimes miserably. But I've listed the best values for each price category that I could find, given the above criteria. The best values are family-run and centrally located, with showers down the hall and no elevator.

Unless I note a difference, the cost of a room includes a continental breakfast, taxes, service, and showers and toilet either in the room or down the hall. This price is usually posted in the room. Before accepting, confirm your understanding of the complete price. The only tip the hotels I've listed would like is a friendly, easy-going guest.The accommodations prices listed in this book should be good through 1994. I appreciate feedback on your hotel experiences.

The 2 to 22 Days Accommodations Description Code

To save space while giving more specific information for people with special concerns, I've described my recommended hotels with a standard code. When there is a range of prices in one category the price will fluctuate with the season, size of room, or length of stay.

S—single room or price for one person using a double.

D—double or twin room. Double beds are usually big enough for non-romantic couples.

T—three-person room (often a double bed with a single bed moved in).

Q—four-adult room (an extra child's bed is usually cheaper).

B—private shower (most likely) or bath in the room. This often means with toilet also. All rooms have a sink. B rooms are often bigger and renovated while the cheaper rooms without B often will be on the top floor or yet to be refurbished. Any room without B has access to a B on the corridor (free unless otherwise noted). Rooms with baths often cost more than rooms with showers. Most B rooms have a WC.

CC—accepts credit cards: V=Visa, M=Mastercard, A=American Express. Many also accept Diners (which I ignored). With no CC mention, assume they accept only cash.

SE—the likelihood that an English-speaking staff person is available is graded A through F.

KF—indicates that a place is particularly "kid-friendly."

EZ—indicates that there is an elevator or rooms on the ground floor for those interested in EZ access.

So, a "DB-140 DM, CC-V, SE-A, EZ" hotel would offer two-person rooms with a private shower or bath for 140 DM, accept only Visa cards or cash, speak very good English, and have an elevator or rooms on the ground floor.

Finding a Room
While you could do this entire trip without reservations, if you want to stay in my best listings, make calling a day or three ahead your standard operating procedure. It's best to call between 9:00 and 10:00 on the day you plan to arrive, when the hotel knows who's checking out and just which rooms will be available. I've taken great pains to list telephone numbers with long distance instructions (see Practical Extras). Use the telephone and the convenient telephone cards. A hotel receptionist will trust you and hold a room until 17:00. Reconfirm by telephone for safety. Don't let these people down. I promised you'd call and cancel if for some reason you won't show up. Don't needlessly confirm rooms through the tourist office; they'll take a commission.

Room lists are always available at local tourist offices, and remaining vacancies are often posted there after hours.

Camping and Hosteling

Campers should get a camping guide for the area. Listings are available in each country, and your hometown travel bookstore has guidebooks for camping Europe. You'll find campgrounds just about wherever you need them. Look for *Campingplatz* signs. Camping is a popular middle-class family way to go among Germans. You'll find that campgrounds are cheap ($4-$5 per person), friendly, safe, more convenient than rustic, and very rarely full.

Youth hostelers can take advantage of the wonderful network of hostels. Follow the signs marked *Jugendherberge*. Triangles and the "tree next to a house" are also youth hostel symbols. Generally, you must have your membership card ($25 per year, sold in most U.S. cities), though sometimes nonmembers are admitted for an extra charge.

Hostels are open to members of all ages (except in Bavaria where a maximum age of 26 is strictly enforced). They usually cost $6 to $15 per night (cheaper for those under 27, plus $4 sheet rental if you don't have your own) and serve good cheap meals or provide kitchen facilities. While many have couple's or family rooms available upon request for a little extra money, plan on beds in segregated dorms—four to twenty per room. Hostels can be idyllic and peaceful, or school groups can raise the rafters. School groups are most common on summer weekends and on school-year weekdays. I like small hostels best. While many hostels may say they're full over the telephone, most hold a few beds for people who drop in, or they can direct you to budget accommodations nearby.

Recommended Guidebooks

This small book is your itinerary handbook. You can do fine with this book alone, but I'd consider supplementing this guidebook with the following books.

Let's Go: Germany, Austria, and Switzerland, written

and updated every year—new editions come out around January—by Harvard students for students, it covers hosteling, camping, and the local youth and nightlife scene better than I do.

A cultural and sightseeing guide—the tall green Michelin guides (Germany, Austria, and Switzerland) have nothing about room and board but everything else you'll ever need to know about the sights, customs, and culture. They are excellent (especially for drivers) and available in English in Europe.

A small German phrase book and dictionary is also helpful. My *Europe Through the Back Door German Phrase Book* (150 pages, published by JMP) is a fun and practical tool for independent budget travelers. With everything from beerhall vocabulary to sample telephone hotel reservation conversations to German tongue twisters, you'll be glad you've got this handy book in your pocket.

My *Europe Through the Back Door* (John Muir Publications, 12th edition, 1994) gives you the basic skills, the foundations that make this demanding 22-day plan possible. Chapters include minimizing jet lag, packing light, driving versus train travel, finding budget beds without reservations, changing money smartly, theft, travel photography, long-distance telephoning in Europe, Ugly Americanism, traveler's toilet trauma, laundry, and itinerary strategies and techniques. The book also includes special articles on forty exciting nooks and undiscovered European crannies that I call "Back Doors."

Other Rick Steves 2 to 22 Days Itinerary Planners—If your trip is bigger than this book, consider my guides to Europe, Britain, France, Italy, Spain/Portugal, and Norway/Sweden/Denmark (all published annually by John Muir).

Europe 101: History and Art for Travelers (John Muir Publications, 1991; by Rick Steves and Gene Openshaw) tells you the story of these cultures in a practical, fun-to-read, 360-page package. It's ideal for those who want to be able to step into a Gothic cathedral and excitedly nudge their partner, saying, "Isn't this a marvelous improvement over Romanesque!"

Mona Winks: Self-Guided Tours of Europe's Top Museums (John Muir Publications, 1993; by Rick Steves and Gene Openshaw) gives you fun, easy-to-follow, self-guided tours of Europe's twenty most exhausting and frightening museums, including (for this tour) the top museums in Munich and Vienna.

Many European bookstores, especially in tourist areas, have good selections of maps. For this tour, I picked up the *Deutschland Auto Atlas* (30 DM, by RV Verlag, 1:200,000 scale) for Germany and the *Österreich Euro-Reiseatlas* (also by RV Verlag, 17 DM, 1:300,000 scale) for Austria. Each of these atlases has good coverage of the entire country with an extensive index and handy maps of all major cities. For Switzerland, I got by with Michelin maps 216 and 217 (or *Die General Karte* maps 1 and 2) with 1:200,000 scale. Throughout the tour you'll be picking up free maps of cities and regions at local tourist offices.

Back Door Manners
I have heard over and over how 2 to 22 Days readers were the most considerate and fun-to-have-as-guests travelers my recommended accommodations dealt with. Thank you for traveling as temporary locals who are sensitive to the culture. It's fun to follow you in my travels.

Vagabondage or Freedom
This book's goal is to free you, not chain you. Defend your spontaneity as you would your mother. Use this book to sort the region's myriad sights into the most interesting, representative, diverse, and efficient 2 or 22 days of travel. Use it to avoid time- and money-wasting mistakes, to get more intimate with Europe by traveling without a tour. Remem-ber, you're traveling as a temporary local person. And use it as a point of departure for shaping your best possible travel experience. Only a real dullard would follow this entire plan exactly as I've laid it out.

Anyone who's read this far has what it takes intellectually to do this tour on their own. Be confident and militantly positive—relish the challenge and rewards of doing your own planning. Judging from all the positive feedback and happy postcards we get from our traveling readers, it's safe to assume you're on your way to a great European vacation—independent, inexpensive—with the finesse of an experienced traveler. Europe—here you come!

Send Me a Postcard, Drop Me a Line

While I do what I can to keep this book accurate and up-to-date, things are always changing. If you enjoy a successful trip with the help of this book and would like to share your discoveries, please send any tips, recommendations, criticisms, or corrections to me at Europe Through the Back Door, Box 2009, Edmonds, WA 98020. To update the book before your trip or share tips, tap into our free computer bulletin board travel information service (206/771-1902:1200 or 2400/8/N/1). All correspondents will receive a two-year subscription to our "Back Door Travel" quarterly newsletter (it's free anyway). Tips actually used will get you a first-class railpass in heaven. Thanks, and *Gute Reise!*

BACK DOOR PHILOSOPHY

AS TAUGHT IN *EUROPE THROUGH THE BACK DOOR*

Travel is intensified living—maximum thrills per minute and one of the last great legal sources of adventure. In many ways, the less you spend, the more you get.

Experiencing the real thing requires candid informality—going "Through the Back Door."

Affording travel is a matter of priorities. Many people who "can't afford a trip" could sell their cars and travel for two years.

You can travel anywhere in the world for $50 a day plus transportation costs. Money has little to do with enjoying your trip. In fact, spending more money builds a thicker wall between you and what you came to see.

A tight budget forces you to travel "close to the ground," meeting and communicating with the people, not relying on service with a purchased smile. Never sacrifice sleep, nutrition, safety, or cleanliness in the name of budget. Simply enjoy the local-style alternatives to expensive hotels and restaurants.

Extroverts have more fun. If your trip is low on magic moments, kick yourself and start making things happen.

If you don't enjoy a place, it's often because you don't know enough about it. Seek the truth. Recognize tourist traps.

A culture is legitimized by its existence. Give a people the benefit of your open mind. Think of things as different but not better or worse.

Of course, travel, like the world, is a series of hills and valleys. Be fanatically positive and militantly optimistic.

Travel is addicting. It can make you a happier American as well as a citizen of the world. Our Earth is home to more than five billion equally important people. It's wonderfully humbling to travel and find that people don't envy Americans. They like us, but with all due respect, they wouldn't trade passports.

Globe-trotting destroys ethnocentricity and encourages the understanding and appreciation of various cultures. Travel changes people. Many travelers toss aside their "hometown blinders," assimilating the best points of different cultures into their own character.

The world is a cultural garden. We're tossing the ultimate salad. Raise your travel dreams to their upright and locked position and join us.

DAY 1 Start in Frankfurt, the most direct and least expensive German destination from the U.S.A. Pick up your rental car or hop on the train and dive into the Middle-Ages via Rothenburg, Germany's best preserved walled town.

DAY 2 Spend all day medievaled in Rothenburg. Walk the wall, see the exquisitely carved altarpiece and the strangely enjoyable medieval crime-and-punishment museum. Be careful . . . this cobbled mall is Germany's best shopping town.

DAY 3 Follow the Romantic Road through picturesque villages, past farmhouses and onion-domed churches south into Bavaria's medieval heartland. After hiking up to the Ehrenberg ruined castle and screaming down a nearby ski slope in an oversized skateboard, catch your breath for an evening of slap-dancing and yodeling in Austria's Tirol

DAY 4 Bavaria's the cookie jar, and no one's looking. After touring "Mad" Ludwig's fairy-tale Neuschwanstein Castle—Europe's most spectacular—stop by the Wies Church, a textbook example of Bavarian rococo bursting with curly curlicues, and browse through Germany's wood-carving capital, Oberammergau.

DAY 5 Work your way north to Munich, possibly riding the lift up the Zugspitze, Germany's tallest mountain, and stopping at Andechs Monastery for beer that would almost make celibacy tolerable. Orient yourself in Munich's old center with its colorful pedestrian mall.

DAY 6 Spend today immersed in Munich's art and history—crown jewels, baroque theater, Wittelsbach palaces, great art, beautiful parks, and gardens. Munich evenings are best spent in frothy beer halls—belching oompah music into rowdy Bavarian atmosphere. Pry big pretzels from no-nonsense buxom beer maids who pull mustard packets from their cleavages.

DAY 7 On the seventh day you'll rest—but only until noon. Then you'll travel south to Salzburg, visiting Hitler's mountain hideaway, Berchtesgaden, on the way. Put on an old miner's outfit (freshly laundered) and tour a salt mine, riding the tiny train into the mountain to slide down long, hopefully splinter-free banisters, cruise subterranean lakes, and learn about old-fashioned salt mining.

DAY 8 Enjoy the sights and castle of Salzburg, Mozart's hometown, before heading for *Sound of Music* country. Spend a very scenic afternoon in the Salzkammergut Lake District (through hills alive with the *S.O.M.*). Then check into a private home in the postcard-pretty, fjord-cuddling town of Hallstatt.

DAY 9 Take a short intermission from fairy-tale Austria for a pilgrimage to the powerful Mauthausen concentration camp. Then follow the Danube through its most romantic section, lined with ruined castles, glorious abbeys, vineyard upon vineyard, and small towns, into Vienna.

DAY 10 Vienna, the easternmost and most exciting historic and cultural city of this tour, was the Habsburg capital. It excels in art, tombs, palaces, pastries, coffee shops, and music. In other words, you'll be very busy today.

DAY 11 After another Vienna morning and the afternoon at the Schönbrunn Palace, Versailles's eastern rival, drive the autobahn five hours west to Innsbruck, sleeping in the nearby village of Hall in Tirol.

DAY 12 Joyride through Austria's Alps into Switzerland. Appenzell—traditional and cozy—is the best first taste of Heidi-land. This is cowbell country. Only a few staggering mountains, but a fine chance to savor Switzerland's small-town ambience.

DAY 13 The Ballenberg Open-Air Folk Museum, a park full of historic buildings from every corner of the country, gives you an intimate walk through Switzerland's diverse culture. From the nearby grand old resort of Interlaken, travel south into the Jungfrau region where a gondola will lift you high into the terrific traffic-free Alpine village of Gimmelwald.

DAY 14 You learn why they say, "If Heaven isn't what it's cracked up to be, send me back to Gimmelwald." You're free all day to frolic and hike, high above the stress and clouds of the real world. Take a vacation from your busy vacation. Recharge your touristic batteries.

DAY 15 After breakfast at 10,000 feet and a morning hike, visit Bern. Stately but human, classy but fun, the Swiss capital offers the most enjoyable look at urban Switzerland. Crossing into French-speaking Switzerland, settle down in Murten . . . Morat, if you're speaking French.

DAY 16 Using Murten, Switzerland's best-preserved medieval walled town as a springboard, tour the highlights of French Switzerland. Explore the romantic Château Chillon on Lake Geneva, see Gruyère cheese made in its spectacularly situated hometown, and resurrect the ruins of an ancient Roman capital, Avenches.

DAY 17 Enjoy an easy morning in Murten before heading for Germany's Black Forest. Tour the region's capital, Freiburg, but spend the night in the charming and overlooked village of Staufen.

DAY 18 The Black Forest is filled with tourists and cuckoo clocks. It's also swimming with soothing mineral spas, Germany's healthiest air and sunniest climate. Enjoy a scenic drive through this legendary forest, stopping at the German clock museum and an open-air folk museum before finding your hotel in Baden-Baden. Today's grand finale is a two-hour "Roman Irish" bath complete with massage.

DAY 19 Tour Baden-Baden's casino. After spending the middle of the day as a 19th-century aristocrat enjoying the parks, shops, and another spa, you'll understand why this place was Europe's leading resort a hundred years ago. Then zip north into the Rhine Valley to settle down in a castle-crowned village.

DAY 20 Today is for storybook Germany. Spend the day cruising the romantic Rhine and climbing through the cream of the Rhine's crenelated crop, mighty Rheinfels Castle above the town of St. Goar.

DAY 21 Explore the misty, swan-speckled Mosel, so much more relaxing than the busy and industrial Rhine. Tour Germany's most exciting medieval castle, Burg Eltz, then turn in your car and catch the train to Köln for a look at its world-class art and Germany's finest Gothic cathedral. Sleep on the train to Berlin or, if you're out of time and money, fly home from Frankfurt tomorrow.

DAY 22 Berlin, once again the capital of a mighty Germany, is a fitting finale for this tour. Enjoy the thrill of walking over The Wall and under Brandenburg Gate. Sample art treasures from Nefertiti to Rembrandt. Ideally, stretch this 22-day book to 23—Berlin can use two days.

Flying home, think back over what you've experienced: the best 22 days Germany, Austria, and Switzerland have to offer. Of course, next year you may want 22 more.

ARRIVE IN FRANKFURT, SET UP IN ROTHENBURG

How much you do today depends on what time your flight arrives. It's best to plan an easy first day or two in Europe. Today's goal is to arrive safely, travel to Rothenburg (pronounced ROE-ten-burg), and get settled. Since most connections from the U.S.A. arrive in the morning, figure on a couple of hours of sightseeing along Germany's Romantic Road before reaching Rothenburg.

Suggested Schedule

Morning arrival at Frankfurt airport. Pick up reserved car, or catch train for the 2-hour ride to Würzburg.

Tour Würzburg Palace (closes at 17:00).

Take Romantic Road from Bad Mergentheim to Rothenburg.

Check into Rothenburg hotel. Quiet evening.

When flying to Europe, you lose a day; if you leave on a Tuesday, you'll land on Wednesday. Call before going to the airport to confirm departure time as scheduled. Expect delays. Bring something to do—a book, a journal, floss, some handwork—to make the wait easy on yourself. Remember, no matter what happens en route, if you arrive in Europe safely on the day you hoped to, consider the flight a smashing success.

To minimize jet lag (body clock adjustment stress):
• Leave healthy and well-rested. Pretend you're leaving a day earlier than you really are. Plan accordingly and enjoy a peaceful last day at home.
• During the flight, minimize stress by eating lightly and avoiding alcohol, caffeine, children, and sugar. Drink juice ("Two glasses, no ice please"). Take walks.
• Sleep through the in-flight movie, or at least close your eyes and fake it.

• After your nap, set your watch ahead to European time. Start adjusting mentally before you land.
• On the day you arrive, keep yourself awake until a reasonable local bedtime. Jet lag hates fresh air, bright light, and exercise. A long evening city walk is helpful.
• You'll probably wake up very early the next morning— but ready to roll.

Landing in Frankfurt

Frankfurt's airport (*Flughafen*), just an 11-minute train ride from downtown (six trips per hour, 5 DM, ride included in the 6-DM all-day city transit pass), is efficient and user-friendly. It has everything an airport could need: showers, baggage check, banks with fair rates open 7:30 to 22:00, a grocery store, a handy train station, a decent waiting lounge where you can sleep overnight, easy rental car pickup, plenty of parking, a hard-to-miss big green meeting point sign, an information booth, a McDonald's that serves beer, and lots of Yankee soldiers. McWelcome to Germany.

Airport telephone directory: general information 069/690 30511, Lufthansa—690 71222, American Airlines—230 591, British Air—250 121, Delta—664 1212, Northwest—666 6611, SAS—694 531, United—605 020.

Upon arrival in Frankfurt, change a couple of hundred dollars into deutsche marks, call your Rothenburg hotel to reserve or reconfirm your room, and leave. Drivers follow the blue autobahn signs for Würzburg.

Train travelers can validate Eurailpasses or buy tickets at the airport station and catch a train directly to Würzburg, connecting to Rothenburg via Steinach. (The Romantic Road bus leaves Frankfurt at 8:00.)

Picking Up Your Car

Your rental car orientation is always rushed, but be sure to understand the basics. Locate the car manual and insurance document, know how to change a tire and what kind of gas to use, and understand the breakdown policy and how to use the local automobile club membership (like our AAA) if it comes with your car rental. Ask the attendant for a list of drop-off offices, any maps he can give you, an autobahn handbook, a list of standard road signs, directions to Rothenburg, and a spare key (or get one copied ASAP). Before you leave, drive around the airport parking lot and get to know your car for five minutes. Work the keys. Try everything. Find problems before you leave.

Transportation: Frankfurt to Rothenburg

The 3-hour drive from the airport to Rothenburg is something even a jet-lagged zombie can handle. The airport is on the Würzburg freeway. It's a 75-mile straight shot to Würzburg; just follow the blue (for autobahn) signs. The Spessart rest stop at Rohrbrunn (tel. 06094/220, open 10:00-13:00 and 14:00-19:00) has a tourist information office (TI), where friendly Herr Ohm can telephone Rothenburg (and speak German) for you. Pick up "Let's Go Bavaria" brochures on Würzburg, Rothenburg, and the Romantic Road, and a Munich map, all free and in English

Leave the freeway at the Heidingsfeld-Würzburg exit. If you're going directly to Rothenburg, follow signs south to Stuttgart/Ulm/road 19, then to Rothenburg via a scenic slice of the Romantic Road. If stopping at Würzburg, follow "Stadtmitte" then "Residenz" signs from the same freeway exit. (*Wo ist . . . ?* means "Where is . . . ?") From downtown Würzburg follow Ulm/road 19 signs to Bad Mergentheim/Rothenburg.

Train travelers may have missed the Romantic Road bus on the day of their arrival, so they'll have to go straight to Rothenburg with a possible stop in Würzburg (the Residenz is a 15-minute walk from the station). The 3½-hour train ride from the airport to Rothenburg goes airport-Frankfurt Hauptbahnhof (central station)-Würzburg-Steinach-Rothenburg, with trains departing from the airport just before the top of each hour, from Frankfurt Central 25 minutes later, arriving in Würzburg in about 2 hours, and on to Rothenburg (after a change in Steinach) The tiny Steinach-Rothenburg train often leaves from the "B" section of track, away from the middle of the station, shortly after the Würzburg train arrives. Don't miss it.

Steinach has no tourism, for good reason. For Romantic Road bus tour schedule details see below

Sightseeing Highlights between Frankfurt and Rothenburg
Frankfurt—While on few sightseeing targets, Frankfurt ıs actually pleasant for a big city and a lot more interesting than killing time at the airport. For a quick look, pick up a city map at the TI in the train station (long hours, tel. 069/212-3-8849), walk down sleazy Kaiserstrasse past Goethe's house (great man, mediocre sight) to Römerberg, Frankfurt's lively market square. A string of museums is just across the river along Schaumainkai (10:00-17:00, closed Monday). Try to avoid driving or sleeping in Frankfurt. Pleasant Rhine towns are just a quick drive or train ride away.

If you must spend the night in Frankfurt, you can sleep near the station at **Hotel Goldener Stern** (D-75 DM, showers-8 DM, Karlsruherstr. 8, tel. 069/233309), **Pension Becker** (S-40 DM, D-60 DM, showers-3 DM; near the Botanical Gardens, 20 minutes walk from the station or U-bahn to Westend, Mendelssohnstr. 92, tel. 069/747992), or at the youth hostel (8-bed rooms, 24 DM a bed with sheets and breakfast for members of any age, bus 46 from station to Frankenstein Place, Deutschherrnufer 12, tel. 069/619058). For a quick meal in the station find the Nordsee cafeteria.

▲▲**Würzburg**—A historic city, though freshly rebuilt since World War II, Würzburg is worth a stop to see its impressive Prince Bishop's Residenz, bubbly baroque chapel (Hofkirche), and sculpted gardens. This is a Franconian Versailles with grand stairways, 3-D art, and a tennis-court-sized fresco by Tiepolo. Tag along with a tour if you can find one in English, or buy the fine little 4.50 DM guidebook (9:00-17:00 April-September, and 10:00-15:30 October-March; closed Monday, last entry a half hour before closing, admission 4.50 DM.) Easy parking is available right there. (TI tel. 0931/37335, offers almost-daily English walks, 11:00, two hours, 10 DM.)

Budget hotels in Würzburg, all between the train station and the palace, in ascending order of comfort and price: **Pension Siegel** (S-50 DM, D-80 DM; just off Kaiserstrasse at Reisbrubengasse 7, tel. 0931/52941), **Hotel Schönleber** (DB-100 DM, CC-VMA, elevator; Theaterstrasse 5, tel. 0931/12068, fax 16012), and **Altstadt Hotel** (DB-110 DM, CC-VM; Theaterstr. 7, tel. 0931/52204, fax 17317).

Romantic Road (Romantische Strasse)—The best way to connect Frankfurt with Munich or Füssen is via the popular Romantic Road. This path winds you past the most beautiful towns and scenery of Germany's medieval heartland. Any tourist office can give you a brochure listing the many interesting baroque palaces, lovely carved altarpieces, and walled medieval cities you'll pass along the way. From Frankfurt in the north to Munich or Füssen in the south, the route includes these highlights:

▲▲**Würzburg** (see above)

▲**Weikersheim**—Palace with fine baroque gardens (luxurious picnic spot), folk museum, and picturesque town square.

▲**Herrgottskapelle**—Tilman Riemenschneider's greatest carved altarpiece in a peaceful church (one mile from Creglingen). Fast and fun Fingerhut (thimble) museum just across the street. The south-bound bus stops here for 15 minutes, long enough to see one or the other. Both open 8:30-18:00, 2 DM.

▲▲▲**Rothenburg ob der Tauber**—See Day 2.

▲**Dinkelsbühl**—Rothenburg's little sister. Twenty towers and gates surround this cute, beautifully preserved walled town. Kinderzeche children's festival turns Dinkelsbühl wonderfully on end each mid-July. (TI tel. 09851/3031.)

Rottenbuch—Impressive church, nondescript village in lovely setting.

▲▲**Wieskirche**—Germany's most glorious baroque-rococo church. In a sweet meadow. Newly restored. Heavenly! North-bound Romantic Road buses stop here for 15 minutes. (See day 4.)

▲▲▲**Neuschwanstein**—"Mad" King Ludwig's Disneyesque castle. (See day 4.)

The Romantic Road drive gives you a good look at rural Germany. My favorite sections are from Weikersheim to Rothenburg and from Landsberg to Füssen. By car, simply follow the green *Romantische Strasse* signs.

By train . . . take the bus. The Europa Bus Company makes the Frankfurt-Munich trip daily in each direction (April-October). A second bus goes from Rothenburg to Füssen daily. Buses arrive in Rothenburg early enough to allow switching over for those wanting to go from Frankfurt to Füssen or vice versa. Buses leave from train stations in towns served by a train. The 11-hour ride costs about $70 but is free with a Eurailpass. Each bus makes stops in Rothenburg (90 minutes) and Dinkelsbühl (45 minutes) and briefly at a few other attractions, and has a guide who hands out brochures and narrates the journey in English. While many claim Eva Braun survives as a Romantic Road bus tour guide, there is no quicker or easier way to travel across Germany and get such a hearty dose of its countryside.

Romantic Road Bus Schedule (daily, April–October)				
8:00	—	Frankfurt	20:15	—
9:45	—	Würzburg	18:25	—
12:15-13:45	14:00	Rothenburg	15:00-16:30	12:30
14:30-15:15	14:45-15:30	Dinkelsbühl	12:25-14:00	11:45
17:15	17:15	Augsburg	10:15	10:15
18:45	—	Munich	9:00	—
—	20:00	Füssen	—	7:30

Bus reservations are free but rarely necessary (except possibly on summer weekends; call 069/790 3256 one day in advance). You can start, stop, and switch over where you like.

Germany (Deutschland)
• United Germany is 136,000 square miles (the size of Montana).
• Population is 77 million (about 650 per square mile, declining slowly).
• The West was 95,000 square miles (like Wyoming) with 61 million people.

Germany

- The East was 41,000 square miles (like Virginia) with 16 million people.
- One deutsche mark (DM) is about $.60; $1 is about 1.6 DM.

Deutschland is energetic, efficient, and organized, and Europe's muscleman—economically and wherever people are lining up. Eighty-five percent of its people live in cities; and average earnings are among the highest on earth. Ninety-seven percent of the workers get a one-month paid vacation, and during the other eleven months they create a gross national product of about one-third that of the United States, and growing. Germany has risen from the ashes of World War II to become the world's fifth-biggest industrial power, ranking fourth in steel output and nuclear power and third in automobile production. Its bustling new cities are designed to make people feel like they belong. It shines culturally, beating out all but two countries in production of books, Nobel laureates, and professors. And think of the Olympic gold medals coming their way next time around.

While its East-West division lasted about forty years, historically, Germany has been and continues to be divided north and south. While northern Germany was barbarian, is Protestant, and assaults life aggressively, southern Germany was Roman, is Catholic, and enjoys a more relaxed tempo of life. The southern German, or Bavarian, dialect is to High (northern) German what the dialect of Alabama or Georgia is to the speech of the northern United States. The American image of Germany is Bavaria (probably because that was "our" sector immediately after the war) where the countryside is most traditional. This historic north-south division is less pronounced these days as Germany becomes a more mobile society. Of course, the big chore facing Germany today is integrating the rotten and wilted economy of what was East Germany into the powerhouse economy of the West. This monumental task has given the West higher taxes (and second thoughts).

Germany's most interesting tourist route today—Rhine, Romantic Road, Bavaria—was yesterday's most important trade route, along which its most prosperous and important medieval cities were located. Germany as a nation is just 120 years old. In 1850, there were 35 independent countries in what is now one Germany. In medieval times, there were over 300, each with its own weights, measures, coinage, king, and lotto. Many were surrounded by what we would call iron curtains. This helps explain Germany's many diverse customs.

Germans eat lunch from 11:30 to 14:30 and dinner between 18:00 and 21:00. Each region has its own gastronomic twist, so order local house specials whenever possible. Pork, fish, and venison are good, and don't miss the bratwurst and sauerkraut. Potatoes are the standard vegetable. Great beers and white wines abound. Try the small local brands. Go with whatever beer is on tap. "Gummi Bears" are a local gumdrop candy with a cult following (beware of imitations—you must see the word "Gummi"), and Nutella is a chocolate nut spread specialty that may change your life.

Banks are generally open from 8:00 to 12:00 and 14:00 to 16:00, other offices from 8:00 to 16:00. Beware: some banks charge per traveler's check. August is a holiday month for workers, but that doesn't really affect us tourists (unless you're on the road on the 15th, when half of Germany is going over the Alps one way and half returning the other).

ROTHENBURG ON THE TAUBER

Today you stay put, get over jet lag, and enjoy Germany's most exciting medieval town. Rothenburg is worth two nights and a whole day. In the Middle Ages, when Frankfurt and Munich were just wide spots on the road, Rothenburg was Germany's second-largest free imperial city with a whopping population of 6,000. Today it's her best-preserved medieval walled town, enjoying tremendous tourist popularity without losing its charm.

Suggested Schedule

7:00	Walk the wall.
8:30	Breakfast.
9:00	Confirm plans at the TI. Climb the tower, visit the city museum and the Medieval Crime and Punishment museum. Buy a picnic.
12:00	Picnic in the castle garden, rest.
13:30	City walking tour (from town square).
16:00	More museums, shop, or walk through the countryside.

Sleep Rothenburg.

Orientation—Rothenburg

To orient yourself in Rothenburg, think of the town map as a human head. Its nose—the castle garden—sticks out to the left, and the neck is the skinny lower part, with the youth hostel and my favorite hotels.

During Rothenburg's heyday, from 1150 to 1400, it was the crossing point of two major trade routes: Tashkent-Paris and Hamburg-Venice. Most of the buildings you'll see were built by 1400. The city started around the long-gone castle (today's castle garden; built in 1142, destroyed in 1356). You can see the shadow of the first town wall, which defines the oldest part of Rothenburg, in its contemporary street plan. A few gates from this wall survive. The richest and therefore biggest houses were in this central part. The commoners built higgledy-piggledy (read:

picturesquely) farther from the center near the present walls. Today, the great trade is tourism; two-thirds of the townspeople are employed serving you. While 2.5 million people visit each year, a mere 500,000 spend the night. Rothenburg is most enjoyable early and late when the tour groups are gone.

Too often, Rothenburg brings out the shopper in visitors before they've had a chance to appreciate the historic city. True, this is a great place to do your German shopping, but first see the town. The TI on the market square offers 90-minute guided tours in English (daily, May-October at 13:30 from the market square, 4 DM). If none are scheduled, you can hire a private guide. For 50 DM, a local historian—who's usually an intriguing character as well—will bring the ramparts alive. Eight hundred years of history are packed between the cobbles. (Manfred Baumann, tel. 09861/4146 and Anita Weinzierl, tel. 09868/7993 are good guides.)

Start your visit by picking up a map, the "sights worth seeing and knowing" brochure (a virtual walking guide to the town; read it all), and information at the TI on the main square (Monday-Friday 9:00-12:00, 14:00-18:00, Saturday 9:00-12:00, 14:00-16:00, closed Sunday, tel. 09861/40492, or tel. 19412 after hours for room finding help). The TI's free "Hotels and Pensions of Rothenburg" map has the most detail and names all streets. Confirm sightseeing plans and ask about the daily 13:30 walking tour and evening entertainment. The travel agency in the TI is a handy place to arrange train and couchette reservations. The best town map is available free at the Friese shop, two doors toward the nose. Telephone code: 09861.

Sightseeing Highlights—Rothenburg

▲▲**Walk the Wall**—Just over a mile around, with great views, and providing a good orientation, this walk can be done by those under six feet tall in less than an hour and requires no special sense of balance. Photographers go through lots of film, especially before breakfast or at sunset when the lighting is best and the crowds are least. The best fortifications are in the Spitaltor (south end). Walk from

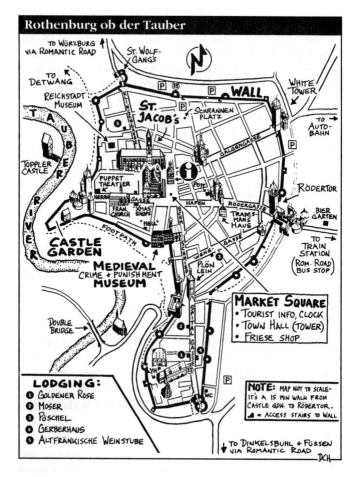

Rothenburg ob der Tauber

TO WÜRZBURG VIA ROMANTIC ROAD
ST. WOLF-GANGS
N
WHITE TOWER
WALL
TO DETWANG
REICHSTADT MUSEUM
ST. JACOB'S
SCHRANNEN PLATZ
GALGENGASSE
TO AUTO-BAHN
TAUBER RIVER
TOPPLER CASTLE
PUPPET THEATER
HERRN GASSE
FRAN. CHURCH
XMAS SHOPS
HEU
POST
HAFEN
RÖDERGASSE
TRADES-MANS HAUS
RÖDERTOR
BIER GARTEN
CASTLE GARDEN
FOOTPATH
GASSE
TO TRAIN STATION (ROM. ROAD) BUS STOP
MEDIEVAL CRIME + PUNISHMENT MUSEUM
PLÖN LEIN
DOUBLE BRIDGE
YH
WC

MARKET SQUARE
- TOURIST INFO, CLOCK
- TOWN HALL (TOWER)
- FRIESE SHOP

LODGING:
❶ GOLDENER ROSE
❷ MOSER
❸ PÖSCHEL
❹ GERBERHAUS
❺ ALTFRÄNKISCHE WEINSTUBE

NOTE: MAP NOT TO SCALE—IT'S A 15 MIN WALK FROM CASTLE GDN. TO RÖDERTOR.
▟ = ACCESS STAIRS TO WALL

↓ TO DINKELSBÜHL + FÜSSEN VIA ROMANTIC ROAD
DCH

there counterclockwise to the forehead. Climb the Rödertor en route. The names you see along the way are people who donated money to repair the wall after WWII.

▲**Rödertor**—The wall tower nearest the train station is the only one you can climb. It's worth the hike up for the view and a fascinating rundown on the bombing of Rothenburg in the last weeks of World War II (the northeast corner of the city was destroyed; photos, English translation, 1 DM, 9:00-17:00, closed off-season).

▲▲**Climb Town Hall Tower**—The best view of Rothenburg and the surrounding countryside and a closeup look at an old tiled roof from the inside (9:30-12:30, 13:00-17:00, off-season Saturday and Sunday 12:00-15:00 only) are yours for 1 DM and a rigorous (214 steps, 180 feet) but interesting climb. Ladies, beware, some men find the view best from the bottom of the ladder just before the top.

▲▲**Herrengasse and the Castle Garden**—Any town's Herrengasse, where the richest patricians and merchants (the *Herren*) lived, is your chance to see its finest old mansions. Wander from the market square down Herrengasse (past the old Rothenburg official measurement rods on the City Hall wall), drop into the lavish front rooms of a ritzy hotel or two. Pop into the Franciscan Church (from 1285, oldest in town, with a Reimenschneider altarpiece; 10:00-12:00, 14:00-16:00, free), continue on down past the old-fashioned puppet theater, through the old gate (notice the tiny after-curfew door in the big door and the hole from which hot tar was poured onto attackers) and into the garden that used to be the castle. (Great Tauber Riviera views at sunset.)

▲▲**Medieval Crime and Punishment Museum**—It's the best of its kind, full of fascinating old legal bits and Kriminal pieces, instruments of punishment and torture, even a special cage—complete with a metal gag—for nags. Exhibits are in English. (Fun cards and posters, daily 9:30-18:00, in winter 14:00-16:00, 5 DM.)

▲**Toy Museum**—Two floors of historic kinder cuteness is a hit with many (just off the market square, downhill from the fountain, Hofbronneng 13; 9:30-18:00 daily, 5 DM, 12 DM per family).

▲▲**St. Jacob's Church**—Here you'll find a glorious 500-year-old wooden altarpiece by Tilman Riemenschneider, located up the stairs and behind the organ. Riemenschneider was the Michelangelo of German woodcarvers. This is the one required art treasure in town (daily 9:00-17:30, off-season 10:00-12:00, 14:00-16:00, 2 DM, free helpful English info sheet).

Meistertrunk Show—Be on the main square at 11:00, 12:00, 13:00, 14:00, 15:00, 20:00, 21:00, or 22:00 for the ritual gathering of the tourists to see the less-than-breathtak-

ing reenactment of the Meistertrunk story.In 1631, the
Catholic army took the Protestant town and was about to
do its rape, pillage, and plunder thing when the mayor
said, "Hey, if I can drink this entire 3-liter tankard of wine
in one gulp, will you leave us alone?" The invading com-
mander, sensing he was dealing with an unbalanced people, said, "Sure." Mayor Nusch drank the whole thing, the
town was saved, and the mayor slept for three days.

Hint: for the best show, don't watch the clock; watch
the open-mouthed tourists gasp as the old windows flip
open. At the late shows, the square flickers with flash
attachments.

▲**Historical Vaults**—Under the town hall tower is a city
history museum that gives a waxy but good look at
medieval Rothenburg and a good-enough replica of the
famous Meistertrunk tankard (well described in English,
9:00-18:00, closed off-season, 2 DM).

Museum of the Imperial City (Reichsstadt Museum)—
This stuffier museum, housed in the former Dominican
Convent, gives a more scholarly look at old Rothenburg
with some fine art and the supposed Meistertrunk tankard,
labeled "Kürfurstenhumpen" (10:00-17:00, in winter 13:00-
16:00, 3 DM).

St. Wolfgang's Church—This fortified Gothic church is
built into the medieval wall at Klingentor (near the "forehead"). Explore its dungeon-like passages below and
check out the shepherd's dance exhibit to see where they
hot-oiled the enemy back in the good old days (10:00-
13:00, 14:00-17:00, closed off-season, 2 DM).

Alt Rothenburger Handwerkerhaus—This 700-year-old
tradesman's house shows the typical living situation of
Rothenburg in its heyday (Alter Stadtgraben 26, near the
Markus Tower; daily 9:00-18:00, closed off-season, 3 DM).

▲**Walk in the Countryside**—Just below the Burggarten
(castle garden) in the Tauber Valley is the cute, skinny,
600-year-old castle/summer home of Mayor Toppler
(13:00-16:00 on Friday, Saturday, and Sunday in summer
only, 2 DM). Intimately furnished, it's well worth a look.
Notice the photo of bombed-out 1945 Rothenburg on the
top floor. Then walk on past the covered bridge and huge

trout to the peaceful village of Detwang. **Detwang** is actually older than Rothenburg, with another Riemenschneider altarpiece in its church (from 968, the second oldest in Franconia). For a scenic return, loop back to Rothenburg through the valley along the river past a café with outdoor tables, great desserts, and a town view to match.

A Franconian Bike Ride—For a fun, breezy look at the countryside around Rothenburg, rent a bike from the train station (12 DM per day, 8 DM with a train pass or ticket, extra gears available for 1 DM each, 5:00-18:30). For a pleasant half-day pedal, bike south down to Detwang via Topplerschloss and Fuchesmill (an old water mill across the street). Go north along the level bike path to Tauberscheckenbach, then huff and puff uphill about twenty minutes to Adelshofen and south back to Rothenburg.

Swimming—Rothenburg has a fine modern recreation center, with an indoor/outdoor pool and a sauna, a few minutes walk down the Dinkelsbühl Road (8:00 or 9:00-20:00, tel. 4565).

Franconian Open-Air Museum—Twenty minutes drive from Rothenburg in the undiscovered "Rothenburgy" town of Bad Windsheim is a small, open-air folk museum that, compared with others in Europe, isn't much. But it's trying very hard and gives you the best look around at traditional rural Franconia (9:00-18:00, closed off-season, 5 DM).

Shopping

Rothenburg is one of Germany's best shopping towns. Do it here, mail it home, and get it out of your hair. Lovely prints, carvings, wineglasses, Christmas tree ornaments, and beer steins are popular.

The Kathe Wohlfahrt Christmas trinkets phenomenon is spreading across the half-timbered reaches of Europe. In Rothenburg, tourists flock to the Kathe Wohlfahrt Kris Kringle Market and the Christmas Village (on either side of Herrengasse, just off the main square). This Christmas wonderland is filled with enough twinkling lights to require a special electric hookup, instant Christmas spirit mood music (best appreciated on a hot day in July), and American and Japanese tourists hungrily filling little

woven shopping baskets with 5-to-10-DM goodies to hang
on their trees. Prices have hefty tour-guide kickbacks built
into them. (Okay, I admit it, my Christmas tree dangles
with a few KW ornaments.)

The Friese shop (just off the market square, west of the
tourist office on the corner across from the public W.C.)
offers a charming contrast. Cuckoo with friendliness, it
gives shoppers with this book tremendous service: a 10
percent discount, 14 percent tax deducted if you have it
mailed, and a free Rothenburg map. Anneliese, who runs
the place with her sons, Frankie and Berni, charges only
her cost to ship things, changes money at the best rates in
town with no extra charge, and lets tired travelers leave
their bags in her back room for free.

For good prints and paintings, and a free shot of
schnapps, visit the Ernst Geissendörfer print shop where
the main square hits Schmiedgasse.

Those who prefer to eat their souvenirs shop the
Bäckerei (bakeries). Their succulent pastries, pies, and
cakes are pleasantly distracting. Skip the good-looking but
bad-tasting "Rothenburger Schneeballs."

Evening Fun and Beer Drinking

The best beer garden for balmy summer evenings is just
outside the wall at the Rödertor (red gate). If this is dead,
as it often is, go a few doors farther out to the alley (left)
just before the Sparekasse for two popular bars and the
hottest disco in town.

For a rare chance to mix it up with locals who aren't
selling anything, bring your favorite slang and tongue-
twisters to the English conversation club (Wednesdays,
20:00-24:00) at Mario's Altefränkische Weinstube. This
dark and smoky pub is an atmospheric hangout any night
but Tuesday, when it's closed (Klosterhof 7, off
Klingengasse, behind St. Jacob's church, tel. 6404).

For mellow ambience, try the beautifully restored Alte
Keller's Weinstube on Alterkellerstrasse under walls fes-
tooned with old toys.

Sleeping in Rothenburg (about 1.6 DM = US$1, postal code: 91541, tel. code: 09861)

Rothenburg is crowded with visitors, including probably Europe's greatest single concentration of Japanese tourists, but when the sun sets, most retreat to big-city high-rise hotels. Room-finding is easy throughout the year. In fact, those who arrive by train may be greeted by the *Zimmer* skimmer trying to waylay those on their way to a reserved room. If you arrive without a reservation, try talking yourself into one of these more desperate B-and-B rooms for a youth hostel price. The first five listings are at the south end of town, 15 minutes from station, a 7-minute (without shopping) walk downhill from the market square. Walk downhill on Schmiedgasse (*gasse* means lane) until it becomes Spitalgasse (Hospital Lane). Throughout this book, unless otherwise indicated, room prices include breakfast.

I stay in **Hotel Goldener Rose** (S-32 DM, D-60 DM, DBWC-80-85 DM in classy annex behind the garden, some triples, SE-B, kid-friendly, EZ in annex, CC-VMA; Spitalgasse 28, tel. 4638, closed in January and February) where scurrying Karin serves breakfast and stately Henni causes many monoglots to dream in fluent Deutsche. The hotel has only one shower for two floors of rooms and the streetside rooms can be noisy, but the rooms are clean and airy and you're surrounded by cobbles, flowers, and red-tiled roofs. The Favetta family also serves good, reasonably priced meals. Remember to keep your key to get in after they close (at the side gate in the alley).

For the best real with-a-local-family, comfortable, and homey experience, stay with **Herr und Frau Moser** (30 DM per person, one double and one triple; Spitalgasse 12, tel. 5971). This charming retired couple speak little English but try very hard. Speak slowly, in clear, simple English.

Pension Pöschel (S-30 DM, D-60; Wenggasse 22, tel. 3430, SE-D) is also friendly, has bright rooms, and is a little closer to the market square. Just across the street, the **Gastehaus Raidel** (D-60 DM, DB-84 DM; Wenggasse 3, tel. 3115) offers bright rooms with cramped facilities down the hall. It's run by grim people who make me want to sing the "Addams Family" theme song, but it works in a pinch.

Hotel Gerberhaus, a classy new hotel in a 500-year-old building, is warmly run by Ingra, who mixes modern comforts into bright and airy rooms while keeping the traditional flavor. Great buffet breakfasts and pleasant garden in back (DB-90 to 140 DM, no CC but takes personal checks, SE-B; Spitalgasse 25, tel. 3055, fax 86555).

Rothenburg's fine youth hostel, the **Rossmühle** (18 DM beds, 5 DM sheets, 8 DM dinners, tel. 4510, reception open 7:00-9:00, 17:00-19:00, 20:00-22:00, will hold rooms until 18:00 if you call, lockup at 23:30) has three to five double bunks per room and is often filled with school groups. This droopy-eyed building is the old town horse-mill (used when the town was under siege and the river-powered mill was inaccessible). Here in Bavaria hosteling is limited to those under 27, except for families traveling with children under 16.

Right on the town square, **Gasthof Marktplatz** (S-35 DM, D-60 DM, DB-75 DM, T-80 DM, TB-100 DM; Grüner Markt 10, tel. 6722, Herr Rosner SE) has simple rooms and a cozy atmosphere. Its cheap rooms have sinks, but are the only rooms listed in this book that have access to absolutely no shower.

Frau Guldemeister rents two simple and plain rooms (DB-60 or 70 DM, breakfast in the room, SE-A, EZ-A; off the Market Square behind the Christmas shop, Pfaffleinsgasschen 10, tel. 8988).

Bohemians with bucks enjoy the **Hotel Altfränkische Weinstube am Klosterhof** (SB-65 DM, DB-90 to 100 DM, TB-120 DM, CC-VM, kid-friendly, SE-A; behind St. Jacob's church, just off Klingengasse at Klosterhof 7, tel. 6404). A young couple, Mario and Erika, run this dark and smoky pub in a 600-year-old building. Upstairs they rent *gemütliche* rooms with upscale Monty Python atmosphere, TVs, modern showers, open-beam ceilings, and "himmel beds" (canopied four-poster "heaven" beds). Their pub is a candle-lit classic, serving hot food until 22:00, closing at 1:00. You're welcome to drop by on Wednesday evenings (20:00-24:00) for the English conversation club.

If money doesn't matter, the **Burg Hotel** (DB-250 DM, SE-A, CC-VMA; Klostergasse 1, on the wall near the castle garden, tel. 5037, fax 1487), with elegance almost unimaginable in a medieval building with a Tauber Valley view and a high-heeled receptionist, offers a good way to spend it.

In the modern world, a block from the train station, you'll find **Pension Willi Then,** run by a cool guy (Willi played the sax in a jazz band for seven years after the war and is a regular at the English language club) on a quiet street (D-65 DM, DB-75 DM, SE-A; across from a handy laundromat at 8 Johannitergasse, tel. 5177).

The town of Detwang, a 15-minute walk below Rothenburg, is loaded with quiet Zimmer. The clean, quiet, and comfortable old **Gasthof zum Schwarzen Lamm** in Detwang (D-80 DM, DB-98 DM, tel. 6727) serves good food, as does the popular and very local-style **Eulenstube** next door. **Gastehaus Alte Schreinerei** (8801 Bettwar, tel. 1541) offers good food and quiet, comfy, reasonable rooms a little farther down the road in Bettwar.

Eating in Rothenburg

Finding a reasonable meal (or a place serving late) in the town center can be tough. Most places serve meals only from 11:30 to 13:30 and 18:00 to 20:00. Galgengasse (Gallows Lane) has two cheap and popular standbys: **Pizzeria Roma** (19 Galgengasse, 11:30-24:00, 10-DM pizzas and normal schnitzel fare) and **Gasthof zum Ochen** (26 Galgengasse, 11:30-13:30, 18:00-20:00, closed Thursday, decent 10-DM meals). **Zum Schmolzer** (corner of Stollengasse and Rosengasse) is a local favorite for its cheap beer and good food. If you need a break from schnitzel, the **Hong Kong China Restaurant**, outside the town near the train tracks (1 Bensenstr., tel. 7377), serves good Chinese food. There are two supermarkets near the wall at Rödertor (the one outside the wall to the left is cheaper).

Itinerary Options
This "two nights and a full day" plan assumes you have a
car. Eurailers taking the Romantic Road bus tour must
leave around 14:00, so you'll have to decide between half
a day or a day and a half here. For sightseeing, half a day
is enough. For a rest after jet lag, a day and a half sounds
better.

Countless renowned travelers have searched for the elusive "untouristy Rothenburg." There are many contenders
(such as Michelstadt, Miltenberg, Bamberg, Bad Windsheim, and Dinkelsbühl), but none holds a candle to the
king of medieval German cuteness. Even with crowds,
over-priced souvenirs, Japanese-speaking night watchmen,
and yes, even with schneeballs, Rothenburg is best. Save
time and mileage, and be satisfied with the winner.

ROMANTIC ROAD TO THE TIROL

Wind through Bavaria's Romantic Road, stopping wherever the cows look friendly or a village fountain beckons. After a glimpse of Europe's most fairy-tale castle, you'll cross into Austria's Tirol to explore the desolate ruins of a medieval castle and finish the day with an evening of slap-dancing, yodeling, and local music.

Suggested Schedule	
7:30	Breakfast.
8:30	Romantic Road, head for Austria.
9:30	Stop in Dinkelsbühl, buy picnic.
10:00	Drive south on Romantic Road, picnicking en route.
14:00	Cross into Austria, check into a hotel in Reutte.
15:00	Luge ride down the ski slope.
16:30	Hike to Ehrenberg ruins.
18:00	Rest and dinner.
20:30	Tirolean folk evening.

Sleep Reutte.
Note: off-season (with no crowd considerations), consider doing Neuschwanstein castle today.

Transportation: Rothenburg to Reutte, Austria
Get an early start to enjoy the quaint hills and rolling villages of what was Germany's major medieval trade route. After a quick stop, dead center, in Dinkelsbühl, cross the baby Danube River (*Donau* in German) and continue south along the Romantic Road to Füssen. Drive by Neuschwanstein Castle just to sweeten your dreams before crossing into Austria to get set up at Reutte.

If detouring past Oberammergau, you can drive through Garmisch, past Germany's highest mountain (the Zugspitze) into Austria via Lermoos and on to Reutte. Or you can take the small scenic shortcut to Reutte past Ludwig's Linderhof and along the windsurfer-strewn Plansee.

Romantic Road

Reutte (pronounced "ROY-teh," rolled "r"), population 5,000, is a relaxed town, far from the international tourist crowd but popular with Germans and Austrians for its climate. Doctors recommend its "grade 1" air. If the weather's good, hike to the mysterious castle ruins and ride the luge. Finish your day off with a slap-dancing bang at a Tirolean folk evening.

Train travelers catch the Romantic Road bus tour from the Rothenburg train station (departures at 13:45 or 14:00). You can catch one bus into Munich (arrives at 18:45) or the other direct to Füssen (arrives at 20:00, long after the last bus to Reutte). Ask about exact times in Rothenburg at the train station or tourist office. If you stake out a seat when the bus arrives, you'll have a better chance of being on it when it leaves two hours later.

Today and tomorrow, you'll cross the German-Austrian border several times. The plan calls for sleeping tonight and tomorrow night just a few miles south of Germany in the Austrian town of Reutte and making a loop tomorrow from Austria back through Germany, returning to your Austrian home base.

Sightseeing Highlights

▲**Dinkelsbühl**—A miniature, second-rate Rothenburg without the mobs but cute enough to merit a short stop. Park near the church in the center, buy a picnic, and browse. You'll find an interesting local museum, a well-preserved medieval wall, towers, gates, and a moat. (TI tel. 09851/90240, cheap rooms at Haus Küffner, tel. 1247, and Zur Linde, tel. 3465, both on Neustädtlein.)

▲▲**Sommerrodelbahn, the Luge**—Near Lermoos, on the Innsbruck-Lermoos-Reutte road you'll find two rare and exciting luge courses. In the summer, these ski slopes are used as luge courses, or Sommerrodelbahn. To try one of Europe's great $5 thrills, take the lift up, grab a sled-like go-cart, and luge down. The concrete bobsled course banks on the corners, and even a novice can go very, very fast. Most are cautious on their first run and speed demons on their second. (Recently, a woman showed me her journal illustrated with her husband's dried 5-inch-long luge scab. He disobeyed the only essential rule of luging: keep both hands on your stick.) No one emerges from the course without a windblown hairdo and a smile-creased face. Both places charge a steep 65 AS per run, with five-trip or ten-trip discount cards; both are open weekends from late May and daily from about mid-June through September and into October if weather permits, from 9:00 or 10:00 until about 17:00. Closed in wet weather. Always telephone before going out.

The small and steep luge: The first course (100-meter drop over 800-meter course) is 6 kilometers beyond Reutte's castle ruins; look for a chairlift on the right and

exit on the tiny road at the yellow Riesenrutschbahn sign
(call ahead, tel. 05674/5350, the local TI at 05674/5354
speaks more English).

The longest luge: The Biberwihr Sommerrodelbahn,
15 minutes closer to Innsbruck, just past Lermoos in
Biberwihr (the first exit after a long tunnel), is a better luge,
the longest in Austria—1,300 meters—but has a shorter season. It opens at 9:00, a good tomorrow-morning alternative
if today is wet. Tel. 05673/2111, local TI tel. 05673/2922.

Just before this luge, behind the Sport und Trachten-
stüberl shop, is a wooden church-dome with a striking
Zugspitze backdrop. If you have sunshine and a camera,
don't miss it.

▲▲**Reutte's Ehrenberg Ruins**—The brooding ruins of
Ehrenberg (two castle ruins atop two neighboring hills),
just outside of Reutte on the road to Lermoos, await sur-
vivors of the luge. These thirteenth-century rock piles are
a great contrast to tomorrow's "modern" castles. Park in
the lot at the base of the hill and hike up; it's a 20-minute
walk to the small (*kleine*) castle for a great view from your
own private ruins. Imagine how proud Count Meinrad II
of Tirol (who built the castle in 1290) would be to know
that his castle repelled 16,000 Swedish soldiers in the
defense of Catholicism in 1632.

You'll find more medieval mystique atop the taller neighboring hill in the big (*gross*) ruins. You can't see anything
from below and almost nothing when you get there, but
these bigger, more desolate and overgrown ruins are a little more romantic (and a lot harder to get to).

The easiest way down is via the small road from the
gully between the two castles. The car park, with a
café/guest house (with a German language flyer about the
castle), is just off the Lermoos/Reutte road. Reutte is a
pleasant 90-minute walk away. The town museum and
many Reutte hotels have sketches of the intact castle.

▲▲**Tiroler Folk Evening**—Ask in your hotel if there's a
Tirolean folk evening tonight. About two evenings a week
in the summer, Reutte or a nearby town puts on an
evening of yodeling, slap-dancing, and Tirolean frolic—

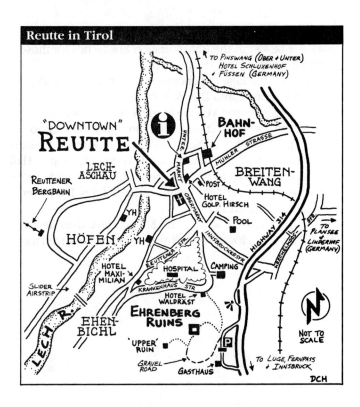

usually worth the charge and a few kilometers drive. Off-season, you'll have to do your own yodeling.

Reutte, Füssen, Neuschwanstein, and Accommodations in the Region
See Day 4.

Itinerary Options
Train travelers may prefer skipping Reutte and taking advantage of the better train and bus connections in Füssen or doing tomorrow's "castle day" as a side trip from Munich. Organized tours do the Bavarian biggies in a day. The Grey Line, tel. 089/5904248, does Neuschwanstein, Linderhof, Oberammergau, and the Wies Church in a busy 10-hour day for 50 DM, departing daily

at 8:30 from near the Munich station. Staying in Reutte may not be worth the transportation headaches for those without wheels.

Remember, the luge experience is possible only on dry days. It fits easily into Day 3, 4, or 5.

If for some reason you do Munich on your way to Reutte, the autobahn from Reutte through Innsbruck to Salzburg takes 5 hours. Stay on it. The small roads basically repeat what you've already seen. You could stop at Hall just past Innsbruck to reserve and pay for your night there for your late arrival after Vienna. (The hotel is 100 meters from the autobahn.)

If you're skipping Vienna, do Munich first, then Reutte, then follow the lovely Lech River Valley into Switzerland.

BAVARIA AND CASTLE DAY

Today you circle through the nutcracker-and-castle corner of Bavaria. After touring Europe's most ornate castle, Ludwig's fantasy called Neuschwanstein, visit Germany's most ornate church, a rococo riot. After a quick look at Oberammergau, Bavaria's wood-carving capital and home of the famous Passion Play, you can tour another of Ludwig's extravagant castles—the more livable Linderhof Palace.

Suggested Schedule—by Car (Home Base: Reutte)

7:30	Breakfast.
8:15	Leave Reutte.
8:45	Tour Neuschwanstein Castle.
11:30	Picnic by the lake (Alpsee).
12:15	Drive to Wies Church and on to Oberammergau.
13:45	Park at Passion Play Theater, take tour.
15:30	Tour Linderhof Castle (or shopping in Oberammergau).
17:15	Drive home to Reutte via Plansee.
18:30	Tirolean folk evening (if not last night).
Sleep	Reutte.

Suggested Schedule—by Train (Home Base: Füssen)

7:30	Breakfast.
8:00	Bus or bike (rent from Füssen station) to Neuschwanstein, tour Ludwig's castles (one or both).
11:00	Lakeside picnic under the castle.
12:00	Bike (along lake, tiny road over border) or bus (via Füssen) to Reutte.
14:00	Hike up to the Ehrenberg ruins. Bike or bus back to Füssen.

Bavaria and Tirol—The Castle Loop

Transportation (60-mile circle)

This day is designed for drivers (instructions are worked into the sightseeing descriptions). More than a day's worth of travel fun is laid out in a circular drive starting in Reutte.

Without your own wheels, it won't all be possible. Local bus service is inexpensive but spotty for sightseeing. Buses from the Füssen station to Neuschwanstein run hourly. Füssen-to-Wies Church buses go twice a day. Oberammergau-to-Linderhof buses run fairly regularly. Hitchhiking is possible, but hitting everything is highly improbable. Without a car, home-base in Munich and take an all-day bus tour or sleep in Füssen or Reutte and skip the Wies Church and Oberammergau. Reutte-Füssen buses depart at 8:35, 13:50, and 17:45 (returning from Füssen to Reutte at 9:30, 13:20, and 17:05). This is great biking country. Most train stations (including Reutte and Füssen) and many hotels rent bikes for around 8 DM a day.

From Reutte, you can bus directly to the castle at Neuschwanstein (11:25-12:00) and return (15:45-16:10). Hourly trains make the 2-hour trip connecting Munich and Füssen.

Reutte
You won't find Reutte in any American guidebook. Its charms are subtle. It never was rich or important. Its castle is ruined, its buildings have paint-on "carvings," its churches are full, its men yodel for each other on birthdays, and lately its energy is spent soaking its Austrian and German guests in gemütlichkeit.

Because most guests stay for a week, the town's attractions are more time-consuming than thrilling. The mountain lift swoops you high above the tree line to an Alpine flower park with special slow-down-and-smell-the-many-local-varieties paths. The town Heimatmuseum (10:00-12:00, 14:00-17:00, closed Monday; in the Green House on Untermarkt, around the corner from Hotel Golden Hirsch) offers a quick look at the local folk culture and the story of the castle, but so do the walls and mantels of most of the hotels.

Reutte has an Olympic-sized swimming pool open from 10:00 to 21:00, which might be a good way to cool off after your castle hikes (off-season 14:00-21:00, closed Monday, 55 AS).

For a major thrill on a sunny day, drop by the tiny airport in Hofen across the river and fly. A small single-prop plane (three people for 30 minutes, 1,200 AS; 60 minutes for 1,900 AS) can buzz the Zugspitze and Ludwig's castles and give you a bird's-eye peek at Reutte's Ehrenberg ruins (that's about the cost of three lift tickets up the Zugspitze, and a lot easier). Or for something more angelic, how about Segelfliegen? For 240 AS, you get 30 minutes in a glider for two (you and the pilot). Just watching the tow rope launch the graceful glider like a giant slow motion rubber-band gun is thrilling (late May through October, 11:00-19:00, in good weather, tel. 05672/3207).

Füssen

Important as the southern terminus of the trade route that is today's tourist trade route called the Romantic Road, Füssen is romantically situated under a renovated castle on the lively Lech River.

Unfortunately, in the summer it's entirely overrun by tourists—of the worst kind. Traffic can be exasperating, but by bike or on foot, it's not bad. The train station (where the Romantic Road bus tour leaves at 7:30 and arrives at 20:00 (daily, April-October) is a few minutes walk from the TI, good rooms, the hostel, and the town center, a cobbled shopping mall. Off-season, the town is a jester's delight.

Halfway between Füssen and the border (as you drive) is the Lechfall, a thunderous look at the river with a handy potty stop.

Sightseeing Highlights—Castle Day Circle

▲▲▲Neuschwanstein and Hohenschwangau Castles (Königsschlösser)—The fairy-tale castle, Neuschwanstein, looks medieval, but it's only about as old as the Eiffel Tower. It was built to suit the whims of Bavaria's King Ludwig II and is a textbook example of the romanticism that was popular in nineteenth-century Europe.

Beat the crowds. See Neuschwanstein, Germany's most popular castle, early in the morning. The castle is open every morning at 9:00; by 10:00, it's packed. Rushed 25-minute English-language tours leave regularly, telling the sad story of Bavaria's "mad" king.

After the tour, climb up to Mary's Bridge to marvel at Ludwig's castle, just as Ludwig did. This bridge was quite an engineering accomplishment a hundred years ago. From the bridge, the frisky can hike even higher to the "Beware—Danger of Death" signs and an even more glorious castle view. For the most interesting (but 15-minute longer and extremely slippery when wet) descent, follow signs to the Pöllat Gorge.

The big, yellow Hohenschwangau Castle nearby was Ludwig's boyhood home. It's more lived-in and historic and actually gives a better glimpse of Ludwig's life. (Both

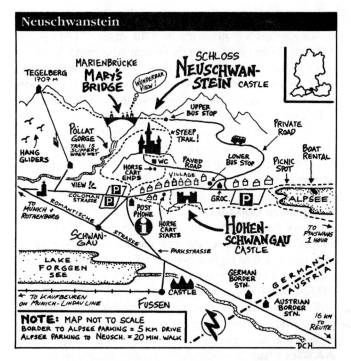

castles cost 8 DM and are open daily 9:00-17:30, November-March 10:00-16:00, tel. 08362/81035. If not enough English-speakers gather, you may have to do Hohenschwangau with a German group.)

The "village" at the foot of the castles was created for and lives off the hungry, shopping tourists who come in droves to Europe's "Disney" castle. The big yellow Bräustüberl restaurant by the lakeside parking lot is cheapest, with food that tastes that way. Next door is a little family-run, open-daily souvenir/grocery store with the makings for a skimpy picnic and a microwave fast-food machine. Picnic in the lakeside park or in one of the old-fashioned rent-by-the-hour rowboats. At the intersection is the bus stop, the post/telephone office, and a helpful TI. Park, if possible, at the closest lot (the lakeside Schloss Parkplatz am Alpsee); they all cost 4 DM. As you'll notice, it's a steep hike to the castle. Buses (3.50 DM up, 5 DM round-trip, dropping you at Mary's Bridge, a steep 10

minutes above the castle) and horse carriages (slower than
walking, stops 5 minutes short of the castle, 7 DM up,
3.50 DM down) go constantly (watch your step). Your
work continues inside the castle as your tour takes you up
and down more than 300 stairs. Signposts and books often
refer to these castles in the German, "Königsschlösser."

To give your castle experience a romantic twist, hike or
bike over from Hotel Schluxenhof in Austria. The mostly
paved lane crosses a lonely German/Austrian border
fence. It's an hour's hike with bus connections back to
Füssen and Reutte or a great circular bike trip. Füssen-
Hohenschwangau buses go twice an hour.

▲**Tegelberg Gondola**—Just north of Neuschwanstein,
you'll see hang gliders hovering like vultures. They
jumped from the top of the Tegelberg gondola. For 22
DM, you can ride high above the castle to the 5,500-foot
summit and back down (last lift at 17:00, tel.
08362/81018). On a clear day, you get great views of the
Alps and Bavaria and the vicarious thrill of watching hang
gliders and parasailers leap into airborne ecstasy. From
there, it's a pleasant 2-hour hike down to Ludwig's castle.

▲▲**Wies Church**—Germany's greatest rococo-style
church, Wieskirche, is newly restored and looking as brilliant as the day it floated down from heaven. With flames
of decoration, overripe but bright, bursting with beauty,
this church is a divine droplet, a curly curlicue, the final
flowering of the baroque movement. The ceiling depicts
the Last Judgment. Walk down the side aisles to get close
to the altar and the wooden statue of Christ that supposedly wept and still attracts countless pilgrims. Take a com-
mune-with-nature-and-smell-the-farm detour back through
the meadow to the car park.

Wies (daily, 7:00-19:00, admission for a donation) is 30
minutes north of Neuschwanstein. Drive north, turn right
at Steingaden, and follow the signs. The northbound
Romantic Road bus tour stops here for 15 minutes. If you
can't visit Wies, other churches that came out of the same
heavenly spray can are Oberammergau's church, Munich's
Asam church, the Würzburg Residenz chapel, or the
splendid (free and nearby) Ettal Monastery.

The Echelsbacher Bridge arches 250 feet over the Pöllat
Gorge on the way from Wies to Oberammergau, where
you hit road 23. Drivers should let their passengers walk
across and meet them at the other side. Any kayakers?
Notice the painting of the traditional village woodcarver
(who used to walk from town to town with his art on his
back) on the first big house on the Oberammergau side, a
shop called Almdorf Ammertal. It has a huge selection of
overpriced carvings and commission-hungry tour guides.
▲**Oberammergau**—The Shirley Temple of Bavarian villages and exploited to the hilt by the tourist trade,
Oberammergau wears way too much makeup. It's worth a
wander only if you're passing through anyway. Browse
through the woodcarvers' shops—small art galleries filled
with very expensive whittled works—or the local Heimat
(folk art) Museum. (TI tel. 08822/1021; off-season, closed
Saturday afternoon and Sunday.)

Visit the church, a poor cousin of the one at Wies. This
church looks richer than it is. Put your hand on the "marble" columns. If they warm up they're painted fakes.
Wander through the graveyard. Ponder the deaths that
two wars dealt Germany. Behind the church are the photos
of three Schneller brothers, all killed within two years in
World War II.

Once each decade, Oberammergau performs the
Passion Play (next show in the year 2000). Five thousand
people a day for 100 summer days attend Oberammergau's all-day dramatic story of Christ's crucifixion. Until
2000, you'll have to settle for reading the book and taking
the theater's 45-minute tours (cheap, in English, regular
departures from 9:30-12:00 and 13:30-16:00) or seeing
Nicodemus tooling around town in his VW.

Gasthaus zum Stern (D-70 DM, DB-80 DM; Dorfstr. 33,
8103 Oberammergau, tel. 08822/867) is friendly, serves
good food and, for this tourist town, is a fine value
(closed Tuesdays and November, will hold a room with a
phone call, English spoken). Oberammergau's modern
youth hostel (16 DM beds, open all year, tel.
08822/4114) is on the river a short walk from the center.

Driving into town, cross the bridge, take the second right, follow "Polizei" signs, and park by the huge gray Passionsspielhaus. Leaving town, head out past the church and turn toward Ettal on road 23. You're 20 miles from Reutte.

▲▲**Linderhof Castle**—This was Mad Ludwig's "home," his most intimate castle. It's small and comfortably exquisite, good enough for a minor god. Set in the woods, 15 minutes from Oberammergau, surrounded by fountains and sculpted, Italian-style gardens, it's the only palace I've toured that actually had me feeling envious. Don't miss the grotto (April-September, 9:00-17:00, off-season 10:00-16:00, fountains often erupt at 17:00, English tours constantly, tel. 08822/3512, 7 DM). Plan for lots of crowds, lots of walking, and a 2-hour stop. There are several buses a day from Füssen and Oberammergau.

▲**Fallershein**—A special treat for those who may have been Kit Carson in a previous life, this extremely remote log cabin village is a 4,000-foot-high, flower-speckled world of serene slopes and cowbells. Thunderstorms roll down the valley like it's God's bowling alley, but the pint-sized church on the high ground, blissfully simple after so much baroque, seems to promise that this huddle of houses will survive and the river and breeze will just keep flowing. The couples sitting on benches are mostly Austrian vacationers who've rented cabins here. Many of them, appreciating the remoteness of Fallershein, are having affairs.

For a rugged chunk of local Alpine peace, spend a night in the local **Matratzenlager Almwirtschaft Fallershein**, run by friendly Kerle Erwin (80 AS per person with breakfast; open, weather permitting, May-November; 27 very cheap beds in a very simple loft dorm, meager plumbing, good inexpensive meals; 6671 Weissenbach 119a, b/Reutte; tel. 05678/5142, rarely answered, and then not in English). Crowded only on weekends. Fallershein is at the end of a miserable 2-kilometer fit-for-jeep-or-rental-car-only gravel road that looks more closed than it is, near Namlos on the Berwang road southwest of Reutte. To avoid cow damage, park 300 meters below the village at the tiny lot before the bridge.

Sleeping in Reutte (11 AS = about $1, zip code: 6600, tel. code: 05672)

Austria's Tirol is easier and cheaper than touristy Bavaria. The town of Reutte, just over the border, is my home base for the area. I choose it because it's not so crowded in peak season, because of the easygoing locals' contagious love of life, because I like Austria's ambience, and out of habit.

The Reutte tourist office (a block in front of the train station; open weekdays 8:30-12:00 and 13:00-17:00 or 18:00, Saturday 8:00-12:00 and, from mid-July to mid-August on Saturday and Sunday afternoons from 16:00-18:00; tel. 05672/2336, or, direct and cheap from Germany, 0043-5672/2336) is very helpful. Go over your sightseeing plans, ask about a folk evening, pick up a city map, ask about discounts with the hotel guest cards. Reutte has no laundromat.

Youth Hostels: Reutte has plenty of reasonable hotels and Zimmer and two excellent little youth hostels. If you've never hosteled and are curious, try one of these. They accept old people and non-members. The down-town hostel doesn't have much personality, but it's clean and rarely full. It serves no meals but has a fine members' kitchen (70 AS per bed; a pleasant 10-minute walk from the town center, follow the Jugendherberge signs to the Kindergarten sign, 6600 Reutte, Prof. Dengelstr. 20, Tirol, open mid-June to late August, tel. 3039).

The **Jugendgastehaus Graben** (120-AS beds with breakfast; A-6600 Reutte-Höfen, Postfach 3, Graben 1, from downtown Reutte, cross the bridge and follow the road left along the river, about 2 miles from the station, tel. 2644) has two to 12 beds per room and includes breakfast, shower, and sheets. Frau Reyman, who keeps the place traditional, homey, clean, and friendly, serves a great dinner. No curfew, open all year, direct bus connection to Neuschwanstein Castle.

Zimmer: The tourist office has a list of over 50 private homes that rent out generally elegant rooms with facilities down the hall, a pleasant communal living room, and breakfast. Most charge 160 AS per person per night but don't like to rent to people staying less than three nights. Making reservations for a stay of one or two nights is difficult and unnecessary. The TI can always find you a room when you arrive (free).

The tiny village of Breitenwang is a 10-minute walk from the Reutte train station and TI. It's older and quieter than Reutte and seems to have all the best central Zimmer These four places are each very comfortable, quiet, kid-friendly; they accept one-nighters, and are within two blocks of the Breitenwang church steeple (SE-D, EZ-B): **Maria Auer** (a charming woman who rents three lovely 300-AS doubles; Kaiser Lothar Strasse 25, tel. 29195), **Inge Hosp** (a more old-fashioned place with 320-AS doubles, a 190-AS single and antlers over the breakfast table; Kaiser Lothar Strasse 36, tel. 2401), across the street is her cousin **Walter Hosp** (D-320 AS; Kaiser Lothar Strasse 29, tel. 5377), and **Helene Haissl** (D-280 AS; Planseestr. 63, tel. 41504).

Hotels: Reutte is popular with Austrians and Germans who come here year after year for a one- or two-week vacation. The hotels are big, elegant, full of comfy carved furnishings and creative ways to spend so much time in one spot. They take great pride in their restaurants, and the owners send their children away to hotel management schools. Breakfast is included and showers are in the room. Your choices are: right in Reutte, out of town in a nearby village, in a quiet meadow with the cows, or in the forest under the castle. (To call Reutte from Germany, dial 0043-5672 and the four-digit number.)

Hotel Goldener Hirsch, a grand old hotel renovated with a mod Tirolean Jugendstil flair, has sliding automatic doors, mini-bars, TV with cable in the room, and one lonely set of antlers. It's located right downtown (2 blocks from the station). They can help with cheaper rooms if they are full or too expensive. The Goldener Hirsch has a fine and reasonable restaurant (not serving on Mondays). For those without a car, this is by far the most convenient hotel (SB-480 AS, DB-800 AS, CC-VMA, SE-A, EZ-A, 3 minutes' walk; 6600 Reutte-Tirol, tel. 2508 and ask for Helmut or Monika, fax 2508-100).

Hotel Maximilian, just down the river a mile or so in the village of Ehenbichl, is the best splurge. It includes the use of bicycles, sauna, ping-pong, a children's playroom, and the friendly service of the Koch family. Daughter Gabi speaks fine English, and waitresses Isölde, Sonja, and Liliane make meals a treat. There always seems to be a special event here, and if you're lucky, you'll hear the Koch family make music, an Edelweiss experience. American guests are made to feel right at home (DB-840 AS, cheaper bigger rooms, CC-VMA, SE-A, far from the train station in the next village but they may pick you up; A-6600 Ehenbichl-Reutte, tel. 2585, fax 2585-54).

Gasthof Schluxenhof gets the "remote old hotel in an idyllic setting" award (SB-380 AS, DB-600 AS, TB-800 AS, modern rustic elegance, buffet breakfast; Family Gstir, A-6600 Pinswang-Reutte, follow the tiny road after the border crossing just before the bridge to Unterpinswang, tel. 05677/8452, fax 845223, brother-in-law Frank speaks English). This refurbished 260-year-old lodge, filled with locals, just off the main road near the village of Pinswang north of Reutte, is a great place for kids—yours and the Gstir grandchildren. Schluxen is the trailhead for an hour's hike over the mountain to Neuschwanstein Castle.

Gasthof-Pension Waldrast (550-650 AS per double; 6600 Ehenbichl, on Ehrenbergstr., a half-mile out of town toward Innsbruck, past the campground, just under the castle, tel. 05672/2443) separates a forest and a meadow and is warmly run by the Huter family. It has big rooms, like living rooms, many with a fine castle view, and it's a good coffee stop if you're hiking into town from the Ehrenberg ruins.

Eating in Reutte

Each of the hotels takes great pleasure in serving fine Austrian food at reasonable prices. Rather than go to a cheap restaurant, I'd order low on their menu. For cheap food, the **Prima** self-serve cafeteria near the station (Mühler Strasse 20; 9:00-19:00, Monday-Friday) and the **Metzgerei Storf Imbiss** (better but open only Monday-Friday 8:30-15:00) above the deli across from the Heimat-museum on Untermarkt Street are the best in town.

Sleeping in Füssen, Germany (1.6 DM = about $1, zip code: 87629, tel. code: 08362)

Füssen, 2 miles from Ludwig's castles, is a cobbled, crenelated, riverside oompah treat but very touristy. It has just about as many rooms as tourists, though. Its tourist office with a free room-finding service is two blocks past the train station (look for *Kurverwaltung*, 8:00-12:00, 14:00-18:00, Saturday 10:00-12:00, 14:00-16:00, Sunday 10:00-12:00, closed off-season weekends, tel. 08362/7077 or 7078, fax 39181). I prefer Reutte, but without your own car, this is a handier home base. (Füssen station to Reutte taxi costs 35 DM.)

All places listed here speak some English and are an easy walk from the train station and the town center. They assured me they are used to travelers getting in after the Romantic Road bus arrives (20:00) and will hold rooms for a telephone promise.

The excellent Germanly run **Füssen youth hostel** (4- to 6-bed rooms, 17 DM for B&B, 7 DM for dinner, 5 DM for sheets, 26 is maximum age, laundry and kitchen facilities; Mariahilferstr. 5, tel. 7754) is a 10-minute walk from town, backtracking from the station. You might rent a bike at the station to get there quick and easy.

Zimmer: Haus Peters (DB-70 DM, QB-112 DM; Augustenstr. 5½ , tel. 7171), Füssen's best value, is an elegant home just a block from the station (toward town, second left). The Peterses are friendly, speak English, and know what travelers like; there is a peaceful garden, a self-serve kitchen, and a good price. The funky old ornately furnished **Pension Garni Elisabeth** (D-70 DM, DB-90, showers-5 DM; Augustenstr. 10, tel. 6275) in a garden just across the street, exudes a chilling Addams-family friendliness. Floors creak and pianos are never played.

Hotels: Hotel Gasthaus zum Hechten offers all the modern conveniences in a traditional shell right under the Füssen castle in the old town pedestrian zone (D-80 DM, DB-95; Ritterstr. 6, tel. 7906, fax 39841).

Gasthof Krone is a rare bit of pre-glitz Füssen also in the pedestrian zone (dumpy halls and stairs but bright, cheery, comfy rooms: S-50 DM, D-88 DM, T-132 DM, 10 percent less for two-night stays, CC-MA; Schrannenplatz 17, tel. 7824).

Bräustüberl (S-50 DM, SB-65 DM, D-90 DM, QB-150 DM; Rupprechtstr. 5, just a block from the station, tel. 7843, fax 38781) has clean and bright rooms in a rather musty old beer-hall-type place filled with locals who know a good value meal.

Inexpensive farmhouse Zimmer abound in the Bavarian countryside around Neuschwanstein and are a great value. Look for Zimmer Frei signs. The going rate is about 60 DM per double including breakfast; you'll see plenty of green vacancy signs. For a Zimmer in a classic Bavarian home within walking distance of Mad Ludwig's place, try **Haus Magdalena** (D-68 DM, DB-80; Brumme Family, Schwangauerstrasse 11, 8959 Schwangau, tel. 08362/81126, SE-B).

REUTTE TO MUNICH

Today you'll drive past (or ride over) Germany's highest peak, possibly stopping for a little more Bavarian sightseeing and lunch at a monastery that serves the best beer in Deutschland, and then arrive in Munich in time to set up, orient, see the center of Bavaria's leading city, and enjoy some beer hall craziness tonight.

Munich, Germany's most livable city, is also one of its most historic, artistic, and entertaining. It's big and growing, with a population of over 1,500,000. Just a little more than a century ago, it was the capital of an independent Bavaria. Its imperial palaces, jewels, and grand boulevards constantly remind visitors that this was once a political as well as a cultural powerhouse.

Suggested Schedule

8:00	Leave Reutte.
9:00	Ride to the summit of the Zugspitze if time, weather, and budget permit.
11:00	Drive to Andechs for lunch. Be very beerful.
14:30	Arrive in Munich, stop at TI, and check into hotel.
15:30	Explore the heart of town, ride scenic tram #19 (or rental bike) to Max Joseph Platz, tour Cuvillies Theater, see 17:00 Glockenspiel show at Marienplatz, shop, browse, stroll through center, drop into Hofbräuhaus.
20:00	Dinner and evening of oompah fun at a beer hall or garden.
Sleep	Munich.

Transportation: Reutte to Munich (90 miles)
Drivers leave Reutte following Innsbruck/Fernpass signs Exit at Lermoos. Get to the Zugspitzebahn via Ehrwald and Obermoos. Signs direct you through Garmisch-Partenkirchen to the Munich autobahn. If you're stopping in Andechs, catch road #2 after Garmisch for Murnau,

Weilheim, and Starnberg. From Andechs, a small road goes to Munich. Otherwise, autobahn into Munich following signs to Zentrum and then Hauptbahnhof (main train station, near most of my recommended hotels).

By train, Munich is 3 hours from Füssen or Reutte (plenty of departures, one connection each).

Sightseeing Highlights—South of Munich
▲▲**Zugspitze**—The tallest point in Germany is a border crossing. Lifts from Austria and Germany go to the 10,000 foot summit of the Zugspitze. Straddle two great nations while enjoying an incredible view. There are restaurants, shops, and telescopes at the summit. The hour-long trip from Garmisch on the German side costs 55 DM (by direct lift or a combo cogwheel train/cable car ride, tel. 08821/7970). From the less crowded Talstation Obermoos, above the Austrian village of Erwald, the new tram zips you to the top in only ten minutes and costs about $5 less (335 AS). The German ascent is easier for those without a car. But buses do connect Erwald village and the Austrian lift twice an hour.

▲▲**Andechs**—A fine baroque church in a Bavarian setting at a monastery that serves hearty food and the best beer in Germany in a carnival atmosphere full of partying locals? That's the Andechs Monastery, crouching quietly with a big smile between two lakes just south of Munich. Come ready to eat chunks of tender pork chain-sawed especially for you, huge and soft pretzels (best I've had), spiraled white radishes, savory sauerkraut, and Andecher monk-made beer that would almost make celibacy tolerable. Everything is served in medieval proportions; two people can split a meal. Great picnic center, too. Open daily 9:00 to 21:00, first-class view, second-class prices (tel. 08807/1048).

To reach Andechs from Munich without a car, take the S-5 train to Herrsching and walk two miles or catch the bus from there

Munich
See Day 6

MUNICH

Spend all day immersed in the art and history of this cultural hub of Germany and then come up for a big breath of good living. With less than two days to see Bavaria's exciting capital, you'll need to be selective and plan carefully. Today will include a mountain of baroque razzle-dazzle, crown jewels, great art, and *Biergarten* fun.

Suggested Schedule

8:00	Breakfast. Consider renting a bike for the day.
9:00	Münchner Stadtmuseum, photo fun at Viktualien Market.
11:00	Tour Residenz and Schatzkammer.
12:30	Picnic in Hofgarten or Viktualien Market (buy picnic here or at Alois Dallmayr). Walk to Alte Pinakothek.
13:30	Alte Pinakothek.
15:30	Free time (modern art or Deutsches Museum).
17:30	If sunny, stroll through Englischer Garten, early dinner or a drink at the Chinese Pagoda.

Note: museums are closed on Monday.

Munich Orientation, Information, Transit

Munich is big—Germany's third-largest city, after Berlin and Hamburg—and growing fast, but nearly all the sights (and my recommended hotels) are within about a 20-minute walk of Marienplatz. Its excellent tourist information office and sleek subway system make life easy for the millions of visitors who come to town each year.

Take full advantage of the TI office in the train station (Monday-Saturday 8:00-20:00, Sundays 11:00-20:00, tel. 089/2391-256 or 257, near street exit at track 11). Have a list of questions ready, confirm your sightseeing plans, and pick up brochures: free city map, subway map; consider buying the 2-DM "Monatsprogram" for a German-language list of sights and calendar of events or the "Young People's Guide" (1 DM, in English, good regard-

less of your age). They have a room-finding service (5 DM).
If the line is worse than your questions are important, skip
your questions, go directly to the cash window and pick up
the map and other brochures. The TI city map, with a
handy downtown inset, is Europe's best. Use it.

The industrious, eager-to-help **EurAide** office (halfway
to the Bahnhof Mission, down track 11, daily May-early
October, 7:30-11:30, 13:00-18:00, closes at 16:30 in May,
089/593889, fax 550-3965) is an American whirlpool of
travel information ideal for Eurailers and budget travelers.
Alan Wissenberg and his staff know your train travel and
accommodations questions and have answers in clear
American English. The German rail company pays them
to help you design your best train travels and you pay
them 6 DM to find the cheapest available rooms in and
around Munich. They also have Dachau and King Ludwig
tours (frustrating without a car), advice on cheap money
changing, transit tickets, a new "Czech Prague Out" train
pass (convenient for Prague-bound Eurailers), and a free
newsletter.

At the other end of the station, near track 30, is **Radius Touristik** (daily, 10:00-18:00, May through mid-October, tel. 596113, run by Englishman Patrick Holder) which rents three-speed bikes (5 DM/hour, 20 DM/day, 25 DM/24 hours, 40 DM/48 hours) and organizes introduction walks of old Munich (14 DM, almost daily, starting at the station at 10:30, getting to Marienplatz for the noon Glockenspiel performance, and finishing at the Viktualien Market in time for lunch). Patrick dispenses all the necessary tourist information (city map, bike routes) and sells *Munich Found* (a good English monthly for English-speaking residents of Munich). Munich—level, compact, with plenty of bike paths—feels good on two wheels. For a quick orientation in the station, use the big wall maps of the train station, Munich, and Bavaria (through the center doorway as you leave the tracks on the left). For a quick rest stop, the Burger King upstairs has toilets as pleasant and accessible as its hamburgers. Sussmann's Internationale Presse (across from track 24) is great for English language books, papers, and magazines including *Munich Found.*

The great Munich tram, bus, and subway system is a sight in itself. Subways are called U- or S-bahns. Eurail passes are good on the S-bahn (actually an underground-while-in-the-city commuter railway). The fares are complicated, and four rides will cost you the same as the 10-DM, "all-day-after-9:00-a.m." pass. Get a pass, validate it in a machine, and you have Munich by the rail for a day (purchase at tourist offices, subway booths, and in machines at most stops). The entire system (bus/tram/subway) works on the same tickets. Taxis are expensive and needless.

The tourist's Munich is circled by a ring road (which was the town wall) marked by four old gates: Karlstor (near the train station), Sendlinger Tor, Isartor (near the river), and Odeonsplatz. Marienplatz is the city center. A great pedestrian-only street cuts this circle in half, running nearly from Karlstor and the train station through Marienplatz to Isartor. Orient yourself along this east-west axis. Most sights are within a few blocks of this people-filled walk.

You'll find Munich's architecture a bit sterile, as most of its historic center was destroyed in World War II and rebuilt in the lean years that followed. Most Munich sights are closed on Monday. Telephone code: 089.

Sightseeing Highlights—Munich
▲▲**Marienplatz and the Pedestrian Zone**—The essence of Munich will slap you in the smile as the escalator takes you out of the underground system and into the sunlit Marienplatz (Mary's Place). Surrounding you is the glory of Munich: great buildings bombed flat and rebuilt, the ornate facades of the new and old City Halls (the Neues Rathaus, built in neo-Gothic style from 1867 to 1910, and the Altes Rathaus), outdoor cafés, and people bustling and lingering like the birds and breeze they share this square with. From here the pedestrian mall (Kaufingerstrasse and Neuhauserstrasse) leads you through a great shopping area past plenty of entertaining street singers, the twin-towering Frauenkirche (built in 1470, rebuilt after World War II), and several fountains, to Karlstor and the train station. The not-very-old Glockenspiel "jousts" on Marienplatz daily through the tourist season at 11:00, 12:00, 17:00, and a shorty at 21:00 (If you liked the Rothenburg Meistertrunk show, you'll love this one!)

▲▲**City Views:** Neues Rathaus (2 DM, elevator from under the Marienplatz Glockenspiel, Monday-Thursday 9:00-16:00, Friday 9:00-13:00). For a totally unobstructed view, but with no elevator, I prefer the St. Peter's church tower just a block away. It's a long climb, much of it with two-way traffic on a one-way staircase, but the view is dynamite (2.50 DM, 9:00-18:00, Sunday 10:00-18:00). Try to be two flights from the top when the bells ring at the top of the hour (and when your friends ask you about your trip, you'll say, "What?"). The highest viewpoint is from a 350-foot-high perch on top of the Frauenkirche (elevator, 4 DM, 10:00-17:00, closed Sunday).

▲▲**Residenz**—For a long hike through rebuilt corridors of gilded imperial Bavarian grandeur, tour the family palace of the Wittelsbachs who ruled Bavaria for more

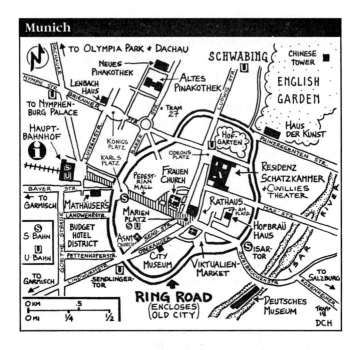

than 700 years (10:00-16:30, closed Monday, 4 DM, enter on Max-Joseph Platz, 3 blocks from Marienplatz). The **Schatzkammer** (treasury) shows off a thousand years of Wittelsbach crowns and knickknacks (same hours, another 4 DM from the same window). You'll see better in Vienna, but this is Bavaria's best.

▲**The Cuvillies Theater**—Attached to the Residenz, this National Theater, designed by Cuvillies, is dazzling enough to send you back to the days of the divine monarchs (Tuesday-Saturday 14:00-17:00, Sunday 10:00-17:00, 3 DM).

▲▲**Münchner Stadtmuseum**—The underrated Munich city museum is a pleasant surprise—great old photography exhibit, life in Munich through the centuries, historic puppets, the story of beer, a huge collection of musical instruments from around the world, and a changing collection of living rooms from 1700 to 1930, often with some fine Jugendstil art. No crowds, bored and playful guards (Tuesday-Saturday 10:00-17:00, Wednesday until

20:30, Sunday 10:00-18:00, closed Monday, 5 DM, free on
Sunday; three blocks off Marienplatz at St. Jakob's Platz 1).
▲▲▲**Alte Pinakothek**—Bavaria's best collection of art is
stored in a pleasing, easy-to-handle museum, strong on
Italian and North European artists, such as Rubens and
Dürer. This, along with Vienna's Kunsthistorisches
Museum, is your best chance to see great European mas-
terpieces on this tour. Spend two hours enjoying a collection that took the Wittelsbach family 400 years to amass
(9:15-16:30, 19:00-21:00 on Tuesday and Thursday, closed
Monday, 6 DM, free on Sunday; U-2 to Königsplatz or
tram #27, tel. 23805-215; friendly sales pitch: self-guided
tours of this museum and Vienna's are among the twenty
included in my *Mona Winks* guidebook).
▲**Haus der Kunst**—Built by Hitler as a temple of Nazi
art, this bold and fascist building now houses modern art,
much of which the Führer censored. It's a fun collection—
Kandinsky, Picasso, Dali, and much more from this century
(9:00-16:30, Thursday evenings 19:00-21:00, closed
Monday, 3.50 DM).
Bayerisches Nationalmuseum—An interesting collection
of Riemenschneider carvings, manger scenes, traditional
living rooms, and old Bavarian houses (9:30-17:00, closed
Monday, 5 DM, free on Sunday; tram #20 or bus 53 or 55
to Prinzregentenstrasse 3).
▲▲**Deutsches Museum**—Germany's answer to our
Smithsonian Institution has everything of scientific and
technical interest from astronomy to zymurgy but can be
disappointing because of its overwhelming size and lack
of English descriptions (there is an English guidebook).
With 10 miles of exhibits, even those on roller skates will
need to be selective. Technical types enjoy lots of hands-
on gadgetry, a state-of-the-art planetarium and an IMAX
theater (Self-serve cafeteria, museum open daily 9:00-
17:00, 8 DM admission; S-Bahn to Isartorplatz).
Schwabing—Munich's artsy, bohemian university district
or "Greenwich Village" has been called "not a place but a
state of mind." All I experienced was a mental lapse. The
bohemians run the boutiques. I think the most colorful
thing about Schwabing is the road leading back down-

town. U-3 or U-6 will take you to the Münchener-Freiheit
Center if you want to wander. Most of the jazz and disco
joints are near Occamstrasse. The Haidhausen neighborhood (U-bahn: Max Weber Platz) is becoming the "new
Schwabing."

▲**Englischer Garten**—One of Europe's great parks,
Munich's "Central Park" is the Continent's largest, laid out
in 1789 by an American. Bike rentals are at the south
entrance, and there's a huge beer garden near the Chinese
Pagoda. Caution: the place is sprinkled with nude sun-
bathers (although a new law requires them to wear
clothes . . . on the tram). A rewarding respite from the
city, especially fun on a bike under the summer sun.

Asam Church—Near the Stadtmuseum, this private
church of the Asam brothers shows off their very popular
baroque-concentrate style. If you missed (or loved) the
Wies Church, visit the gooey drippy masterpiece by
Bavaria's top two rococonuts.

The Centre of Unusual Museums is a collection of
mediocre but occasionally interesting one-room museums
featuring goofy topics such as padlocks, Easter bunnies,
chamber pots, and so on (daily 10:00-18:00; near
Marienplatz and Isartor at Westenriederstr. 26; not worth
the 8 DM).

▲**Olympic Grounds**—Munich's great 1972 Olympic sta-
dium and sports complex is now a lush park offering a
tower (commanding but boring view from 820 feet, 8:00-
24:00, 5 DM), an excellent swimming pool (7:00-22:30,
Monday from 10:00, Thursday closed at 18:00, 5 DM), a
good look at its striking "cobweb" style of architecture,
and plenty of sun, grass, and picnic potential. Take U-3 or
U-2 to Olympiazentrum.

BMW Museum—The BMW headquarters, located in a
striking building across the street from the Olympic
Grounds, offers free factory tours (normally one a day in
English) and a 5 DM museum (tel. 389-53307, closed
much of August). The museum is popular with car buffs

**Organized bus tours of the city and nearby country-
side**—Panorama Tours (at the station, tel. 591504) offers
all-day tours of Neuschwanstein and Linderhof (68 DM)

and 1-hour city orientation bus tours (at 10:00, 11:30, and 14:30, 15 DM). EurAide does a train/bus Neuschwanstein-Linderhof-Wies Church day tour (transportation only, 70 DM, 54 DM with a train pass). Renate Suerbaum (tel. 283374, 130 DM tours) is a good local guide.

▲▲**Nymphenburg Palace**—This royal summer palace is impressive, but if you've already seen the Residenz, it's only mediocre. If you do tour it, don't miss King Ludwig's "Gallery of Beauties"—a room stacked with portraits of Bavaria's loveliest women—according to Ludwig (who had a thing about big noses). The palace park, good for a royal stroll, contains the tiny Amalienburg Palace, a rococo jewel of a hunting lodge by Cuvillies. The sleigh and coach collection (Marstallmuseum) is especially interesting for "Mad" Ludwig fans (10:00-12:30 and 13:30-16:00, closed Monday, shorter hours October-March, admission 5 DM, use the little English guidebook, tel. 179080, reasonable cafeteria; S-bahn to Laim, then bus 41 or 68 or walk).

▲▲**Dachau**—Since you'll visit the even more powerful Mauthausen concentration camp, I haven't worked Dachau into the schedule. But if you won't be going to Mauthausen on your way to Vienna, visit Dachau. Dachau was the first Nazi concentration camp (1933). Today it's the most accessible camp to travelers and a very effective voice from our recent but grisly past, warning and pleading "Never Again," the memorial's theme. This is a valuable experience and when approached thoughtfully, well worth the trouble. In fact, it may change your life. See it. Feel it. Read and think about it. After this most powerful sightseeing experience, many people gain more respect for history and the dangers of not keeping tabs on their government.

On arrival, pick up the mini-guide and note when the next documentary film in English will be shown (25 minutes, normally at 11:30 and 15:30). The museum and the movie are exceptional. Notice the Expressionist fascist-inspired art near the theater, where you'll also find English books, slides, and a WC. Outside, be sure to see the reconstructed barracks and the memorial shrines at the far end (9:00-17:00, closed Monday; S-bahn 2, direction

Petershausen, to Dachau, then bus 722, Dachau-Ost, from
the station to "Gedenkstätte.") If you're driving, follow
Dachauerstrasse from downtown Munich. If lost, signs to
Augsburg will lead to signs to Dachau. Then follow the
KZ-Gedenkstätte signs. (Note: Dachau is easier than
Mauthausen for train travelers. Transportation instruction
sheet at the Munich TI. Guided walks from EurAide.) The
town of Dachau (TI tel. 08131/84566) is more pleasant
than its unfortunate image.

Oktoberfest
When King Ludwig I had a marriage party in 1810 it was
such a success that they made it an annual bash. These
days the Oktoberfest starts on the third Saturday in
September with an opening parade of more than 6,000
participants and fills eight huge beer tents with about
6,000 people each. Sixteen days and a million gallons of
beer later, they roast the last ox.

While you can always find a festival in Munich's beer
halls, the entire city celebrates each fall with this mother
of all keggers. It's crowded, but if you arrive in the morning (except Friday or Saturday), the TI will be able to find
you a room.

The fairgrounds known as the Wies'n (a few blocks
from the station) erupts in a frenzy of rides, dancing,
strangers strolling arm-in-arm down rows of picnic tables,
while the beer god stirs tons of beer, pretzels, and wurst
in a bubbling caldron of fun. The "three loops" roller
coaster must be the wildest on earth (do it before the beer
drinking). During the fair, the city functions even better
than normal, and it's a good time to sightsee even if beer
hall rowdiness isn't your cup of tea. The Fasching carnival
time (early January to mid-February) is nearly as crazy.

**Sleeping in Munich (1.6 DM = about US$1, tel. code:
089)**
There are no cheap beds in Munich. Youth hostels strictly
enforce their 26-year-old age limit, and side-tripping in is
a bad value. But there are plenty of decent, moderately
priced rooms, most located within a few blocks of the

Hauptbahnhof (central train station). August, September, and early October are most crowded, but conventions can clog the city on any day. Call ahead and reserve one of the places I've listed below. Receptionists usually speak English, know what's available by 9:00, and will hold a room for your arrival later that day. Otherwise, use the TI.

Budget hotels, offering 80- to 90-DM doubles with breakfast, no elevator, and a shower down the hall, cluster in the area immediately south of the station. It's seedy after dark (erotic cinemas, bar-nacles with lingerie tongues, men with moustaches in the shadows) but dangerous only to those in search of trouble. Still, I've listed places in more polite neighborhoods, generally a 5- or 10-minute walk from the station and handy to the center. Those farthest from the station are most pleasant. There are some very bad values to be had if you (or the TI) just choose one out of the blue. I've listed places in order of closeness to the station. All prices include breakfast.

Jugendhotel Marienherberge (S-32 DM, 27 DM per bed in 2- to 6-bed rooms, open 8:00-24:00; a block from the station at Goethestr. 9, tel. 555891, SE-C) is a pleasant, friendly convent accepting young women only (loosely enforced 25-year age limit). If you qualify, sleep here (and reserve by phone in advance).

Hotel Gebhardt (D-95 DM, DB-120 DM, T-120 DM, TB-160 DM, Q-150 DM, QB-170 DM, CC-VMA, SE-A; Goethestr. 38, Munich, four blocks from the station, tel 539446, fax 53982663) offers a decent combination of neighborhood, comfort, and price surrounded by cold institutional hotel plastic and plaster.

YMCA (CVJM), open to people of all ages and sexes (D-80 DM, T-108 DM, a bed in a shared triple-36 DM; Landwehrstr. 13, 80336 Munich, has an elevator, SE-A, tel 5521410, fax 5504282), has modern, simple rooms and cheap dinners (served 18:00-21:00, Tuesday-Friday).

Hotel Pension Erika (D-70 DM, DB-95 DM, TB-120 DM, CC-VMA; Landwehrstr. 8, tel. 554327) is skinny, squeaky, and as bright as dingy yellow can be. Its cheap doubles are a rare value.

Hotel Pension Luna (D-95 DM, DB-110 DM, T-125 DM, TB-140 DM, CC-VMA, SE-B, lots of stairs; 5 Land-wehrstrasse, tel. 597833, fax 523 2561) employs a loving touch to give a dumpy building quiet, bright, and cheery rooms.

Hotel Pension Zöllner (small twin-85 DM, big double-95 DM, DB-104 DM; near Karlstor at Sonnenstr. 10, tel. 554035, front rooms may be noisy) is plain, clean, and concrete on the big ring road between the station and the old center.

Hotel Pension Utzelmann (S-50 DM, D-90 DM, DB-110 DM, T-120 DM, TB-150 DM; Pettenkoferstr. 6, tel 594889) has huge rooms, especially the curiously cheap room 6. Each lacey room is richly furnished. It's in an extremely decent neighborhood a 10-minute walk from the station, a block off Sendlinger Tor. Easy parking.

Hotel Uhland (DB-150, more during Octoberfest and festivals, TB-180 DM, all with WC, CC-VMA, EZ-A, SE-A, reserve with CC #, huge breakfast; 1 Uhlandstr., 80336 Munich, near the Theresienwiese Oktoberfest grounds, 10-minute walk from the station, tel. 539277, fax 531114), a mansion with sliding glass doors and a garden, is a worth-while splurge. Easy parking.

Pension Mariandl (D-95 DM, CC-VMA, 42 DM per person in larger rooms, prices inflate during festivals; Goethestr. 51, tel. 534108, SE-B, will hold rooms until 18:00) is an uppity place in an old, formerly elegant mansion with peeling vinyl floors, weak lights, and yellow corridors. The rooms are basic but fine, the neighborhood is peaceful and residential, and the classy dining hall plays free classical music Monday through Friday with dinner.

Pension Diana (D-98 DM, T-132 DM, Q-172, CC-VA, SE-C; Altheimer Eck 15, tel. 2603107, fax 263934, run by Mr. Geza Szabo, a Hungarian), 70 steps up and no eleva-tor, 17 bright and airy doubles, and two power showers, is an environment perfect for retired and married nuns. In the old center, a block off the pedestrian mall (through the green "Arcade").

Pension Linder (S-55 DM, D-95 DM, DB-120 DM; Dultstr. 1—just off Sendlinger Strasse, 80331 Munich, tel

263413, Marion Sinzinger SE-D) is clean, quiet, modern, with pastel bouquet rooms hiding behind a concrete stairway. Along with the Diana, the most central of my listings, it's across the street from the city museum, a few blocks from Marienplatz.

Hostels: Munich's youth hostels charge 20 to 25 DM with sheets and breakfast and strictly limit admission to YH members who are under 27. The **Burg Schwaneck hostel** (30 minutes from the center, S-bahn to Pullach, then walk 10 minutes to Burgweg 4, tel. 7930643) is a renovated castle. Other hostels are at Miesingstrassse 4 (U-bahn: Thalkirchen, tel. 7236560) and Wendl-Dietrichstr. 20 (U-bahn to Rothreuzplatz, tel. 131156, theft problem)

"The Tent," Munich's **International Youth Camp Kapuzinerhölzl**, offers up to 400 places on the wooden floor of a huge circus tent with a mattress, blankets, good showers, and free tea in the morning for 6 DM to anyone under 25 (flexible). It's a fun experience—kind of a cross between Woodstock (if anyone under 24 knows what that was) and a slumber party. Call 1414300 (recorded message before 17:00) before heading out to it. No curfew. Cool ping-pong-and-frisbee atmosphere throughout the day. Take U-bahn 1 to Rotkreuzplatz, catch tram #12 to Botanischer Garten (direction Amalienburgstrasse), and follow the youthful crowd down Franz-Schrank-strasse to the big tent. This is near the Nymphenburg Palace. Open late June through August. There is a theft problem, so sleep on your bag or leave it at the station.

Eating in Munich

Munich's most memorable budget food is in the beer halls. You have two basic choices: famous touristy places with music or mellower beer gardens with Germans. The touristy ones have great beer, reasonable food, live music and are right downtown. These days Germans go there for the entertainment—to sing "Country Roads," see how Texas girls party, and watch salarymen from Tokyo chug beer. The music-every-night atmosphere is thick; the fat and shiny-leather band has even church mice standing up and conducting three-quarter time with a breadstick.

Meals are inexpensive (for a light 9-DM meal, I like the
local favorite, Schweinswurst and Kraut); huge, liter beers
called *ein Mass* (or "ein pitcher" in English) are 9 DM;
white radishes are salted and cut in delicate spirals; and
surly beer-maids pull mustard packets from their cleavages.
You can order your beer "*Helles*" (light, what you'll get if
you say "ein beer"), "*Dunkle*" (dark) or "*Radler*" (half
lemonade, half light beer). Notice the vomitoriums in the
WC.

The most famous beer hall, the **Hofbräuhaus** (Platzl 9,
near Marienplatz, tel. 221676, music for lunch and dinner),
is most touristy. But check it out; it's fun to see 200
Japanese people drinking beer in a German beer hall.
(They have a gimmicky folk evening upstairs in the
"Festsaal" nightly at 20:00, 8 DM, tel. 290136-10, food and
drinks are sold from the same menu.) My long-time
favorite, **Mathäser Bierstadt** (tel. 592896, Bayerstrasse 5,
halfway between the train station and Karlstor, music after
17:00) has joined the Hofbräuhaus as the tour-group beer
hall. For typical Bavarian fast food try the self-serve at
Mathäser's entry.

The **Weisses Bräuhaus** (Tal 10, between Marienplatz
and Isartor) is more local and features the local fizzy
"wheat beer." Hitler met with fellow fascists here in 1920
when his Nazi party had yet to ferment. The **Augustiner
Beer Garden** (across from the train tracks, three blocks
from the station away from the center on Arnulfstrasse) is
a sprawling haven for local beer-lovers on a balmy
evening. Upstairs in the tiny **Jodlerwirt** (4 Altenhof-
strasse, between the Hofbräuhaus and Marienplatz, after
19:00, closed Sunday) is a woodsy, smart-aleck, yodeling
kind of pub. For a classier evening stewed in antlers, eat
under a tree or inside at the **Nürnberger Bratwurst
Glöckl am Dom** (Frauenplatz 9, under the twin-domed
cathedral, tel. 22 03 85, closed Sunday).

For outdoor atmosphere and a cheap meal, spend an
evening at the **Englischer Garten's Chinese Pagoda**
(Chinesischer Turm) **Biergarten**. You're welcome to BYO
food and grab a table or buy from the picnic stall
(*Brotzeit*) right there. Don't bother to phone ahead: there

are six thousand seats! For similar BYOF atmosphere right behind Mairienplatz, eat at the Viktualien market's beer garden. Lunch or dinner here taps you into the about the best budget eating in town. Countless stalls surround the beer garden selling wurst, sandwiches, produce, and so on.

The classiest picnic of the tour can be purchased in the historic, elegant, and expensive **Alois Dallmayr** delicatessen at 14 Dienerstrasse just behind the Rathaus (9:00-18:30, Saturday 9:00-14:00, closed Sunday). Wander through this dieter's purgatory, put together a royal picnic, and eat it in the nearby, adequately royal Hofgarten. To save money, browse at Dallmayr's, but buy in the basement of the Kaufhof across Marienplatz.

MUNICH TO SALZBURG

After some last sightseeing or exploring in Munich, you'll take the autobahn two hours south back into Austria, setting up in Salzburg by mid-afternoon. Today's sightseeing plan is flexible. There are four major sights. You can pick two—the Nymphenburg Palace and the Deutsches Museum in Munich (see Sightseeing, Day 6) or the Berchtesgaden Salt Mines and the Hellbrunn Castle near Salzburg. Speedsters with a car and enough coffee could do three, but I'd rather do two and get comfortably set up to take a rest before a hopefully music-filled Salzburg evening.

Suggested Schedule	
9:00	Check out of hotel. Tour Nymphenburg Palace or the Deutsches Museum.
11:30	Drive south, picnicking at Chiemsee rest stop.
14:00	Tour the Berchtesgaden Salt Mines or the Hellbrunn Castle.
17:00	Arrive in Salzburg, visit TI, check into hotel.
19:30	Stroll through gardens to Augustiner Keller (wild) or St. Peter's Keller (subdued) for dinner, with a floodlit city-from-the-bridge view for dessert.
22:00	Wander the streets of old Salzburg.

Transportation: Munich to Salzburg (100 miles)
From the train station, Bayerstrasse leads to autobahn signs to Salzburg. You'll pass Chiemsee on your left. (Ludwig's third castle, Schloss Herrenchiemsee, is on the island in the lake. Boats go from Prien.)

After crossing the border, stay on the autobahn, taking the Süd Salzburg exit in the direction of Anif. This road leads you north into town, passing first the Schloss (and zoo) Hellbrunn and then the TI and a great park-and-ride service. Get sightseeing information and a 24-hour bus ticket from the TI (9:00-20:00 daily), park your car (free) and catch the shuttle bus (every 5 minutes) into town. Mozart never drove in the old town, and neither should you. If you don't believe in P&R, the easiest, cheapest, and most central parking lot is the giant 1,500-car Altstadt lot in the tunnel under the Mönchsberg (150 AS per day). Your hotel may have parking passes.

By train, it's an easy 90-minute shot to Salzburg. Use the Salzburg station TI. Hellbrunn buses go twice an hour (bus 55, buy the 24-hour pass, 20-minute ride). Berchtesgaden is a direct train ride from Munich with an easy, scenic, and more-direct-than-train bus connection into Salzburg.

Sightseeing Highlights on the Road to Salzburg

▲**Hitler's First Autobahn Rest Stop**—At Chiemsee you can see the first autobahn rest stop. It was built during Hitler's rule and still has its *Deutschland über alles* frescoes. It's now an American armed forces recreation center and hotel. Drop in for a glimpse at how the other half lives.

Take the Felden exit off the Munich-Salzburg autobahn, cross over the autobahn, follow the winding road between the freeway and the lake for half a mile, past the campground into U.S. military land, to a large lakeside hotel. Enter near the pillars where the sign says "AFRC Chiemsee hotel check-in." A plaque outside the door tells the Nazi history, and a friendly receptionist inside will direct you past the cafeteria to the large dining hall with its 1938 murals depicting good hardworking Nazis from every walk of life.

Homesick Yankees are welcome to use the cafeteria (three meals every day, cheap, dollars or marks) and U.S. mail service there. Pick up a free Salzburg tourist map and stamps at the postcard shop. Any taxpayer is welcome to eat and hang around, but you've got to be a military taxpayer to sleep there.

▲**Berchtesgaden**—This Alpine resort just across the German border flaunts its attractions very effectively, and you may find yourself in a traffic jam of desperate tourists looking for ways to turn their money into fun. From the

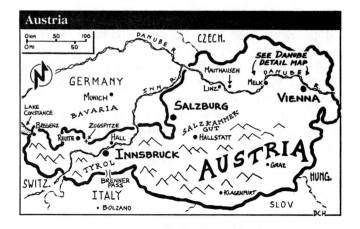

station and the helpful TI (tel. 08652/5011), buses go to the idyllic Königsee (2-hour scenic cruises, four per hour, stopovers anywhere, 16 DM, tel. 08652/4026) and the salt mines (a 30-minute walk otherwise).

The salt mines are open daily 8:30 to 17:00 (winter, Monday-Friday, 12:30-15:30, tel. 08652/60020). For 15 DM, you put on the traditional miners' outfits, get on funny little trains, and zip deep into the mountain. For 60 minutes you'll cruise subterranean lakes; slide speedily down two long, slick wooden banisters; and learn how they mined salt so long ago. Call for crowd avoidance advice. You can buy a ticket early and browse through the town until your tour time.

Hitler's famous (but overrated) "Eagle's Nest" towered high above Berchtesgaden. Now Kehlstein and Obersalzberg are open to visitors, but little remains of Hitler's Alpine retreat, which he visited only five times. The bus ride up the private road and the lift to the top cost about 22 DM. If the weather's cloudy, as it often is in the morning, you'll Nazi a thing.

Berchtesgaden caters to long-term German guests. During peak season, it's not worth the headaches for the speedy tourist.

Hellbrunn Castle and Other Salzburg Sights
See Day 8.

Austria (Österreich, the Kingdom of the East)

- 32,000 square miles (the size of South Carolina, or two Switzerlands).
- 7.6 million people (235 per square mile and holding, 85 percent Catholic).
- About 11 AS = US$1. Figure a dime each.

During the grand old Habsburg days, Austria was Europe's most powerful empire. Its royalty built a giant kingdom of more than 50 million people by making love, not war (having lots of children and marrying them into the other royal houses of Europe).

Today this small, landlocked country does more to cling to its elegant past than any other in Europe. The waltz is still the rage. Austrians are very sociable; more so than anywhere else, it's important to greet people you pass on the streets or meet in shops. The Austrian's version of "Hi" is a cheerful *Grüss Gott* (may God greet you). You'll get the correct pronunciation after the first volley—listen and copy.

The Austrian schilling (S or AS) is divided into 100 groschen (g). Divide prices by ten to get approximate costs in dollars (e.g., 420 AS is $42). About 7 AS = 1 DM. While merchants and waiters near the border are happy to accept DM, you'll save money if you use schilling. While they speak German, accept German currency (at least in Salzburg, Innsbruck, and Reutte), and talked about unity with Germany long before Hitler ever said "*Anschluss*," the Austrians cherish their distinct cultural and historical traditions. They are not Germans. Austria is mellow and relaxed compared to Deutschland. *Gemütlichkeit* is the local word for this special Austrian cozy-and-easy approach to life. It's good living—whether engulfed in mountain beauty or bathed in lavish high culture. The people stroll as if every day were Sunday, topping things off with a visit to a coffee or pastry shop.

It must be nice to be past your prime—no longer troubled by being powerful, able to kick back and be as happy as St. Francis's birds in the clean, untroubled mountain air. While the Austrians make less money than their neighbors, they enjoy a short work week and a long life span. Austria was a neutral country throughout the cold war. It's now free to get closer to Europe's economic community.

Austrians eat on about the same schedule we do. Treats include *Wiener Schnitzel* (breaded veal cutlet), *Knödel* (dumplings), *Apfelstrudel,* and fancy desserts like the *Sachertorte,* Vienna's famous chocolate cake. Service is included in restaurant bills.

Shops are open from 8:00 to 17:00 or 18:00. Banks keep roughly the same hours but usually close for lunch.

Salzburg Orientation

With a well-preserved old town, gardens, churches, and lush surroundings, set under Europe's biggest intact medieval castle, and forever smiling to the tunes of Mozart and *The Sound of Music,* Salzburg knows how to be popular. Eight million tourists crawl its cobbles each year. That's a lot of Mozart balls.

This city of 150,000 (Austria's fourth largest) is divided into old and new. The old town, sitting between the Salzach River and the 1,600-foot-high hill called Mönchsberg, is a bundle of Baroque holding all the charm and most of the tourists.

Salzburg is served by a fine bus system (info tel. 87 21 45). Single-ride tickets are sold on the bus for 20 AS. Twenty-four-hour passes cost 27 AS. The 24-hour "Ticket 1" pass includes the lifts up to the castle and the Mönchs‚ berg elevator for 52 AS. These are sold at the TI and at local Tabak shops. Salzburg is bike-friendly and the train station rents good bikes all day until midnight for 45 AS (double if you have no train ticket or pass, no deposit required, go to counter #3 to pay, then pick it up at "left luggage").

The helpful tourist office (at the train station, on Mozartplatz in the old center, and on the freeway entrance to the city, tel. 847568 or 88987) is your essential first stop. Ask for the "hotel plan" map, a transit map, a list of sights with current hours, the "Youth in Salzburg" booklet, and a schedule of events. Book a concert upon arrival.

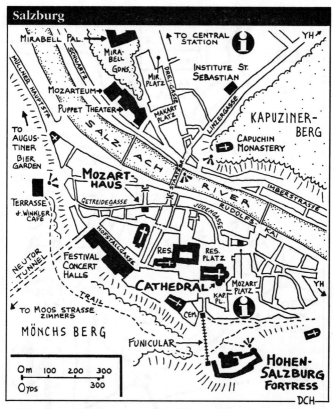

The American Express office (Mozartplatz 5, open
Monday-Friday 9:00-17:30, Saturday 9:00-12:00, tel. 842501)
will hold mail for their check or card users. Salzburg's Old
Town postal code is A-5020. Telephone code: 0662.

Sightseeing Highlights—Salzburg and Beyond
▲**Salzburg Cathedral** (daily 8:00-17:00, free) claims to be
the first baroque building north of the Alps. It's modeled
after St. Peter's and is three-quarters the size of Europe's
biggest church. Back then, the bishop of Salzburg was
number-two man in the Church hierarchy and Salzburg
fancied itself as the "Northern Rome." Check out its 6,000-
pipe organ. Sunday Mass (10:00) is famous for its music.
For a fee you can tour the excavation site under the
church and the Dom Museum in the church.

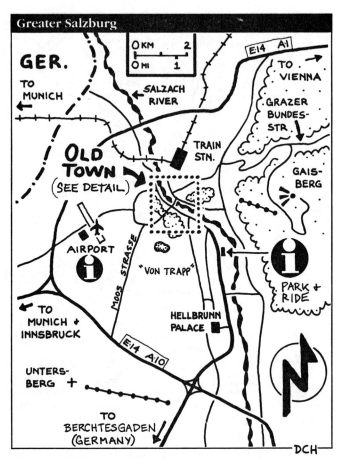

Greater Salzburg

Residenz—It was Archbishop Wolf Dietrich (not Mozart and Julie Andrews) who had the greatest impact on Salzburg. His grandiose vision of Salzburg shaped the city into the Baroque beauty you'll see today. His palace, the Residenz, next to the cathedral is impressive—unless you've seen any others. Admission is by tour only (hourly 10:00-15:00, 40 minutes of German only except in July and August, 40 AS).

▲**Carillon**—The bell tower on Mozartplatz chimes throughout the day. The man behind the bells gives fascinating 20-minute tours daily at 10:45 and 17:45 except in bad weather. You'll actually be up on top among 35 bells as the big barrel turns, the music flies, and you learn what a "dingbat" is. Buy your 20-AS ticket 10 minutes early.

▲**Getreidegasse**—Old Salzburg's lively and colorful main drag, famous for its many old wrought-iron signs, still looks much as it did in Mozart's day.

▲**Mozart's Birthplace (Geburtshaus, 1756)**—Maybe it's just me, but I find that the birthplaces of famous people are usually as dead as they are. But this best Mozart sight in town is almost a pilgrimage, and if you're a fan, you'll have to check it out. It's right in the old town on colorful Getreidegasse, #9 (daily 9:00-19:00, shorter hours off-season, 50 AS).

▲**Hohensalzburg Fortress**—This castle, one of Europe's mightiest, dominates Salzburg's skyline. The interior is so-so unless you catch a tour. Unfortunately, the disorganized castle crew doesn't really know when or if there will be one in English. The basic entry fee (20 AS) gives you only the view and the courtyard. Don't buy the 25-AS museum-and-tour ticket until you know there will be one in English. The museum has the noisiest floorboards in Europe. Even so the prince had a chastity belt. You can see it next to other gruesome torture devices that need no explanation.

Upstairs is a mediocre military museum offering a chance to see photos of nice looking young Nazi officers whose government convinced them that their operation was a just cause.

The funicular zips you effortlessly to the castle (28 AS round-trip, free with transit pass, rides leave constantly). The castle is open daily, 9:00 to 19:00, less in off-season.

▲**Mirabell Gardens and Palace (*Schloss*)**—The bubbly gardens are always open and free, but to properly enjoy the lavish Mirabell Palace, get a ticket to a *Schlosskonzerte*. Baroque music flying around a baroque hall is a happy bird in the right cage. Tickets are around 270 AS (cheaper at the palace and for students) and rarely sold out (tel. 872788).

▲**City Walking Tour**—A great 1-hour guided walking tour of the old town leaves from the TI at Mozartplatz (80 AS, 12:15, Monday-Saturday, May-October, tel. 847568).

While walking on your own, be sure to browse through St. Peter's Cemetery (at the base of the castle lift, tours of early Christian catacombs, this was where the Trapp family hid out in the *S.O.M.*) and through the open-air market on Universitätsplatz.

And for a most enjoyable approach to the castle, consider riding the elevator to the Café Winkler and walking 20 minutes through the woods high above the city to Festung Hohensalzburg (stay on the high trails or you'll have a needless climb back up to the castle).

▲*Sound of Music* **Tour**—I took this tour skeptically (as part of my research chores) and liked it. It includes a quick but good general city tour, stops for a luge ride (in season, fair weather, 25 AS extra), hits all the *S.O.M.* spots (including the stately home, gazebo, and the wedding church), and shows you a lovely stretch of the Salzkammergut.

The Salzburg Panorama Tours Company charges 300 AS for the 4-hour, English-only tour (from Mirabellplatz daily at 9:30 and 14:00, tel. 874029 for a reservation and a free hotel pickup if you like, travelers with this book who buy their ticket at the Mirabellplatz ticket booth get a 10 percent discount on this and any other tour they do). This is worthwhile for *S.O.M.* fans without a car or who won't otherwise be going into the Salzkammergut. Warning: Many think rolling through the Austrian country with 30 Americans singing "Do, a Deer" is pretty schmaltzy. There are several similar and very competitive tour companies which offer every conceivable tour from Salzburg. Hotels have their brochures and push them for a healthy commission.

▲**Hellbrunn Castle**—The attraction here is a garden full of clever trick fountains and the sadistic joy the tour guide gets by soaking his tourists. The archbishop's seventeenth-century palace is not worth a look. His baroque garden, one of the oldest in Europe, is pretty enough, and now features the "I Am 16, Going on 17" gazebo. The burned-out tri-lingual tour guides sound like every night their wives have to remind them "one language is enough" (9:00-18:00 daily, fewer hours off-season, tel. 841696, 50 AS for the 40-minute tour and admission; 3 miles south of Salzburg, bus 55 from downtown). It's a lot of trouble for a few water tricks.

▲▲**Salzburg Festival**—Each summer from late July to the end of August, Salzburg hosts its famous Salzburger Festspiele, founded in 1920 to employ Vienna musicians in the summer. This fun and festive time is crowded, but (except for a few August weekends) there are plenty of beds and tickets available the day of the concert. Salzburg is busy throughout the year with 1,600 classical performances in its palaces and churches annually (ticket office on Mozartplatz; contact the Austrian National Tourist Office in the U.S.A. for specifics on this year's festival schedule and tickets). I have never planned in advance and have enjoyed great concerts with every visit. While you may find folk evenings twice a week in the summer, Innsbruck is better for these.

Sleeping in Salzburg (11 AS = about $1, zip code: 5020, tel. code: 0662)

Finding a room in Salzburg, even during the Music Festival, is usually easy. The tourist offices have pamphlets listing all the pensions, hostels, and private rooms in town. Or, for a couple of dollars, they'll find you an inexpensive bed in a private home in the area of your choice. If you want dorm-style budget alternatives, ask for their list of ten youth hostels and student dorms. Some English is spoken and breakfast is included at all my listings. Most will hold a room with a phone call and more expensive places charge more during July, August, and festivals (as indicated).

Rooms on Linzergasse: The first three listings are on lower Linzergasse, directly across the bridge from Mozartville and a 10-minute walk from the station. Its bustling crowds of shoppers overwhelm the few shy cars that venture on to it.

Institute St. Sebastian (145 AS dorm beds, 380 AS doubles, breakfast is 35 AS extra if served, guests with sheets save 25 AS; Linzergasse 41, enter through arch at #37, tel. 871386 or 882606, reception open 8:00-12:00, 15:00-22:00) is a friendly, clean, historic convent. Mozart's mom is buried in the courtyard, and they usually have rooms available.

Hotel zum Jungen Fuchs (S-220 AS, D-380 AS, T-450, free showers down hall; across from Institute St. Sebastian at Linzergasse 54, tel. 875496), a troglodyte's delight, is wonderfully located in a funky, dumpy old building, very plain but clean, with a tired, elderly management that serves no breakfast and little else.

Hotel Pension Goldene Krone (D-700 to 750 AS, DB-850 to 900 AS, TB-1100 to 1200 AS, EZ-A; Linzergasse 48, tel. 872300) is big, modern, and quiet, with comforts rare in this price range.

Gasthaus Ganslhof (DB-680 to 780, EZ-A; Vogelweiderstr. 6, a 10-minute walk up Linzergasse from the old town, tel. 873853, fax 87385323) is clean, reasonable, central, and comfortable. It's back in the real world, with Motel 6 ambience and a parking lot.

Two plain and decent old places just behind the train station but a 15-minute walk from the sightseeing action on a slightly sleazy street: **Gasthof Jahn** (D-520 to 600 AS, DB-640 to 720 AS, TB-800 to 870 AS; Elisabethstr. 31, tel. 871405) and **Pension Adlerhof** (D-490 to 570 AS, DB-650 to 720 AS, T-740 to 790 AS, TB-890 to 950 AS, public shower is a hike away; Elisabethstr. 25, tel. 875236, fax 8736636, quirky staff).

Places in or above the Old Town
Gasthaus "Zur Goldenen Ente" (DB-900 or 980 AS, 100 AS more in high season, CC-VMA; Goldgasse 10 in the old center, tel. 845622, fax 8456229) is a great splurge if you'd like to sleep in a 600-year-old building above a fine restaurant as central as you can be on a pedestrian street in old Salzburg. Somehow the modern and comfortable rooms fit into this building's medieval-style stone arches and narrow stairs. The breakfast is buffet-big, they give a parking permit for the old town (*Steifgasse*), and hold a room if you leave your credit card number. For dinner, try their roast *Ente* (duck).

Gasthof Hinterbrühl (S-350 AS, D-450 AS, plus optional 50 AS breakfast; on a village-like square just under the castle at Schanzlgasse 12, tel. 846798, SE-C) is a smoky, ramshackle old place with sleepable rooms, a handy location, and not a tourist in sight.

Naturfreundehaus (D-250 AS, 110 AS per person in 4- to 6-bed dorms, 45 AS breakfast, 70 AS dinner with city view; Mönchsberg 19, two minutes from the top of the 21-AS round-trip Mönchsberg elevator, tel. 841729, 23:00 curfew, open May-October) is a local version of a mountaineer's hut. It's a great budget alternative guarded by the chirping birds and snuggled in the remains of a fifteenth-century castle wall overlooking Salzburg with a magnificent old town and mountain view. High above the old town, it's the stone house to the left of the glass Café Winkler.

Youth Hostels: Salzburg has more than its share of hostels (and tourists). The TI has a complete listing (with directions from the station) and there are nearly always beds available. The most fun, handy, and American is **Gottfried's International Youth Hotel** (beds in a double-160 AS, quad-140 AS, or 6- to 8-bed dorm-120 AS include sheets; 5 blocks from the station towards the center at Paracelsusstr. 9, tel. 87 96 49). This impressively run place speaks English first, has cheap meals, lockers, a laundry, tour discounts, no curfew, and welcomes anyone.

Bed and Breakfasts: Salzburg has about 60 homes renting out rooms for around 200 AS per person. These are generally roomy, modern, very comfortable, and come with a good breakfast. Many charge extra for those staying only one or two nights. Off-season, competition is tough and you can consider it a buyer's market. Most are a bus ride from town, but with the cheap 24-hour pass and the frequent service, this shouldn't keep you away. Unsavory Zimmer skimmers lurk at the station. If you have a reservation, ignore them. If you need a place . . . they need a customer. Many places will pick you up at the station.

Brigitte Lenglachner (S-270 AS, bunk bed D-390 AS, D-450 AS, DB-500 AS, T650 AS, two nights minimum; in a chirpy neighborhood a 10-minute walk from the station, cross the pedestrian Pioneer bridge, turn right past park and second left to Scheibenweg 8, tel. 43 80 44) fills her big traditional house with a warm welcome, lots of tourist information, and American tourists.

Moosstrasse, south of Mönchsberg, is lined with
Zimmer. Those farther out are farmhouses. From the station, catch bus 1 and change to bus 60 after you cross the
river. From the old town, it's bus 60. The first three get
lots of Americans and work hard to keep you singing
"The Lonely Goatherd." **Maria Gassner** (D-400 AS, 500
AS, and 600 AS, one night okay; Moosstr. 126-B, tel.
824990, five clean, comfortable rooms in her modern
house, can often pick you up at the station). **Gästehaus
Blobergerhof** (D-400 to 500 AS; Hammerauerstr. 4,
Querstrasse zur Moosstrasse, tel. 830227) is a pleasant
farmhouse run by Inge Keuschnigg. **Frau Kernstock** (D-
440 to 500 AS; further out at Karolingerstr. 29, buses 27
and 77, tel. 827469). **Helga Bankhammer** (D-400 AS;
Moosstr. 77, tel. 830067) offers two rooms in her house
and three in the old but elegant barn.

Eating in Salzburg
Salzburg boasts many inexpensive, fun, and atmospheric
places to eat. My favorites are the big cellars with their
smoky Old World atmosphere, heavy medieval arches,
time-darkened paintings, many antlers, and hearty meals.
These places are famous with visitors but also enjoyed by
the locals.

Gasthaus "Zum Wilder Mann" (enter from
Getreidegasse 20 or Griesgasse 17, tel. 841787, food
served 11:00-21:00) is the place if the weather's bad and
you're in the mood for Hofbräu atmosphere in one small
well-antlered room and a hearty cheap meal at a shared
table, 2 minutes from Mozart's place. For a quick 100-AS
lunch, get the Bauernschmaus, a mountain of dumpling,
kraut, and peasant's meats.

Stieglkeller (50 yards uphill from the lift to the castle,
tel. 84 26 81), a huge, atmospheric institution with several
rustic rooms and outdoor garden seating offering a great
rooftop view of the old town, is an inexpensive way to
get really schnitzeled.

Krimplestätter (Müllner Hauptstr. 31, 10 minutes north
of the old town near the river) employs 500 years of experience serving authentic old Austrian food in its authentic
old Austrian interior or in its cheery garden. For fine food

with a wild finale, eat here and drink at the nearby Augustiner Bräustübl.

Augustiner Bräustübl (Augustinergasse 4, walk through the Mirabellgarten, over the Müllnersteg bridge and ask for "Müllnerbräu," its local nickname, 1,000 seats, open daily 15:00-23:00). This monk-run brewery is so rustic and crude that I hesitate to show my true colors by recommending it, but I must. It's like a Munich beer hall with no music but the volume turned up, a historic setting with beer-sloshed smoke-stained halls, and a pleasant outdoor beer garden serving another fine monastic brew. Local students mix with tourists eating hearty slabs of schnitzel with their fingers or cold meals from the self-serve picnic counter. It'll bring out the barbarian in you. For dessert, enjoy the incomparable floodlit view of old Salzburg from the nearby pedestrian bridge.

Stiftskeller St. Peter (next to St. Peter's church at the foot of Mönchsberg, outdoor and indoor seating, tel. 8412680) has been in business for over a thousand years. It's classier, more central, not too expensive, and your best splurge for traditional Austrian cuisine in medieval sauce. The "Monastery Pot" (hearty soup in a bowl made of dark bread) is cheap and filling. But if you start singing "The hills are alive . . . ," they'll throw you out.

Café Haydn Stube (1 Mirabellplatz at the entry to the Aicherpassage, Monday-Friday 9:30-20:00), run by the local music school, is cheap and very popular with students. The **Mensa Aicherpassage** (hiding in the basement, Monday-Friday, 11:30-14:00) serves even cheaper meals.

Picnics: Classy Salzburg delis serve good, cheap, sit-down lunches on weekdays. Have them make you a sandwich or something hot, toss in a carrot, a piece of fruit, yogurt, and a box of milk and sit at a small table with the local lunch crowd. **Frauenberger** (8:00-14:00, 15:00-18:00, closed Monday and Saturday afternoon and Sunday; across from 16 Linzergasse) is friendly, picnic-ready, and cheap. The University Square, just behind Mozart's house, hosts a bustling produce market daily (except Sunday).

You'll see a mountainous sweet souffle served all over town. The memorable "Salzberger Nockerl" is worth a try.

SALZBURG AND THE SALZKAMMERGUT

Sift through the crowds and enjoy the sights of Salzburg. Then head for *Sound of Music* country—the Salzkammergut Lake District—settling down in the postcard-pretty, fjord-cuddling town of Hallstatt.

Suggested Schedule

8:30	Good morning Salzburg hike from Café Winkler to castle, tour Hohensalzburg.
10:45	Visit the Glockenspiel as it performs.
13:00	Drive into the Lake District.
15:00	Afternoon free in Hallstatt (Eurailers may stay in Salzburg and take 14:00 *Sound of Music* Tour for a look at the lakes).

Sleep in Hallstatt.

Transportation: Salzburg to Hallstatt (50 miles)

Drivers can get advice from their hotel on the best route to St. Gilgen. It may be easiest to get on the Munich-Wein autobahn (blue signs), head for Vienna, exit at Thalgau and follow signs to Hof, Fuschl and St. Gilgen. Soon the "hills are alive," and you're surrounded by the loveliness that has turned on everyone from Emperor Franz Josef to Julie Andrews. To us English-speakers, this is *The Sound of Music* country (alias the Salzkammergut Lake District).

The road to Hallstatt leads first past Fuschlsee (mediocre Sommerrodlebahn summer luge ride, 28 AS, open April to mid-October when dry 10:00-17:00, at Fuschl an See), to St. Gilgen (pleasant but touristy), to Bad Ischl (the center of the Salzkammergut with a spa, salt mine tour, casino, the emperor's villa if you need a Habsburg history fix, and a good tourist office, tel. 06132/3520), and along Hallstattersee to Hallstatt.

Hallstatt is basically traffic-free. Park in the middle of the tunnel at the P-1 sign and waterfall. If this is full, try the lakeside lot (P-2, pleasant 5-minute lakeside walk from town center) just after the tunnel. If you're traveling off-season and staying downtown, you can drive in and park by the boat dock (your hotel "guest card" makes you a temporary resident, giving you permission).

While the Salzkammergut is well-served by trains and buses, Eurailers in a hurry can see it from the window of the *Sound of Music* bus tour (described in Day 7), spend the night in Salzburg again, and take the early train toward Vienna. Those riding the train into the Salzkammergut are well-rewarded. The ride to Hallstatt is gorgeous. *Stefanie* (a boat) meets you at the station and glides across the lake into town (20 AS, with each train). From Hallstatt, Vienna-bound trains get you to Melk on the Danube in 4 hours with one change.

Sightseeing Highlights in Salzburg area (see Day 7)
▲**Bad Dürnberg Salzbergwerke**—Like its neighbors, this salt-mine tour above the town of Hallein, 8 miles from Salzburg, respects only the German-speakers. You'll get information sheets or headphones but none of the jokes. Still, it's a fun experience—wearing white overalls, sliding down the sleek wooden chutes, and crossing underground from Austria into Germany (daily 9:00-17:00, easy bus and train connections from Salzburg).

▲▲**Salzkammergut**—This is Austria's "commune with nature" country. Idyllic, majestic, but not rugged, it's a gentle land of lakes, forested mountains, storybook villages, rich in hiking opportunities, inexpensive rooms in private homes, and cheap youth hostels. While you could easily make this area the focus of your trip, you're just sneaking it in quickly for a representative taste and a pleasant and restful evening.

▲▲▲**Hallstatt**—Your target is Hallstatt, a town whose photograph draws desirous gasps when I show it to my travel classes. Lovable Hallstatt is a tiny town bullied onto a ledge between a selfish mountain and a swan-ruled lake with a waterfall ripping furiously through its middle. It can be toured on foot in about 10 minutes. The TI (tel. 06134/208, open daily in summer, often closed for lunch) can find you a room. A hotel "guest card" gives you free parking and sightseeing discounts.

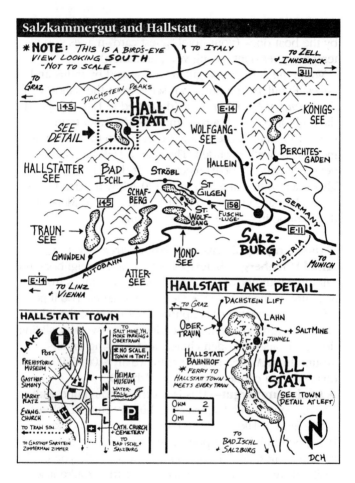

The town is one of Europe's oldest, going back centuries before Christ. The humble Prehistory Museum adjacent to the TI is interesting since little Hallstatt was the important salt-mining hub of a culture which spread from France to the Balkans during what archaeologists call the "Hallstatt Period" (800-400 BC). Back then, Celtic tribes dug for precious salt, and Hallstatt was, as its name means, the "salt place." Your 35-AS Prehistory Museum ticket gets you into the Heimat (Folk Culture) Museum around the corner (10:00-18:00 in summer). It's cute but barely worth the trouble. The Janu sport shop across from the TI recently dug into a prehistoric site and now its basement is another small museum.

From near the boat dock, hike up the covered wooden stairway to the church. The church is lovely (500-year-old altars and frescoes) but the cemetery will rot your flesh. Space is so limited in Hallstatt that bones get only 12 peaceful buried years before making way for the freshly dead. The result is a fascinating chapel of bones (10:00-18:00, 10 AS) in the cemetery. Each skull is lovingly named, dated, and decorated, with the men getting ivy and the women roses. They stopped this practice in the 1960s, about the same time the Catholic Church began permitting cremation.

If you have yet to do a salt mine, Hallstatt's is as good as any. You'll ride a frighteningly steep funicular high above the town (90 AS, round-trip), take a 10-minute hike, do the same old miners'-clothes, underground-train, and slide-the-banisters routine as at Berchtesgaden. And you'll listen to an English tape-recorded tour while your guide speaks German (125 AS, daily, 9:30-16:30, closing early off-season, no children under 4). The well-publicized ancient Celtic graveyard excavation sites, nearby, are really dead.

The charm of Hallstatt is the village and lakeside setting. Go there to relax, nibble, wander, and paddle. In August, tourist crowds trample much of Hallstatt's charm. "Schmuck" means jewelry.

Mountain lovers, hikers, and spelunkers can keep busy for days using Hallstatt as their home base. Get information from the TI on the various caves with their ice formations, the thunderous rivers, mountain lifts, nearby walks, and harder hikes. With a car, consider hiking around nearby Altaussee (2-3 hours) or along Grundlsee to Tolpitzsee. Regular buses connect Hallstatt with Gosausee for a pleasant walk. The TI can recommend a great 2-day hike with an overnight in a nearby mountain hut.

Sleeping in Hallstatt (11 AS = about $1, zip code: A-4830, tel. code: 06134)
The TI can almost always find you a room. July and August can be tight. Early August is worst. A bed in a pri-

vate home costs about 180 AS with breakfast (less if you
stay longer). It's hard to get a one-night reservation. But if
you drop in and they have a spot, they're happy to have
you. All prices include breakfast, lots of stairs, and a silent
night. "*Zimmer mit Aussicht?*" means "room with view?"
. . . worth asking for.

Gasthof Simony (500-800 AS doubles depending upon
the plumbing, view, season, and length of stay, 250 AS for
third person, cheaper for families, tel. 231, SE-B) is my
stocking-feet-tidy 500-year-old favorite, right on the square
with a lake view, balconies, creaky wood floors, slip-
slidey rag rugs, antique furniture, lake-front garden, and a
huge breakfast. Call friendly Susan Scheutz for a reservation.

Pension Seethaler (200 AS per person, 180 AS if you
stay more than one night, in S, D, T, or Q, no extra for
great views; Dr Morton weg 22, tel. 421, SE-D) is a simple
old lodge with 45 beds, perched a little above the lake on
the parking-lot side of town.

Pension Sarstein (D-400 AS, DB-520 AS, plus 30 AS
each for one-night stays in summer; Gosaumühlstr. 83, tel.
217) has 25 beds in a charming building a few minutes
walk along the lake from the center, with a view, run by
friendly Frau Fisher. You can swim from her lakeside garden. Her sister, friendly Frau Zimmermann (175 AS per
person B&B in a double or triple, can be musty;
Gosaumühlstr. 69, tel. 309), runs a small Zimmer in a 500-
year-old ramshackle house with low beams, time-polished
wood, and fine lake views just down the street. These
elderly ladies speak almost no English, but you'll find
yourself caught up in their charm and laughing together
like old friends.

Helga Lenz (150 AS per person in 2-, 3-, or 4-bedded
rooms, gives family discounts, welcomes one-nighters;
high above the paddle-boat dock at Hallberg 17, tel. 508,
SE-B) has a big, sprawling, woodsy house on top of the
town with great lake and town views and a neat garden
perch. Ideal for those who sleep well in tree houses.

Gasthaus Zauner (DB-800 to 1000 AS; Marktplatz 51,
tel. 246, fax 2468) is a business machine offering more

normal hotel rooms on the main square, with a restaurant specializing in grilled food. You'll eat better at Gasthaus Weisses Lamm.

The **Gasthaus Mühle Naturfreunde-Herberge** (135 AS per bed with sheets in 2- to 20-bed coed dorms, 35 AS breakfast, cheaper if you BYO hostel sheet, run by Ferdinand; Kirchenweg 36 just below the tunnel car park, tel. 318) has the best cheap beds in town and is clearly the place to eat well on a budget. Their wonderful pizzas are big enough for two. Closed in November. Restaurant closed on Wednesdays. ("Nature's friends' houses" are found throughout the Alps. Like mountaineers' huts, they're a good, fun, and basic bargain.)

The **youth hostel** (90 AS beds in 2- to 17-bed rooms, extra for sheets and breakfast, Salzbergstr. 50, just below the salt-mine lift, 5 minutes walk past the tunnel, tel. 681 or 279) is clean, without character, and open May through September.

The nearby village of Obertraun is a peaceful alternative to Hallstatt in August. You'll find plenty of Zimmer and a luxurious youth hostel (tel. 06131/360).

Itinerary Options
If you prefer rivers to lakes and have had enough of Salzburg by noon, hit the road for the Danube River valley and spend the night in Melk in an entirely different, more Eastern-feeling world on a river that could float you all the way to Ukraine.

HALLSTATT TO VIENNA

Today, assuming you can pull yourself out of Hallstatt, you'll head to this tour's easternmost point. Speed non-stop to the Danube River, where you'll tour the powerful Mauthausen concentration camp and explore the romantic ruined castles, vineyards, glorious abbeys, and scenery of the Danube River valley. By dinner time, you'll be checked into your hotel and ready to experience Paris's eastern rival, the Habsburg capital—Vienna (Wien).

Suggested Schedule

8:00	Hallstatt (or Salzburg) early departure.
10:00	Tour Mauthausen concentration camp.
12:00	Danube Valley or autobahn to Melk. Picnic and tour at the abbey; drive, bike, or cruise to Krems and into Wien.
17:00	Arrive in Wien; visit tourist information office.
18:00	Check into your hotel.
19:00	Stroll through center with *A to Z* book. Dinner downtown, late wine at Brezl-Gwölb.

Transportation: Hallstatt to Vienna (210 miles)
Forget easygoing Austria—today is very demanding (unless you can splice in an extra day, which Hallstatt and the Wachau Valley could easily gobble up). Drivers leave Hallstatt early. Follow scenic route 145 through Gmunden to the autobahn and head east. After Linz, take exit #155, Enns, and follow the Mauthausen signs (8 km from the freeway). You'll go quickly through the village of Windpassing, cross the Donau (Danube, hum "dut duh da da da, dee dee, doo doo"), go through Mauthausen town, and follow signs to Ehemaliges KZ-lager. From Maut-hausen, the speedy route is the autobahn to Melk, but the curvy, scenic route 3 along the river is worth the nausea.

This region, from Persenbeug to Melk, is Nibelung-engau, the fourth- and fifth-century home of the legendary Nibelung tribe, dramatized in Wagner's opera. Next stop:

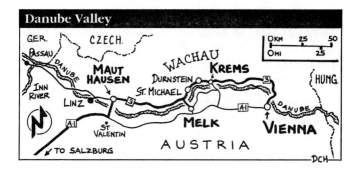

Danube Valley

Melk's great abbey. Cross the bridge and follow the signs
not into town (Zentrum Melk) but to Stift Melk, the
Benediktinerstift (Benedictine abbey).

The most scenic stretch of the Donau is the Wachau
Valley, lying between Melk and Krems. From Melk (get a
Vienna map at the TI), cross the river again (signs to
Donaubrucke) and stay on route 3. After Krems, it hits the
autobahn (A22), and you'll barrel right into Vienna's traffic

Navigating in Vienna, if you understand the Ring and
Gürtel, isn't bad. Study the map and see the two ring
roads looping out from the Donau. As you approach the
city, you'll cross the North Bridge and land right on the
Gürtel, or outer ring. You can continue along the Danube
canal to the inner ring, called the Ringstrasse (clockwise
traffic only). Circle around either thoroughfare until you
reach the "spoke" street you need.

Train travelers in a hurry may skip Mauthausen
(Dachau, outside of Munich, has easier public access) and
take the train straight to Melk where you can tour the
abbey and picnic on the scenic Melk-to-Krems Danube
River cruise. A local train goes from St. Vincent to
Mauthausen station (3 miles from camp, get map from station attendant, camp is #9). You can rent a bike there or
catch the local bus that goes to base of the hill a mile
from the camp, where it's easy to hitch a ride up.

From the attractive town of Krems, hourly 60-minute
trains go into Vienna (it's a 15-minute walk from the
Krems boat dock to the train station). The 16:30 boat goes
all the way to Vienna, arriving at 20:15.

If you take the train directly into Vienna (3 hours from Salzburg), you can easily do the Wachau train/boat excursion as a day trip later on. Remember, the 6-knot flow of the Donau makes downstream (eastbound) trips about a third faster.

Sightseeing Highlights—Danube Valley

▲▲▲Mauthausen Concentration Camp—More powerful and less tourist-oriented than Dachau, this slave labor and death camp functioned from 1938 to 1945 "for the exploitation and extermination of Hitler's opponents." Over half of its 206,000 quarry-working prisoners were killed here. Set in a strangely beautiful setting next to the Danube in a now-still and overgrown quarry, Mauthausen is open daily from 8:00 to 18:00 (20 AS, last entry at 17:00, closes from mid-December through January and at 16:00 off-season). The camp barracks house a museum (some English labels, but the 20-AS English guidebook gives a complete translation) and shows a graphic 45-minute movie (top of each hour, ask for an English showing if necessary, don't wait for the next showing, just slip in). The most emotionally moving rooms and the gas chamber are downstairs. The spirits of the victims of these horrors can still be felt. Outside the camp each victim's country has erected a gripping memorial. Many yellowed photos sport fresh flowers. Walk to the barbed wire memorial overlooking the quarry and the "stairway of death."

By visiting a concentration camp and putting ourselves through this emotional wringer, we heed and respect the fervent wish of the victims of this fascism—that we "never forget." Many people forget by choosing not to know.

▲Melk—Sleepy and elegant under its huge abbey that seems to police the Danube, the town of Melk offers a pleasant stop before the bustle of Vienna. The helpful TI, near the traffic-free main square, has ideas for sightseeing in the area (nearby castle, bike rides along the river, and so on). Melk is on the main Salzburg-to-Vienna train line and autobahn. And it's the starting point for the Wachau (Danube) Valley bike or boat trip. (Melk TI, 9:00-12:00, 15:00-18:00, Saturday and Sunday 9:00-14:00, tel. 02752/2307.)

Melk makes a fine overnight stop. **Hotel Fürst** (DB-580 AS; Rathausplatz 3-5, A-3390 Melk, tel. 02752/2343) is a fluffy, creaky old place with 15 rooms, run by the Madar family, right on the traffic-free main square with a fountain out your door and the abbey hovering overhead. **Gasthof Goldener Stern** (D-440 AS, cheaper 3- to 5-bed rooms; Sterngasse 17, A-3390, Melk, tel. 02752/2214, SE-D) is traditional and also quiet and cozy on a pedestrian street in the center. **Gasthof Baumgartner** (D-300 AS, across from the station, tel. 02752/2419) is pretty dumpy but cheap. The modern **youth hostel** (145 AS beds in quads with sheets and breakfast, easygoing about membership, tel. 02752/2681) is a few minutes walk from the station.

▲▲**Melk Abbey (Benediktinerstift)**—The newly restored abbey beaming proudly over the Danube Valley is one of Europe's great sights. Freshly painted and gilded throughout, it's a baroque dream, a lily alone. Its lavish library, church, palace rooms, and the great Danube view from the abbey balcony are most interesting sights on the 45-minute tour. German tours are available constantly, English tours only with groups of 20 or more (45 AS, 55 AS with a tour, daily 9:00-18:00). Call 02752/2312 to find out when the next English group is scheduled; there are often English tours at 11:30 and at 15:00, and you are welcome to tag along. The abbey garden, café, and charming village below make waiting for a tour pleasant.

▲▲**Wachau (Danube) Valley**—By car, bike, or boat, the 38-kilometer stretch of the Danube between Melk and Krems is as pretty as they come. The boat goes four times daily in season (see below). Those without a car can take advantage of the boat line's generous bike-and-cruise program: 35-AS bike rentals; you can pick them up and drop them at different docks and take your bike onto the boat. The bikes are usually one-speeds; you may get better bikes at the train station. Pedal along the north bank (just off the main road, the "bike in a red border" signs mean no biking) following the TI's "Cycle Track" brochure. It's about a 2.5-hour pedal to Krems where you can drop the bike. You can go half and half by trading in the boat for a bike or vice versa at the Durnstein or Spitz dock.

Boats (3-hour ride, 384 AS, free with Eurailpass) leave
Melk for Krems at 10:00, 14:00, 14:50, and 15:30 (May–
September). Call the DDSG boat company's office,
0732/771090 in Linz or 0222/21750-451 in Vienna, or the
Melk TI at 02752/2307-0 to confirm these times.

Art buffs will recognize the town of **Willendorf** as the
place where the oldest piece of European art was found.
A few blocks off the river (follow the signs to Venus) you
can see the monument where the well-endowed, 30,000-
year-old fertility symbol, the Venus of Willendorf, was dis-
covered. (She's now in Vienna's Natural History Museum.)

This is the Danube's wine road. You'll see wine gardens
all along the river. Those hanging out a wreath of straw or
greenery are inviting you in to taste. St. Michael has a
small wine garden and an old tower you can climb for a
view. In local slang, someone who's feeling his wine is
"blue." Blue Danube?

Durnstein is a touristic flypaper luring hordes of visitors with its traffic-free quaintness and its one claim to
fame (and fortune): Richard the Lion-Hearted was impris-
oned here in 1193. You can probably sleep in his bed-
room.

Krems is a gem of a town. From the boat dock, walk
a few blocks to the TI (pick up a town map and a Vienna
map if you don't have them). Then walk into the traffic-
free, shopper's-wonderland old town. If nothing else, it's
a pleasant stroll to the station (hourly trains, a 1-hour ride
into Vienna's Franz Josef Bahnhof). The local TI (9:00–
18:00, less in winter, tel. 02732/82676) can find you a cheap
bed in a private home (200 AS B&B) if you decide to sidetrip into the big city from this small-town alternative.

Vienna
See Day 10.

VIENNA

Vienna is a head without a body. Built to rule the once-grand Habsburg Empire—Europe's largest—she started and lost World War I, and with it her far-flung holdings. Today, you'll find a grand capital of 1.7 million people (20 percent of Austria's population) ruling a relatively small and insignificant country. Culturally, historically, and from a sightseeing point of view, this city is the sum of its illustrious past. The city of Freud, Kafka, Brahms, a gaggle of Strausses, Maria Theresa's many children, and a dynasty of Holy Roman emperors is right up there with Paris, London, and Rome. Last night you got oriented. Today, attack.

Suggested Schedule

9:00	Ride tram #1 or #2 360 degrees around the Ringstrasse. Get off at City Hall and walk through Hofburg Gardens to the Opera (check Opera House tour schedule, consider standing-room seats for tonight's performance).
10:30	Catch the "Getting Acquainted" city orientation tour.
12:00	Stroll the Naschmarkt, buy a picnic to eat with Mozart in the Burggarten (or eat at Rozenberg behind the Opera).
14:00	Take the Opera tour.
15:00	Kunsthistorisches Museum (English tour).
17:00	Tram #2 to the Kursalon in the Stadtpark for the free waltz concert (16:00-18:00).
19:00	Choose from among: classical music, Heuriger wine garden, the Prater amusement park, or an evening in the old town.

Vienna Orientation

Vienna, or Wien (pronounced "veen") in German, is so big, busy, and culturally complex that a little chaos would be understandable. Even though administrative districts of

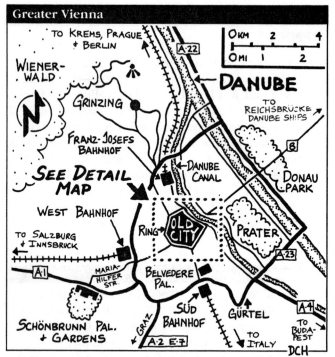

the city are called *Bezirke*, the place is orderly and has gone to great lengths to make life easy—if not cheap—for its visitors.

Vienna is bordered on three sides by the Vienna woods (Wienerwald) and the Danube. To the southeast is industrial sprawl. The Alps, which arc across Europe from Marseilles, end with Vienna's wooded hills. These provide a popular playground for walking and new-wine drinking. This greenery's momentum carries on into the city. You'll notice over half of Vienna is park land, filled with ponds, gardens, trees, and statue memories of Austria's glory days.

Think of the city map as a target. The bull's-eye is the cathedral, the first circle is the *Ring* and the second is the *Gürtel*. The old town snuggles around towering St. Stephan's cathedral south of the Donau, bound tightly by the Ringstrasse. The Ring, marking what was the city wall, circles the first Bezirk. The Gürtel, a broader ring road, contains the rest of downtown (Bezirke 2 through 9). Addresses start with the Bezirk followed by street and street number. Any address higher than the 9th Bezirk is beyond the Gürtel, far from the center. The middle two digits of Vienna postal codes show the district, or Bezirk. The address "7, Lindengasse 4" means in the seventh district, #4 on Linden Street. Its postal code would be 1070. Nearly all your sightseeing will be done in the core first district or along the Ringstrasse. As a tourist, concern yourself only with this small old center, and sprawling Vienna suddenly becomes manageable.

Vienna's often-crowded tourist offices, located in each train station, at the freeway entrances, and behind the Opera House at Kärntnerstrasse 38 (daily 9:00-19:00, later in the stations, tel. 0222/513 8892 or 211140) are excellent. They find rooms (35 AS fee) and provide visitors with a library of free pamphlets on whatever they need. Stop here first with a list of needs and questions, to confirm your sightseeing plans, and to pick up the free city map (with a small guidebook's worth of local information including transit deals and emergency numbers); the museum brochure (listing hours, telephone numbers, and handicap accessibility); walking tour schedule; the monthly program of concerts, walks, and other events; the fact-filled *Youth Scene* magazine; and the essential, 30-AS *Vienna from A to Z* book (which is all you need to see the town). Every important building has a numbered flag banner that keys into this guidebook. Every city should spoil its visitors like this. *A to Z* numbers are keyed into the TI's city map. When lost, find one of the "famous building flags" and match its number to your map. If you're at a "famous building" check the map to see what other key numbers are nearby, then check the *A to Z* book to see if you want to drop by.

Vienna has a fine transit system of buses, trams, and sleek, easy subways. To simplify the complicated fare system (even though it may not pay for itself), buy the 24-hour (45 AS) or 72-hour (115 AS) subway/bus/tram pass at any Tabak shop. I use it mostly to zip along the Ring (tram #1 or #2). A transit map (15 AS) is available at transit ticket windows. Without a pass, blocks of five tickets for 75 AS are cheaper than 20-AS individual tickets (each good for one journey with necessary changes). Eight-strip all-day, 235-AS transit passes can be shared (for instance, four people for two days each). Vienna's comfortable, honest, and easy-to-flag-down taxis start at 22 AS and mount quickly; you'll pay about 60 AS for a 5-minute ride Don't drive in Vienna. Ask at your hotel where to park your car and leave it there. Nights and weekends are wide open. Blue lines mean limited parking. Many streets allow unlimited parking. Several people told me that out-of-country cars can ignore parking tickets. Parking garages abound (around 200 AS per day).

Vienna has two main train stations: Westbahnhof serving most of Europe; and Südbahnhof serving Italy, the former Yugoslavia, and Greece. Tram #58 connects the Westbahnhof with the center, tram D takes you from the Südbahnhof downtown, and tram #18 connects the two stations. Trains to Krems and the Wachau Valley leave from a third station, the Franz Josef Bahnhof. For train information, call 1717.

Vienna is slowly expanding its telephone system. A digit will be inserted in the second place. If a number is wrong, dial 1611 for assistance. Also, Vienna's phones let you dial right through to the extension. Dial numbers with a dash (like many fax numbers) straight through. Note that Vienna's telephone code changes: 0222 (from inside Austria) and 1 (from outside Austria).

Sightseeing Highlights—Vienna

▲**Ringstrasse**—In the 1860s, Emperor Franz Josef had the city's ingrown medieval wall torn down and replaced with a grand boulevard 190 feet wide arcing nearly 3 miles around the city's core. One of Europe's great streets, it's lined with many of the city's top sights. Trams #1 and #2 circle the whole route and so should you.

▲▲**St. Stephan's Cathedral**—Stephansdom is the Gothic needle around which Vienna spins. With hundreds of years of history carved in its walls and buried in its crypt (open eight times a day, tel. 515 52 526), the cathedral is a fascinating starting point for a city walk. Tours of the

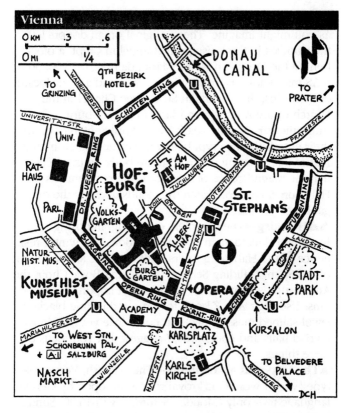

church are in German only, the 50-minute daily mass is impressive (schedule near the entry), and the crowded lift to the north tower (daily 9:00-18:00) shows you a big bell but a bad view. A great view is only 343 tightly wound steps away, up the spiral staircase to the watchman's lookout, 246 feet above the postcard stand (south tower, daily 9:00-17:30). From the top, figure out the town, using your *Vienna from A to Z* to locate the famous sights. The church is nearly always open.

Stephansplatz around the square is colorful and lively. And at the nearby *Graben* (ditch) street, topnotch street entertainment dances around an exotic plague monument. The cathedral museum (Dom und Diözesan Museum, 10:00-16:00, Thursday until 18:00, Sunday until 13:00, closed Monday) is at Stephansplatz 6.

Visiting the remains of the Habsburgs is not as easy as you might imagine. These original organ donors left their bodies in the Kaisergruft (Capuchin Crypt, a block behind the Opera on Neuer Markt, daily 9:30-16:00, 30 AS, 5 AS map with a Habsburg family tree and a chart locating each coffin), their hearts in St. George Chapel in the church of the Augustinian friars (in the Hofburg, Augustinerstr. 3, daily 10:00-18:00, April-September), and their entrails in the crypt below the cathedral. Don't tripe. Rather than chasing down all these body parts, remember that the magnificence of this city is the real remains of the Habsburgs. Pan up. Watch the clouds glide by the ornate gables of Vienna.

▲▲**Hofburg**—The complex, confusing, imposing Imperial Palace demands your attention. The winter residence of the Habsburg rulers until 1918, it's still the home of the Spanish Riding School, the Vienna Boys' Choir, the Austrian president's office, and several important museums. Use your *A to Z* book to sort out this time-blackened, jewel-stained mess. While you could lose yourself in its myriad halls and courtyards, I suggest that you focus on three things:

▲**The Imperial Apartments**—These lavish, Versailles-type "wish I were God" royal rooms are open by German-language tour only (Monday-Saturday 8:30-16:00, Sunday 8:30-12:30, entrance from courtyard under the dome of St. Michael's Gate, Michaelerplatz, tel. 587 555 4515). Be sure that every eager, wide-eyed English-speaker in your group politely lets your guide know you're dying to hear some English. This is a small downtown version of the grander (and more tour-worthy) Schönbrunn Palace.

▲▲**Treasury**—The Weltliche and Geistliche Schatzkammer (secular and religious treasure room) is one of the world's great collections of historical jewels, with the 1,000-year-old crown of the Holy Roman Emperor (10:00-18:00, closed Tuesday).

▲**The Neue Burg**, or new palace, is the last (from this century, built for Franz Ferdinand but never used) and most impressive addition to the palace. Its grand facade arches around Heldenplatz (the horse and buggy depot).

Check it out quickly, not only to see its fine armory, musical instruments, and classical statuary from ancient Ephesus, but also just to wander among those royal Habsburg halls, stairways, and painted ceilings (10:00-16:00, closed Tuesday).

▲▲▲**Opera**—The Staatsoper facing the Ring, just up from Stephansdom and next to the TI, is a central point for any visitor. While the critical reception of the building 130 years ago led the architect to commit suicide, and it's been rebuilt since the World War II bombings, it's a dazzling place. (By 40-minute tour only, daily in English, July and August at 10:00, 11:00, 13:00, 14:00, and 15:00; other months, afternoons only; 40 AS. Tours are often canceled for rehearsals and shows, so check the posted schedule or call 51444-2613.)

The **Vienna State Opera**, with the Vienna Philharmonic Orchestra in the pit, is one of the world's top opera houses. There are performances almost nightly, except in July and August, with shows normally sold out. If you really want to see a performance and it's sold out, try for one of 500 *Stehplatz* (standing-room spots; the 20-AS downstairs spots are best, otherwise it's 15 AS higher up). Join the Stehplatz line-up at the Abendkasse side door where the number of available places is posted. The ticket window opens an hour before each performance. Buy your place at the padded leaning rail. If your spot isn't numbered, tie your belt or scarf to it and you can slip out for a snack and return to enjoy the performance.

▲▲▲**The Kunsthistorisches Museum**—This museum has the most exciting and varied collection of paintings on this tour, with the great Habsburg collection of work by Dürer, Rubens, Titian, Raphael, and especially Brueghel. There's also a fine collection of Egyptian and classical art and applied arts including a divine golden salt shaker by Cellini. There are often English tours at 11:00 and 15:00 (if you forgot to pack the chapter from *Mona Winks*). The paintings are hung on one easy floor, and clear charts keep you on course (Tuesday-Sunday, 10:00-18:00, closed Monday, parts of the picture gallery are often open on Tuesday and Friday from 18:00-21:00, tel. 52177-489;

95 AS, 50 AS for students and seniors over 60). Picnic or
nap in the lovely park outside. The Natural History museum (twin building facing the art museum) has moon
rocks, dinosaur stuff, and the Venus of Willendorf—at
30,000 years old, the world's eldest sex symbol.

▲**Academy of Fine Arts**—This small but exciting collection includes works by Bosch, Botticelli, and Rubens, a
Venice series by Guardi, and a self-portrait by 15-year-old
Van Dyck (3 minutes from the Opera at Schillerplatz 3,
Tuesday, Thursday, and Friday 10:00-14:00, Wednesday
10:00-13:00 and 15:00-18:00, Saturday and Sunday 9:00-
13:00, tel. 5881-6225).

▲**Albertina Collection of Graphic Arts**—This lovely
collection of etchings by many of the masters offers a
behind-the-scenes appreciation of artists like Raphael,
Dürer, and Rubens. Unfortunately, only copies are dis-
played (across the street from the Opera at Augustinerstr.
1, Monday, Tuesday, and Thursday 10:00-16:00,
Wednesday 10:00-18:00, Friday 10:00-14:00, Saturday and
Sunday 10:00-13:00, closed Sunday in July and August, tel.
53483; the rustic, fast, and cheap Augustiner cellar restaurant is downstairs.)

▲**Belvedere Palace**—The elegant palace of Prince
Eugene of Savoy (the still-much-appreciated conqueror of
the Turks) houses the Austrian Gallery of nineteenth- and
twentieth-century art. Skip the lower palace and focus on
the garden and the top floor of the upper palace (*Oberes
Belvedere*) for a winning view of the city and a fine collection of Jugendstil art, Klimt, and Kokoschka (Tuesday-
Sunday 10:00-17:00, entrance at Prince Eugen Strasse 27).

▲▲▲**Schönbrunn Palace**—Schloss Schönbrunn, the
Habsburg's summer residence, is second only to Versailles
in all of Europe. Located far from the center, it was the
Habsburgs' summer residence. It is big—1,441 rooms—but
don't worry, only 40 rooms are shown to the public.
(8:30-17:00, until 16:30 off-season. English tours leave
between 10:00 and 16:30; check the schedule near the
ticket kiosk. Saturday and Sunday are most crowded;
12:00 to 14:00, and after 16:00 are least crowded, tel.
81113, 80 AS including the required tour, no reductions.)

The little 30-AS guidebook, with an unnecessary room-by-room description, is a good souvenir. Pass any waiting time around the corner in the four light, happy Bergl rooms—gaily painted for Maria Theresa by Bergl (including an interesting palace history exhibit) or at the impressive coach museum (Wagenburg, 30 AS). The sculpted gardens and Gloriette Park are open until dusk, free; long walk to Gloriette for nothing but a fine city view.

▲**Jugendstil**—Vienna gave birth to its own curvaceous brand of Art Nouveau around the turn of the century. Jugendstil art and architecture is popular around Europe these days, and many come to Vienna solely in search of it. The TI has a brochure laying out Vienna's twentieth-century architecture. The best of Vienna's scattered Jugendstil sights are in the Belvedere collection, the Karlsplatz "Golden Cabbage" subway stop, and the clock on Höher Market. The Museum of Applied Arts is disappointing.

KunstHausWien—This modern art museum features the work of local painter/environmentalist Hundertwasser (daily 10:00-19:00, 3, Weissgerberst. 13, tel. 7120491). Nearby, the one-with-nature **Hundertwasserhaus** is a complex of 50 lived-in apartments. This was built in the 1980s as a breath of architectural fresh air in a city of blocky, suicidally predictable apartment complexes. It's not open to visitors but worth a look for its fun-loving exterior and the Hundertwasser festival of shops across the street (3rd district, at Löwengasse and Kegelgasse).

▲**City Park**—Vienna's Stadtpark is a waltzing world of gardens, memorials to local musicians, ponds, peacocks, music in bandstands, and local people escaping the city. Notice the Jugendstil entry at the Stadtpark subway station. The Kursalon orchestra plays Strauss waltzes daily in summer from 16:00 to 18:00 and from 20:00 to 23:00. You can buy an expensive cup of coffee for a front row seat or join the local senior citizens and ants on the grass for free.

▲**Prater**—Vienna's sprawling amusement park tempts any visitor with its huge (220-foot-high, 9:00-23:00 in summer), famous, and lazy Ferris wheel called the Riesenrad, endless food places, and rides like the roller coaster, bumper cars, and Lilliputian Railroad. This is a fun, goofy place to share the evening with thousands of Viennese (subway: Praterstern). For a family local-style dinner, eat at Schweizerhaus or Wieselburger Bierinsel.

Naschmarkt—Vienna's ye olde produce market bustles daily, near the Opera along Wienzeile Street. It's likeably seedy and surrounded by sausage stands, cafés, and theaters. Each Saturday it's infested by a huge flea market (Monday-Friday 6:00-18:30, Saturday 6:00-13:00).

City Tours—Vienna offers many organized city tours. Consider its guided walks (90 minutes, many to choose from daily, 110 AS, tel. 51450, brochure at TI) and the "Getting Acquainted" bus tour (daily from the Opera at 10:30, 11:45, 15:00, and, in summer, 16:30, no reservations necessary, tel. 712 46 830). This 75-minute introduction to the city covers a surprising amount of ground for 190 AS. Cut out of the tour at the Upper Belvedere if you'd like to see its collection of Klimt and Art Nouveau. Eva Prochaska (tel. 513 5294, 1, Weihburggasse 13-15) is an excellent private guide who charges 1,100 AS for a half-day.

Sunbathing—The Austrians, like most Europeans, worship the sun. Their lavish swimming centers are as much for tanning as for swimming. The Krapfenwaldbad, in the high-class 19th district, is renowned as the gathering point for the best-looking topless locals. For the best man-made island beach scene, head for the "Danube Sea," Vienna's 20 miles of beach along the Danube Island (subway: Donauinsel).

▲▲Music—Vienna is Europe's music capital. It's music *con brio* from October through June, with things reaching a symphonic climax during the Vienna Festival each May and June. Sadly, in July and August, the Boys' Choir, the Opera, and many more music companies are—like you—on vacation. But the "Summer of Music" festival (special brochure at TI, tel. 4000-8400 for information, tickets at Rathaus office) assures that even in the summer you'll find lots of top-notch classical music. Anyone with a yen for classical music can get good tickets virtually any day of the year upon arrival in Vienna. There's a box office next to the TI behind the Opera. Anything booked in advance or through a box office comes with a stiff 22 percent booking fee. If you call the theater, they can advise you on the availability of (cheaper) tickets at the door. Vienna takes care of its starving artists (and tourists) by offering lots of standing-room places to top-notch music and opera nearly free.

For a trip back into Vienna's glory days of music, spend a Wednesday, Friday, or Saturday evening (early May until mid-October) at the Wiener Mozart Konzerte. The orchestra, clad in historic costumes and looking better than it sounds, performs Mozart's greatest hits including his famous opera arias. This is a fun evening.

The Vienna Boys' Choir—The boys sing at mass in the Imperial Chapel of the Hofburg (entrance at Schweizerhof) at 9:15 each Sunday except from July through mid-September. Seats (50-220 AS) must be reserved at least two months in advance but standing room is free and open to whoever lines up first. Concerts are also given Fridays at 15:30 in May, June, September, and October (320-400 AS, fax 011-43-1-5871268 from USA). They're nice kids but, for my taste, not worth all the commotion.

Spanish Riding School—Performances are normally sold out in advance, but training sessions (only a little less boring) are open to the public (February-June and September-October, Tuesday-Saturday from 10:00-12:00, 70 AS at the door, Josefsplatz in the Hofburg, long line).

▲**Wine Gardens**—The Heurige is a uniquely Viennese institution celebrating (and drinking) the *Heuriger*, or new wine. It all started when the Habsburgs let Vienna's vintners sell their own new wine tax-free for 300 days a year. Several hundred families opened up Heurigen wine-garden restaurants clustering around the edge of Vienna, and a tradition was born. Today they do their best to maintain their old village atmosphere, serving the homemade new wine (the last vintage, until November 11th) with light meals and strolling musicians. For the whole story and a complete listing with maps and descriptions of each district, get and use the TI's *Heurige in Wien* brochure.

Of the many Heurigen suburbs, Grinzing is the most famous and touristy. **Neustift am Walde** (bus 35A) is a

local favorite with plenty of tourists but much of its original charm intact. **Weinbau Wolff** (on the main street at
Rathstr. 46, tel. 442335) has a great buffet spread, hundreds of outdoor tables, and the right ambience. **Haus
Zimmermann** (bus 35A to Mitterwurzergasse 20, tel.
441207) is a local favorite, more remote, low key, and
without music. For more crowds and music with your
meal, visit Beethoven's home in Heiligenstadt (tel. 371287,
tram #37 to last stop and walk 10 minutes to Pfarrplatz).
At any of these places you'll fill your plate at a self-serve
cold-cut buffet. Waitresses will then take your wine order
(30 AS per quarter liter). Many locals claim it takes several
years of practice to distinguish between Heuriger and
vinegar. For a near-Heurigen experience right downtown,
drop by **Gigerl Stadtheuriger** (described under "eating,"
below).

▲**The Viennese Coffeehouse**—In Vienna, the living
room is the coffeehouse down the street. This tradition is
just another example of the Viennese expertise in good
living. Each of Vienna's many long-established (and sometimes even legendary) coffeehouses has its individual
character. They offer newspapers, pastries, sofas, elegance, and a "take all the time you want" charm, for the
price of a cup of coffee. You may want to order *brauner*
(with a little milk) rather than *schwarzer* (black).
Some of my favorites are: **Café Hawelka** (1, Dorotheergasse 6, closed Tuesday, just off the Graben) with a rumpled "brooding Trotsky" atmosphere, paintings on the
walls by struggling artists who couldn't pay, a saloon
wood flavor, chalkboard menu, smoked velvet couches,
international selection of newspapers, and a phone that
rings for regulars; the **Central** (1, Herrengasse 14,
Jugendstil decor, great topfen strudel); the Jugendstil **Café
Sperl** (6, Gumpendorfer 11, just off Naschmarkt); and the
basic, untouristy **Café Ritter** (6, Mariahilferstr. 73, near
several of my recommended hotels).

Honorable Mention—There's much, much more. The
city museum brochure lists them all. If you're into
Esperanto, undertakers, tobacco, clowns, firefighting, or
the homes of dead composers, you'll find them all in

Vienna. Several good museums that try very hard but are submerged in the greatness of Vienna include: Historical Museum of the City of Vienna (Karlsplatz, Tuesday-Sunday 9:00-16:30); Folkloric Museum of Austria (8, Laudongasse 15, tel. 43 89 05); and the Museum of Military History (Heeresgeschichtliches museum, at 3, Arsenal, Objekt 18, 10:00-16:00, closed Friday, one of Europe's best if you like swords and shields). The Jesuit Church (9 on your city map, on Dr. Ignaz Seipel Platz) has a fascinating false dome painted on its ceiling. Mariahilferstrasse, with over 2,000 shops, is the best-value shopping street. This is the first place most tourists from Eastern Europe stop. For a walk in the Vienna Woods catch the U-4 subway to Heiligenstadt then bus 38A to Kahlenberg for great city views, woodsy restaurants and plenty of trails. Waluliso is a famous peacenik you'll probably see floating around the tourist centers in a white angel-of-peace toga, ringing a tinkly bell and calling for peace. His name stands for water, air, light, and sun. He seems a bit crazy, but, when you read the newspapers, so do we all. So do we all.

Dishonorable Mention—Considering the tough competition and your limited sightseeing time, you need to be selective. Be sure to miss these overrated sights: Spanish Riding School Practice Session (crowded in summer); the homes of Freud, Haydn, and Mozart, and all 47 of Beethoven's residences (many famous people chose to live in Vienna—unless you're a devotee, the houses are as dead as their former residents); City Hall tours (the interior is as plain as the exterior is ornate); Museum of Applied Arts (disappointing garage sale of Jugendstil furniture); and Demels Café (with a slow and steady flow of gawking Americans).

Nightlife

If old music or new wine isn't your thing, Vienna has plenty of alternatives. For an up-to-date rundown on fun after dark, get the TI's free *Youth Scene* magazine. An area known as the Bermuda *Dreieck* (Triangle), north of the cathedral between Rotenturmstrasse and Judengasse, is the hot local night-spot with lots of classy pubs or *Beisles*

(such as Krah Krah, Salzamt, and Roter Engel) and popular music spots (such as the disco P1 at Rotgasse 3, tel.
535 9995, and Jazzland at Franz Josefs-Kai 29, tel. 533
2575). **Tunnel**, popular with local students, features live
music and cheap meals (daily 11:00-02:00, a 10-minute
walk behind the Rathaus at 8, Florianigasse 39, tel.
423465).

A Side Trip East?
Vienna is the natural springboard for a quick trip to
Prague and Budapest. Visas are no longer required. Train
tickets are purchased easily at any travel agency
(Budapest, 3 hours, 520 AS round-trip, free with Eurail;
Prague, 5 hours, 580 AS round-trip, less with Eurail).
Intropa, next to the TI on Kärntnerstrasse is an efficient
place to get train tickets, as well as tours, and concert tick-
ets (with the 22 percent fee).

Sleeping in Vienna (11 AS = about $1, tel. code within Austria: 0222, from outside: 1)
Plan to spend 160 AS for a hostel bed or 500 AS for the
cheapest pension or hotel double with breakfast. Beds in
a central private homes are cozier but no cheaper than
simple pensions. In the summer, call a few days in
advance. All places listed speak English and most will
hold a room without a deposit if you promise to arrive
before 17:00. Be wary of people hustling tourists at the
train stations. I've chosen three handy and central locations. Unless otherwise noted, prices include breakfast.
(Street addresses start with the district. Postal code is 1XX0
with XX being the district.)

Between the Opera and the Westbahnhof
These are scattered near Mariahilferstrasse, about half way
between the Westbahnhof and the Opera, a 10- to-15-
minute walk (or quick subway or tram ride) from either in
a fun, comfortable, and vibrant area filled with local
shops, cafés, and Viennese being very Viennese.
   Privatzimmer F. Kaled (D-500 AS, DB-600 AS, T-750
AS, 150 AS for extra bed, optional 50 AS breakfast in bed;
7, Lindengasse 42, tel. 939013), a unique find, is lovingly

run by Tina and Fred Kaled. It's bright, airy, homey, quiet, and has TVs (with CNN) in each room. Hardworking Tina is a mini tourist information service. (Being Hungarian, she has good contacts for people visiting Budapest.) If you leave your credit card number, she'll hold a room for late arrivals.

Privatzimmer Maria Pribojszki (D-500, T-700; 7, Lindengasse 39, tel. 939006, SE-D) rents four rooms with kitchen privileges in a comfortable apartment.

Pension Lindenhof (D-580 AS, DB-800 AS, showers 20 AS; 7, Lindengasse 4, tel. 930498, fax 937362) is well-worn but clean, filled with plants, and run with Bulgarian strictness.

Pension Reimer (DB-580 to 680 AS, TB-850 AS, optional breakfast is 55 AS; 7, Kirchengasse 18, tel. 936162) muffles its charm with locks everywhere and a pay elevator. Except for a few small ones, most of its rooms are large and comfortable.

Pension Esterhazy (D-470; 6, Nelkengasse 3, tel. 58 75 159) run with a man's touch, has wacky colors, rumpled carpets, a claustrophobic and musty hallway, clean basic rooms, a shower down the hall, no breakfast, but a great location.

Privatzimmer Hilde Wolf (D-470 AS, big optional breakfast 35 AS, 20 AS showers, no smoking; 4, Schleifmühlgasse 7, tel. 586 5103, reserve by telephone and credit card number) just off Naschmarkt and Karlsplatz, is a homey place one floor above an ugly entry, with huge rooms like old libraries. Hilde loves her work and even offers to babysit if traveling parents need a break. Her helpful husband, Otto, speaks English.

Hospiz CVJM (S-320 AS, SB-360 AS, D-560 AS, DB-640 AS, T-810 AS, TB-900 AS, Q-1040 AS, QB-1120 AS, CC-VM; 2 blocks from the Westbahnhof at 7, Kenyongasse 15, tel. 931304, fax 931304-13) is big, sterile, quiet, old-institutional and well-run, as you'd expect a YMCA to be.

Jugendherberg Myrthengasse/Neustiftgasse (IYHF hostel, 140 AS with sheets and breakfast in 2-, 4-, or 6-bed rooms, plus 40 AS for non-members; 7, Myrthengasse 7, tel. 523429, fax 5235849) is actually two hostels side by

side. Both are new, cheery, and well-run, have a 1:00 curfew, will hold a rooms until 16:00, and offer 60-AS meals.
The second hostel, on Neustiftgasse (tel. 5237462) has 10
first-come first-served doubles renting at dorm prices (D-
280 AS).

Across the street is **Believe It Or Not** (160 AS per bed,
110 AS from November-April; Myrthengasse 10, no sign,
ring apt #14, tel. 526 4658), a friendly and basic place with
one big co-ed dorm for ten travelers. Run by an entrepreneurial and charming Pole named Gosha. Locked up from
10:30 to 12:30, kitchen facilities, no curfew, snorers sleep
here at their own risk.

Turmherberge "Don Bosco" (60 AS dorm beds, 25 AS
for sheets, 40 AS extra for those without IYHF cards; 3,
Lechnerstr. 12, tel. 713 1494) is far away but I stayed there
in 1973 and it's still the cheapest place in Vienna.
Catholic-run, closed 12:00-17:00, open to people of any
sex from March-November, tram #18 from either train station to Stadionbrücke.

Northwest of the Ring in the 8th and 9th Bezirk
This area is quieter and more elegant. Freud lived here;
no one knows why. The first two are a couple blocks
behind the Rathaus (City Hall, subway stop: Rathaus). The
others are a short walk off the Ring (near subway stop:
Schottentor).

Pension Andreas (SB-580 AS, DB-780 AS, big DBWC-
950 AS, CC-A, elevator; 8, Schlösselgasse 11, tel. 423488,
fax 423488-50), run by a gracious woman named Sevil,
this well-located, classy, quiet place is a worthwhile
splurge.

Pension Columbia (D-630 AS, DB-670 AS; 8,
Kochgasse 9, tram #5 from Westbahnhof, bus 13A from
Südbahnhof, lots of stairs, tel. 426757) offers huge rooms
and classy (if dog-eared) Old-World elegance rare in this
price range.

Pension Samwald (S-390 AS, SB-430 AS, D-560, DB-
590, TB-770 AS, cheaper off-season, 10 percent extra for
one-nighters; 9, Hörlgasse 4, tel. 347407 or fax 2785739) is
well-worn, well-run, and in a great locale, with tatty chan-

deliers, hardwood floors, skimpy breakfasts, high ceilings, low prices, and an elevator. A few of the cheap doubles are depressingly small. This place is popular with groups (260 to 280 AS per person).

Pension Franz (DB-990 AS, there's a 200-AS discount promised in 1994 for those with this book; 9, Währingerstr. 12, tel. 343637, fax 343637-23, CC-VMA, elevator) is a lush, dark, palace of a place offering spacious, richly decorated rooms and a first-class breakfast.

Pension Falstaff (D-540 AS, DB-650 AS; 9, Müllnergasse 5, tel. 349127, fax 3491864) is clean, basic, flimsy, and efficient. A little farther from the Ring.

Hotel Goldener Bär (D-610 AS, DB-720, CC-V; 9, Türkenstr. 27, tel. 345111, fax 3103944-22) is a well-located slumber mill with 35 small, stark, and simple rooms.

Porzellaneum der Wiener Universität (160 AS per bed in singles, doubles, and quads, open July-September; 9, Porzellangasse 30, between the Ring and Franz Josefs Bahnhof, tram D to Fürstengasse, tel. 347282). This is one of many student dorms that are rented as *Saisonhotel* to travelers from July through September, usually for around 420 AS per double. The TI brochure lists them all.

Within the Ring, in the Old City Center
Better and more expensive than my other listings, these places are listed in other guidebooks, speak English, and tend to fill up. All take easy telephone reservations, so call well ahead. The first three, in the shadow of St. Stephan's cathedral, on or near the Graben where the elegance of Old Vienna strums happily over the cobbles, cost a bit more but are worth the splurge. The subway zips direct from the Westbahnhof to Stephansplatz. The last two listings are near the Opera (Subway: Karlsplatz) just off the famous Kärntner Strasse near the tourist office and 3 minutes from the cathedral.

At **Pension Nossek** (SBWC-550 AS, DBWC-900 to 950 AS; 1, Graben 17, tel. 533 7041, fax 535 3646) an elevator takes you above any street noise into a family-run world where the dog and children seem to be placed among the lace and flowers by an interior designer. Street musicians, a pedestrian mall filled with cafés, and the plague monument are just outside your door.

Pension Aclon (D-760 AS, DB-1020 AS, T-1080 AS, TB-1400, Q-1400, QB-1780; 1, Dorotheergasse 6-8, tel. 512 79 400, fax 513 8751), quiet, elegant, family-run, a block off the Graben, is a memorable 100-year-old elevator ride above my favorite Vienna café.

Pension Pertschy (DB-1,000 to 1,100 AS, CC-VM; 1, Habsburgergasse 5, tel. 53449, fax 5344949) is more hotelesque than the others with more energy put into the lobby than its rooms. It's a bit musty.

Pension Suzanne (DB-930 to 1,130; 1, Walfischgasse 4, tel. 513 2507, fax 5132500), as baroque and doily as you'll find in this price range, is wonderfully located a few yards from the Opera. Suzanne is professional, quiet, and friendly with pink elegance bouncing on every bed.

Hotel zur Wiener Staatsoper (SB-850 AS, DB-1150 AS, TB-1400 AS, CC-VMA; 1, Krugerstr. 11, tel. 513 1274, fax 513 1274-15) is quiet, rich and hotelesque, a great value for this locale and ideal for people whose hotel taste is a cut above mine.

Eating in Vienna

The Viennese appreciate the fine points of life, and right up there with the waltz is eating. The city has many atmospheric restaurants. As you ponder the menus, remember that Vienna's diverse empire may be gone but its flavor lingers. You'll find Slavic and Eastern European specialties here along with wonderful desserts and local wine.

On nearly every corner you can find a colorful *Beisl* (Viennese tavern) filled with poetry teachers and their students, couples loving without touching, housewives on their way home from cello lessons, and waiters who thoroughly enjoy serving hearty food and good drink at an affordable price.

These **Wine Cellars** are fun, touristic but typical, in the old center of town with painless prices and lots of smoke.

Esterhazykeller is an inexpensive, rowdy, smoky self-service cellar (16:00-21:00, at Haarhof near Am Hof, off Naglergasse). **Augustinerkeller** is fun, inexpensive, and, like the Esterhazykeller, touristy (10:00-24:00, next to the Opera under the Albertina Museum on Augustinerstrasse). **Figlmüller** is a popular Beisl famous for its giant schnitzels (one can easily feed two) near St. Stephan's cathedral (just down the 6 Stephansplatz alley at Wollzeile 5). **Zu den Drei Hacken** served great inexpensive goulash with atmosphere, at 1, Singerstrasse 28. Also check out the **Pürstner** restaurant spilling onto the sidewalk 1 block away at Riemergasse 10. **Melker Stiftskeller**, the least touristy, is a deep and rustic cellar with hearty, inexpensive meals and new wine (open 17:00-24:00, closed Sunday and Monday, half way between Am Hof and the Schottentor subway stop at Schottengasse 3, tel. 5335530).

For a near "Heuriger" experience (a la Grinzing, see above) without leaving the center, eat at **Gigerl Stadtheuriger** (near the cathedral, a block off Kärntnerstr. at Rauhensteingasse 3, tel. 5134431). Just point to what looks good (cold cuts, spinach strudel, good salads, all sold by the weight) and choose from many local wines. Other atmospheric or otherwise memorable eateries within a 5-minute walk of the cathedral: **Brezel-Gwölb**, a wonderful wine cellar with outdoor dining on a quiet square, serves delicious, moderately priced light meals, fine Krautsuppe, and local dishes. It's ideal for a romantic late glass of wine (11:30-1:00 daily, at Ledererhof 9, off Am Hof). Around the corner, **Zum Scherer Sitz u. Stehbeisl** (Judenplatz 7, near Am Hof, Monday-Saturday 11:00-1:00, Sunday 17:00-24:00) is just as untouristy, with indoor or outdoor seating, a soothing woody atmosphere, intriguing decor, local specialties.

For a fast, light and central lunch: **Rosenberger Markt Restaurant** is a popular highway chain that opened an elegant super branch a block towards the cathedral from the opera. This place is brilliant: inexpensive, friendly, and efficient, with special theme rooms to dine in, offering a fresh and healthy cornucopia of food and drink and a

cheery break from the heavy, smoky, traditional eateries
(lots of fruits and vegetables, 11:00-23:00, Maysedergasse
2, just off Kärntner Strasse).

Buffet Trzesniewski is justly famous for its elegant and
cheap finger sandwiches (8 AS) and small beers (8 AS).
Three sandwiches and a *kleines Bier* (Pfiff) make a fun,
light lunch (just off the Graben, across from the brooding
Café Hawelka, on Dorotheergasse, Monday-Friday, 9:00-
19:30, Saturday 9:00-13:00).

Naschmarkt, a couple of minutes from the Opera, is
Vienna's best Old World market (6:30-18:00, Saturday until
13:00, closed Sunday) with very fresh produce, plenty of
cheap eateries, cafés, and sausage stands. For about the
cheapest hot meal in town, lunch at the nearby **Technical
University's Mensa** (cafeteria) in the huge, modern, light
green building just past Karlsplatz at Wiedner Hauptstrasse
8-19, second floor (Monday-Friday, 12:00-14:00). Anyone
is welcome to eat here with a world of students. The
snack bar is less crowded but the bigger mensa on the
same floor has a more interesting selection.

Three interesting drinks to try are *Grüner Veltliner* (dry,
green wine, any time), *Sturm* (very very new wine,
autumn only), and *Traubenmost* (a heavenly grape juice
on the verge of wine, autumn only, sometimes just called
Most). The local red wine (called "Portuguese") is pretty
good. Since the Austrian wine is often very sweet, remember the word *Trocken* (German for dry). You can order
your wine in a quarter-liter (*viertel*) and an eighth-liter
(*achtel*). Beer comes in a "*Krugel*" (.5 liter), "*Seidel*" (.3
liter) or a tiny "*Pfiff*" (.8 liter). See the special sightseeing
sections on wine gardens and coffeehouses, above.

VIENNA TO THE TIROL

After some last-minute sightseeing and scurry time in
Vienna, spend the early afternoon visiting the magnificent
Schönbrunn Palace, then hit the autobahn for a long, non-
stop drive westward to the Tirol. Spend the night in a
small town just outside Innsbruck before carrying on into
Switzerland tomorrow.

Suggested Schedule

9:00	St. Stephan's Cathedral.
10:00	Tour treasury and Hofburg or browse and shop Kärntner Strasse, Naschmarkt, or Mariahilferstrasse.
12:00	Check out of hotel, picnic at Schönbrunn.
13:00	Tour Schönbrunn Palace.
15:00	Hit the autobahn for a 5-hour drive to near Innsbruck.
20:00	Arrive at Hall in Tirol.
Sleep	Hall.

Transportation: Vienna to Hall in Tirol (280 miles)
To leave Vienna, follow the signs past the Westbahnhof to
Schloss Schönbrunn, which is directly on the way to the
West A-1 autobahn to Linz. The king had plenty of parking. Leave by 15:00, beating rush hour, and follow the
autobahn signs to West A-1, passing Linz and Salzburg,
nipping through Germany, turning right onto route 93 in
the direction of Kufstein, Innsbruck, and Austria at the
Dreieck Inntal (autobahn intersection). Crossing back into
Austria, you'll follow the scenic Inn River valley, stopping
5 miles east of Innsbruck at Hall in Tirol. There's an autobahn tourist information station just before Hall (10:00-
22:00 daily in season, working for the town's hotels but
still helpful). This 5-hour ride is nonstop autobahn all the
way.

Eurailers can enjoy the rest of today in Vienna and
catch the overnight train straight to Switzerland. There's a

nightly 21:00 departure from the Westbahnhof (train information, tel. 7200), getting into Zürich at 8:30. Reserve a bed (*Liege-platz*) at the station when you arrive in Vienna.

Hall in Tirol

Hall was a rich salt-mining center when Innsbruck was just a humble bridge (*Brücke*) town on the Inn River. Hall actually has a larger Old Town than does its sprawling neighbor, Innsbruck.

Take a lovely "gee, it's great to be alive" walk through easygoing Hall. From Gasthof Badl (just off the autobahn one stop before Innsbruck in Hall), walk over the old pedestrian bridge into town. The first old building you'll see is Hasegg Castle (pick up a map and a list of town sights). This was the town mint. Hall has a colorful morning scene before the daily tour buses arrive. The Hall-Innsbruck bus leaves four times an hour (#4, from just over the big bridge, 15 minutes, 26 AS). Sleepy Hall closes down tight on Sunday and for its daily siesta.

Back when salt was money, Hall was loaded. If the salt mines of the Salzburg area were too crowded, expensive, or time-consuming, try catching a tour (call first) of Hall's Bergbaumuseum, where the town has reconstructed one of its original salt mines, complete with pits, shafts, drills, tools, and the climax of any salt-mine tour—the slippery wooden slide (open by tour only, April-October, on the hour except for noon from 10:00 to 17:00, closed Sunday, tel. 05223/6269). The TI also organizes town walks in English which include the salt museum (10:00 and 14:00, 2 hours, 50 AS).

To give your trip a special splash check out Hall's magnificent *Freischwimmbad*, a huge outdoor pool with four diving boards, a giant lap pool, and a kiddies' pool, all surrounded by a lush garden, a sauna, minigolf, and lounging locals (35 AS).

Sleeping and Eating in Hall

The problem with today's plan is that you'll arrive late in a popular little town. Call in a reservation. Hall's TI (9:00-12:00 and 14:00-18:00, Saturday until 12:00, closed

Sunday, tel. 05223/6269) can find you a room from their list of Zimmer, Pension, and Gasthäuser. Zimmer charge about 140 AS per person but generally don't accept one-night stays. Gasthof Badl has Hall and Innsbruck maps and information in English. If they're full they can help you find another place.

Gasthof Badl (SB-370 AS, DB-640 AS, TB-910 AS, QB-1180 AS, CC-VM, elevator; Innsbruck 4, A-6060, Hall in Tirol, tel. 05223/6784, fax 67843, SE-A) is a big, comfortable, friendly place run by sunny Frau Steiner and her daughter, Sonja. It's easy to find, immediately off the Hall in Tirol freeway exit with an orange-lit "Bed" sign. It's not cheap, but take it for the convenience, the big breakfast, and the fact that they'll hold a room for a phone call. Freeway noise is no problem.

For a cheaper room in a private home, **Frieda Tollinger** (150 AS per person with breakfast; Schopper-weg 8, across the river from Badl, tel. 41366, SE-F) rents out three rooms and accepts one-nighters.

Since autobahn rest stop food isn't great and you'll probably be short on time, consider a rolling picnic dinner for tonight. Hall's kitchens close early but Gasthof Badl's restaurant serves excellent dinners (from 120 AS) until 22:00.

For your Tirolean folk fun, Innsbruck offers an entertaining evening of slap-dancing and yodeling nearly every summer night.

FROM THE TIROL TO SWITZERLAND'S APPENZELL

After an easy morning in the town of Hall, a Tirolean mountain joyride, or a look at Innsbruck, you'll picnic at Innsbruck's Olympic ski jump. Then it's three Alpine hours on the autobahn to Switzerland's moo-mellow, storybook-friendly Appenzell, the warm, intimate side of the land of staggering icy Alps.

Suggested Schedule

8:00	Walk through Hall.
10:00	Visit Innsbruck (picnic at the Olympic ski jump on your way out of town or skip Innsbruck and drive and hike to Walderalm for lunch).
13:00	Drive to Switzerland.
16:00	Cross the border, stop at the Stoss viewpoint.
17:00	Set up in or near Appenzell or catch lift to Ebenalp and spend the night in the mountain hut.
20:00	Appenzeller folk evening? Reconfirm tomorrow's reservation at Walter's hotel (required).

Transportation—Hall to Appenzell (130 miles)
This morning, after a walk through Hall, you have two choices: a look at Innsbruck or a high-Alp experience. If it's sunny, I'd skip the city and do the Hinterhornalm/ Walderalm trip.

For the rainy-day city option, autobahn from Hall to the Innsbruck Ost exit, and follow the signs to Zentrum, then Kongresshaus, and park as close to the old center on the river (Hofgarden) as you can. City bus #4 goes regularly from Hall to Innsbruck in 15 stress-free minutes.

Just south of Innsbruck is the Olympic ski jump (from the autobahn take the Innsbruck Süd exit and follow signs to "Bergisel"). Park at the end of the road near the Andreas Hofer Memorial (an Austrian patriot, killed fighting

Napoleon) and climb to the empty, grassy stands for a panoramic picnic.

Leaving Innsbruck (from ski jump, go down into town along huge cemetery, thoughtfully placed just beyond the jump landing, and follow blue A12, Garmisch, Arlberg signs), head west on the autobahn (direction: Bregenz). The 8-mile-long Arlberg tunnel saves you 30 minutes but costs 150 AS and lots of scenery. For a joyride and to save a few bucks, skip the tunnel, exiting at St. Anton, and go via Stuben.

After the speedy Arlberg tunnel, you're 30 minutes from Switzerland. Pass Feldkirch (and another long tunnel) and exit the autobahn at Rankweil/Feldkirch Nord, following signs for Altstätten and Meiningen (CH). Crossing the baby Rhine River, you leave Austria. From there it's an easy scenic drive through Altstätten and Gais to Appenzell. At the Swiss border you must buy an annual road-use permit for 300 AS or 30 SF if you want to use the Swiss auto-bahns (you do). It's easy to slip across the border without buying one. But anyone driving on a Swiss autobahn without this tax sticker is likely to be cop-stopped and fined.

By train, I'd streamline things by overnighting it from Vienna to Zürich, taking the 3-hour train ride to Brienz, spending the afternoon in Ballenberg, and getting into the Interlaken region for dinner. Swiss trains (even to do the recommended Appenzell sightseeing) are great, and you'll have plenty of English-speaking help at each station.

Sightseeing Highlights—Western Austria
▲▲**Alpine Side Trip by Car to Hinterhornalm**—In Gnadenwald, a village sandwiched between Hall and its Alps, pay a 50-AS toll, pick up a brochure, then corkscrew your way up the mountain. Marveling at the crazy amount of energy put into such a remote road project, you'll finally end up at the rustic Hinterhornalm Berg restaurant (offering three simple 300-AS double rooms and a precarious dorm hut or *Lager* with 130 AS beds with sheets and a cliff-hanger of a view, tel. 05223/2170, crowded on summer weekends, closed through winter). Hinterhornalm is a

hang-gliding springboard. On good days, it's a butterfly
nest.

From there it's a level 20-minute walk to the Walderalm
farm, where you can wander around a working dairy farm
that shares its meadow with the clouds. The cows ramble
along ridgetop lanes surrounded by cut-glass peaks. The
lady of the farm serves soup, sandwiches, and drinks
(very fresh milk in the afternoon) on rough plank tables.
Below you spreads the Inn River Valley and, in the distance, Innsbruck.

▲**Innsbruck**—After Salzburg and Vienna, Innsbruck
(population 150,000) is stale strudel. If you do stop, the
Golden Roof (Goldenes Dachl, 2,657 gilded copper tiles,
built by Emperor Maximilian in 1496 as an impressive
viewing spot for his medieval spectacles) is the historic
center of town. From this square you'll see the baroque-
style Helblinghaus, the city tower (climb it for a great
view, 18 AS), the new Olympics museum with exciting
action videos for winter-sports lovers (24 AS, 9:30-17:30
daily, 32 AS combo tower/Olympics ticket) and, if you
stand just under the Olympics museum sign and look
down the street, you'll see Innsbruck's Olympic ski jump.

Nearby are the palace (Hofburg), the church (Hofkirche),
and the Tiroler Volkskunst Museum. This museum (40 AS,
open in season 9:00-17:00 daily, closed Sunday afternoon)
offers the best look anywhere at traditional Tirolean
lifestyles, with fascinating exhibits ranging from wedding
dresses and babies' cribs to nativity scenes. The upper
floors have Tirolean homes through the ages. (Hard to
appreciate without the English guidebook.)

A popular mountain-sports center and home of the 1964
and 1976 Winter Olympics, Innsbruck is surrounded by
150 mountain lifts, 1,250 miles of trails, and 250 hikers'
huts. If it's sunny, consider riding the lift right out of the
city to the mountaintops above (300 AS, 15 percent less if
ticket purchased at TI). Those who stay three nights
become members of Club Innsbruck and can take advantage of free guided hikes, bike tours, and lots of discounts.

Innsbruck's Alpenzoo is one of its most popular attractions (understandable when the competition is the Golden

Roof). You can ride the funicular up to the zoo (free if you buy your zoo ticket before boarding) and get a look at all the animals that hide out in the Alps—wildcats, owls, elk, vultures, and more (60 AS, daily 9:00-18:00). Innsbruck hotels host nightly folk evenings (200 AS, 21:00) throughout the summer. You can buy tickets (and even see the show for free on a continuous video) at the TI. (TI open daily 8:00-19:00, until 22:00 at the train station, 3 blocks in front of the Golden Roof, tel. 0512/5356.)

Side Trip over Brennerpass into Italy?—A short swing into Italy is fast and easy and would give your trip an exciting new twist (45-minute drive, easy border crossing, no problem with car, Austrian shillings accepted in the border region). To get there take the great Europa Bridge over Brennerpass. It's expensive (about $15), but in 30 minutes you'll be at the border. (Note: traffic can be heavy on summer weekends.) In Italy, drive to the colorful market town of Vipiteno/Sterzing. Just south of town, down a small road next to the autobahn, is the Reifenstein Castle. The lady who lives there gives tours at 9:30, 10:30, 14:00, and 15:00. She speaks German, Italian, and a little English. It's a unique and wonderfully preserved medieval castle (tel. from Austria 00-39-472/765879).

Venice—Imagine parking your car in Innsbruck and catching the night train ($60) to Venice for a day or two. Parking is easy near the station, and a day in Venice (with two nights in a row on the train) gives a fun twist to any half-timbered schnitzel tour.

Side Trip through Liechtenstein?—If you must see the tiny and touristy country of Liechtenstein, take this 30-minute detour: from Feldkirch south on E77, drive through Schaan to Vaduz, the capital. Park near the City Hall, post office, and tourist office. Passports can be stamped (for a small fee) in the tourist office. Stamp collectors make a beeline for the post office across the street while the prince looks down on his 4-by-12-mile country from his castle, a 20-minute hike above Vaduz (it's closed but offers a fine view; catch the trail from Café Berg). Liechtenstein's banks (open until 16:30) sell Swiss francs at uniform and good rates. To leave, cross the Rhine at

Rotenboden, immediately get on the autobahn heading north from Sevelen to the Oberriet exit, and check another country off your list.

SWITZERLAND (Schweiz, Suisse, Svizzera)

• 16,000 square miles (half the size of Ireland, or 13 Rhode Islands).
• About 6 million people (400 people per square mile, declining slightly).
• One Swiss Franc = about US$.70, 1.5 SF = about US$1.

Switzerland is Europe's richest, best-organized, and most mountainous country. Like Boy Scouts, the Swiss count cleanliness, neatness, punctuality, tolerance, independence, thrift, and hard work as virtues, and they love pocket-knives. They appreciate the awesome nature that surrounds them and are proud of their little country's many achievements.

The high average Swiss income, a great social security system, and their strong currency, not to mention the Alps, give them plenty to be thankful for.

Switzerland, 40 percent of which is uninhabitable rocks, lakes, and rugged Alps, has distinct cultural regions and customs. Two-thirds of the people speak German, 20 percent French, 10 percent Italian, and a small group of people in the southeast speak Romansch, a direct descendant of ancient Latin. Within these four language groups, there are many dialects. The sing-songy Swiss German, the spoken dialect, is quite a bit different from High German, which is Switzerland's written German. An interest in these regional distinctions will win the hearts of locals you meet. As you travel from one valley to the next, notice changes in architecture and customs.

Historically, Switzerland is one of the oldest democracies. Born when three states, or cantons, united in 1291, the Confederation Helvetica as it was called in Roman times (the "CH" decal on cars doesn't stand for chocolate) grew to the 23 of today. The government is decentralized, and cantonal loyalty is very strong.

Switzerland loves its neutrality and stayed out of both world wars, but it is far from lax defensively. Every fit

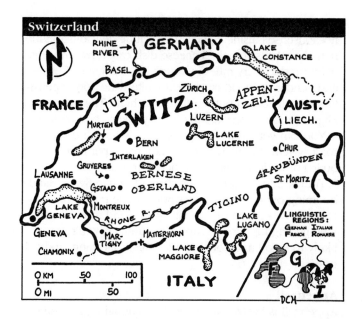

man serves in the army and stays in the reserve. Each house has a gun and a bomb shelter. There are 600,000 rifles in homes and 12,000 heavy guns in place. Swiss vacuum-packed emergency army bread, which lasts two years, is said to also function as a weapon. Airstrips hide inside mountains behind Batmobile doors. With the push of a button, all road, rail, and bridge entries to the country can be destroyed, changing Switzerland into a formidable mountain fortress. Notice the explosive patches checkerboarding the roads at key points like mountain summits (and hope no one invades until you get past). Sentiments are changing, and in 1989, Switzerland came close to voting away its entire military. August 1 is the very festive Swiss national holiday.

Switzerland has a low inflation rate and a strong franc. Dormitory accommodations are plentiful and inexpensive, groceries are reasonable, and hiking is free, but Alpine lifts and souvenirs are expensive. Shops throughout the land thrill tourists with carved, woven, and clanging mountain knickknacks, clocks, watches, and Swiss Army knives (Victorinox is the best brand).

The Swiss eat when we do and enjoy a straightforward, no-nonsense cuisine. Specialties include delicious fondue, rich chocolates, a melted cheese dish called *raclette*, fresh dairy products (try müesli yogurt), 100 varieties of cheese, and Fendant, a good crisp local white wine, too expensive to sell well abroad but worth a taste here. The Co-op and Migros grocery stores are the hungry hiker's best budget bet.

You can get anywhere quickly on Switzerland's fine road system (the world's most expensive per mile to build) or on its scenic and efficient trains.

Tourist information offices abound. While Switzerland's booming big cities are cosmopolitan, the traditional culture survives in the Alpine villages. Spend most of your time getting high in the Alps. On Sundays, you're most likely to enjoy traditional sports, music, clothing, and culture.

Appenzell

Appenzell is Switzerland's most traditional region—and the butt of much local humor because of it. This is Landsgemeinde country, where entire villages would meet in town squares to vote (featured on most post card racks). Until 1991, the women of Appenzell couldn't vote on local issues. A gentle beauty blankets the region overlooked by the 8,200-foot peak, Säntis. As you drive, you'll enjoy an ever-changing parade of finely carved chalets, traditional villages, and cows moaning "milk me." While farmers' daughters make hay in bikinis, old ladies walk the steep roads with scythes, looking as if they just pushed the grim reaper down the hill.

If you're here in early September there's a good chance you'll get in on—or at least have your road blocked by—the ceremonial procession of flower-bedecked cows and whistling herders in traditional, formal outfits. The festive march down from the high pastures is a spontaneous move by the herding families, and when they finally do burst into town (a slow-motion Swiss Pamplona), the people become children again, dropping everything and running into the streets. When locals are asked about their cheese, they clench their fists as they say, "It's the best."

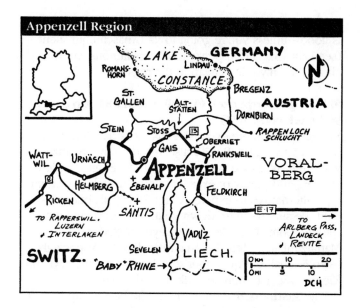

Appenzell Region

From picturesque Altstätten, you'll wind up a steep mountain pass and your world becomes H.O.-gauge. Park at the summit at the tiny Stoss railroad station. Cross to the chapel and walk through the meadow, past munching cows, to the monument that celebrates a local Appenzeller victory over Habsburg Austria. From this spectacular spot you can see the Rhine Valley, Liechtenstein, and the mountains of Vorarlberg back in Austria. This is an appropriate first stop in fiercely independent Switzerland. Enjoy the sun and the wind; stretch out on the stone for a snooze or a picnic. Back by the chapel, the 300-year-old Wirtschaftz Stoss Inn is a rude place for a drink, snack, or rest stop (W.C. in the hallway).

Now carry on through Gais and into Appenzell town. This is the most "typical" town around, where the kids play "barn," not "house," while mom and dad watch yodeling on TV. Tourist Information (9:00-12:00, 14:00-17:00, Saturday 9:00-12:00, tel. 071/874111) is on the main street, Hauptgasse, next to the City Hall. Ask about an Appenzeller folk evening (most nights, July-September, often free, dinner usually optional). Try to see one of these shows tonight. The little folk museum next to the TI is good—unless you're going to its Urnäsch equivalent (see Day 13). The Appenzeller *bier* is famous, good, and about the only thing cheap in the region.

Sleeping in Appenzell (1.5 SF = about $1, zip code: 9050, tel. code: 071)

Switzerland is more expensive than Austria. Doubles under $50 are rare. But it's also wonderfully organized, with an easy phone system, helpful TIs, English widely spoken, and plenty of excellent youth hostels and dorm-type alternatives to expensive hotels. If your budget is tight, be sure to chase down youth hostels (many with "family rooms") and keep your eyes peeled for Matratzenlagers (literally, "mattress dorm"). Appenzell town is small but quite touristy. Hotels are expensive; the Zimmer are a 10-minute walk from the center.

The **Gasthaus Hof** offers by far the best cheap beds in town in its modern Matratzenlager (20 SF per bed in 6- to 8-bed rooms with breakfast, sheets 6 SF more; centrally located just off the Landsgemeindeplatz, tel. 872210, Herr Dörig). Outside of peak times, you'll be sleeping alone in a warehouse of bunkbeds. Gasthaus Hof serves good 20-SF *Rösti*, the area's cheesy potato specialty.

Hotel Adler (D-90 SF, DB-120 to 130 SF, CC-VMA, elevator; a block from the TI, just over the bridge, tel. 871389, fax 871365, SE-A), above a delicious café in a fine location, offers three kinds of rooms: modern, newly refurbished traditional Appenzeller, or old and basic.

Hotel Taube is also good (D-90 SF, DB-120 SF, CC-VMA; between the station and the main street, Hirschengasse 8, tel. 871149). The only inexpensive hotel in town, **Pension Union** (D-70 SF, DB-80 SF; between the station and the main street, tel. 871420, SE-F) is a peaceful, grandfatherly old place.

Haus Lydia (D-75 SF; Eggerstandenstr. 53, CH 9050 Appenzell, east of the center over the bridge and past the Esso station, tel. 874233) is an Appenzell-style home filled with tourist information and a woodsy folk atmosphere, on the edge of town with a garden and a powerful mountain view. This wonderful 6-room Zimmer is run by Frau Mock-Inauen.

Johann Ebneter speaks English and runs a friendly and modern Zimmer in the same area (D-75 SF; Mooshaldenstr. 14, tel. 873487).

Ebenalp (a thin-air alternative to Appenzell town)

While the Appenzell region's forte is the folk culture rather than staggering peaks, it is presided over by 8,200-foot-high Säntis Peak. Säntis is accessible by lift but for a more backdoor experience, ride the lift from Wasserauen, 5 miles south of Appenzell town, to Ebenalp: 5,000 feet, with a sneak preview of the cave church and guest house on the way up, a sweeping view of the entire region all the way to Lake Constance (Bodensee) from the top, and an interesting 90-minute hike down through a prehistoric cave, a hermit's home (now a tiny museum, always open), Wildkirchli, a 400-year-old cave church (hermit monks lived there from 1658-1853), and a 150-year-old guesthouse built precariously into the cliffside (originally used by pilgrims who climbed here to have the hermit pray for them, now Berggasthaus Ascher, see below). These are perched together on a sunny ledge a 12-minute hike below the top of the lift. From this perch you can almost hear the cows munching on the far side of the valley. The hike down is steep but a joy. In the distance, below Säntis, is your destination, the Seealpsee (lake). Only the parasailers, like neon jellyfish, tag your world twentieth-century. The Ebenalp lift runs twice an hour until 19:00 in July and August, 18:00 in June and September, otherwise the last lift is at 17:00 (19 SF round-trip, 12 SF one-way, pick up the free one-page hiking map, tel. 071/881212)

There's no real reason to sleep in Appenzell town. The Ebenalp lift in Wasserauen is a few minutes' drive or train ride south. For a more memorable experience, stay in the **Berggasthaus Ascher** (13 SF for a dorm bed, blankets but no sheets required or provided, 9 SF for breakfast, good dinners, run by Claudia and Bennie Knechtle-Wyss

and their five little children; 9057 Weissbad, 12 minutes by
steep trail below top of lift, tel. 071/881142, open daily
May-October). Their 150-year-old house has only rain
water and no shower. While it's often festive and can
sleep 40 people (literally four hikers to three mattresses),
if you come outside a weekend you'll normally get a small
woody dorm to yourself. The hut is actually built onto the
cliffside; its back wall is the rock. From the toilet you can
study this alpine architecture. Sip your coffee on the deck,
behind drips from the gnarly overhang a hundred yards
above. The goats have their cliff hut adjacent. The guest-
book goes back to 1941 and the piano, in the comfortable
dining/living room, was brought in by helicopter. For a
great 45-minute pre-dinner check-out-the-goats hike, take
the high trail towards the lake; circle clockwise back up
the peak to the lift and down the way you originally
came.

Less atmospheric and more normal is the **Berg
Gasthaus Ebenalp**, just above the lift (23 SF dorm bed
with breakfast, D-72 SF, family Sutter, tel. 071/881194).
From Wasserauen at the base of the lift, you can walk 30
minutes uphill to **Berggasthaus Seealpsee**, situated on an
idyllic alpine lake by the same name (D-70 SF, loft dorm
beds-10 SF plus 10 SF for breakfast, Dörig family; 9057
Weissbad, tel. 071/881140).

APPENZELL TO THE BERNER OBERLAND

After a few short stops in cowbell country, drive three scenic hours to the Interlaken area, spending the afternoon at Switzerland's greatest open-air folk museum, Ballenberg. Climb through traditional houses from every corner of this diverse country and sample the handicrafts and baking in action. After a look at Interlaken, drive deep into the heart of the Alps and ride the gondola to the stop just this side of heaven—Gimmelwald.

Suggested Schedule

8:00	Joyride through Appenzell, cheese tour in Stein.
10:00	Drive direct to Ballenberg, picnic en route or late at Ballenberg.
14:00	Ballenberg Museum. (If it's sunny, consider hiking today and returning for the museum.)
17:00	Drive to Interlaken, quick "travel chores stop" in Interlaken. Drive to Stechelberg for 18:55 lift.
19:00	Check into Walter's Hotel Mittaghorn in Gimmelwald.
19:30	Dinnertime at Walter's.

Transportation: Appenzell to Interlaken (120 miles)
It's a 3-hour drive from Appenzell to Ballenberg and another hour from there to the Gimmelwald lift. Head west out of Appenzell town on the Urnäsch road, taking the first right (after about 2 miles, easy to miss, sign to Herisau/Wattwil) to Stein. In Stein, Schaukäserei signs direct you to a big, modern building. From there, wind scenically south to Urnäsch and down the small road (signs to Hemberg) to Wattwil. Somewhere along the Urnäsch-Hemberg road stop to ask an old local if this is the way to Wattwil (or San Jose), just to hear the local dialect and to see the healthy outdoor twinkle in his or her eyes up close. Drive through Ricken, into the town of

Rapperswil, following green signs to Zurich over the long lake bridge, and southward following blue signs to Einsiedeln and Gotthard. You'll go through the town of Schwyz, the historic core of Switzerland that gave its name to the country.

From Brunnen, one of the busiest, most expensive to build, and most impressive roads in Switzerland wings you along the Urnersee. It's dangerously scenic, so stop at the parking place after the first tunnel (on right, opposite Stoos turnoff) where you can enjoy the view and a rare Turkish toilet. Follow signs to Gotthard through Flüelen, then autobahn for Luzern, vanishing into a long tunnel that should make you feel a little better about your 30-SF autobahn sticker. Exit at the Stans-Nord exit (signs to Interlaken). Go along the Alpnachersee south toward Sarnen. Continue past Sarnensee to Brienzwiller before Brienz. A sign at Brienzwiller will direct you to the Ballenberg Freilicht (Swiss Open-Air) Museum/Ballenberg Ost. You can park here, but I prefer the west entrance, a few minutes down the road near Brienz.

From Brienzwiller, save 20 minutes by taking the new autobahn to Interlaken along the south side of Lake Brienz. Cruise through the old resort town down Interlaken's main street from the Ost Bahnhof, past the cow field with a great Eiger-Jungfrau view on your left and grand old hotels, the TI, post office, and banks on your right, to the West Bahnhof at the opposite end of town. Park there.

To get to Gimmelwald (from downtown Interlaken or from the autobahn), follow signs south to Lauterbrunnen, pass through Lauterbrunnen town, noticing the train station on your left and the funicular across the street on your right, and drive to the head of the Stechelberg valley, a glacier-cut cradle of Swissness, where you'll see the base of the Schilthornbahn (a big gray gondola station). This parking lot is safe and free. Allow 30 minutes to drive from Interlaken to the Stechelberg gondola parking lot. Ride the 18:55 lift (7 SF, two trips an hour at :25 and :55; get off at first stop, walk into the village, hard right at PTT, signs direct you up the path, 5 minutes) to Gimmelwald.

A steep 300-yard climb brings you to the chalet marked simply "Hotel." This is Walter Mittler's Hotel Mittaghorn. You have arrived.

Eurailers, take the Zürich-Luzern-Brünig-Brienzwiller train. At the Brienzwiller station, check your bag, note when trains depart for Interlaken, buy your Ballenberg ticket, and follow the footpath into the museum. Carry on later by train to Interlaken-Ost (East).

While most major trains leave from Interlaken-West station, private trains (not covered by Eurailpass) go from the Interlaken-East station into the Jungfrau region. Ask at the station about discount passes and special fares. Spend some time in Interlaken before buying your ticket to Lauterbrunnen. It's a pleasant walk between the East and West stations.

Take the train from Interlaken Ost to Lauterbrunnen, cross the street to catch the funicular to Mürren. You'll ride up to Grütschalp where a special scenic train (*panorama fahrt* in German) rolls you along the cliff into Mürren. From there, walk an easy, paved 40 minutes downhill or walk 10 minutes across town to catch the gondola (7 SF and a 5-minute steep uphill backtrack) to Hotel Mittaghorn. If you walk, turn left out of the station and walk through the town, keeping eyes open for the left turn (yellow sign) down to Gimmelwald. Your hotel will greet you at the edge of Gimmelwald. A good bad-weather option (or vice versa) is to ride the post bus from Lauterbrunnen (leaves at 5 minutes past the hour) to the base of the Stechelberg-Schilthorn gondola and ride up to Gimmelwald from there. The hike from Stechelberg to Gimmelwald is well marked and as enjoyable as a steep 2-hour hike can be. (Note that for a week in early May and for three weeks in mid-November, the Schilthornbahn is closed for servicing. During this time, Gimmelwald is a serious headache to get to and Hotel Mittaghorn is closed. Schilthornbahn tel. 036/231444 or 552141.)

Sightseeing Highlights—On the Road to Gimmelwald
▲▲**Stein**—The Appenzell Showcase Cheese Dairy (Schaukäserei) is open daily from 8:00 to 19:00 (cheese

making normally 9:00-11:00 and 13:00-15:00). It's fast, free, and well explained in the free English brochure (with cheese recipes). The lady at the cheese counter loves to cut the cheese so you can enjoy small samples. They also have yogurt and cheap boxes of cold iced tea for sale. The TI and a great folk (*Volkskunde*) museum are next door (10:00-17:00, closed for lunch and on Monday, may open a little early if you ask nicely, 7 SF, borrow English booklet, tel. 071/591159). This is the ultimate cow-culture museum with old-fashioned cheese-making demonstrations, peasant houses, fascinating and complex embroidering machinery, lots of cow art, and folk craft demonstrations daily in the summer. If you missed the cows on parade, this moo-seum is the next best thing.

▲**Urnäsch**—An appealing one-street town, which has my nomination for Europe's cutest museum. The Appenzeller Museum (on the town square, open 13:30-17:00 daily in summer, less in spring and fall, closed in winter; 4 SF, good English description brochure, will open for groups of five or more if you call the director at 581487 or 582322) brings this region's folk customs to life. Warm and homey, it's a happy little honeycomb of Appenzeller culture. The Gasthaus Ochsen, three doors down from the museum, is a fine traditional hotel (D-80 SF, tel. 071/581117) with good food, low ceilings, and wonderful atmosphere. Peek into its old restaurant.

▲**Einsiedeln**—Just a few minutes off the road south of Rapperswil is the "Alpine Lourdes," Switzerland's most important pilgrimage church. The interior's bubble-gum Baroque is awesome.

▲▲▲**Ballenberg**—The Swiss Open-Air Museum Ballenberg is a rich collection of traditional and historic farmhouses from every region of the country. Each house is carefully furnished, and many feature a traditional craftsperson at work. The sprawling 50-acre park, laid out roughly as a huge Swiss map, is a natural preserve providing a wonderful setting for this culture-on-a-lazy-Susan look at Switzerland.

The Thurgau house (#621) has an interesting wattle-and-daub (half-timbered construction) display and a fun bread museum upstairs. Use the 2-SF map/guide. The more expensive picture book is a better souvenir than guide. Open daily 10:00 to 17:00, April through October, 12 SF entry, half-price after 16:00 (houses close at 17:00, park stays open later), craft demonstration schedules are listed just inside the entry, 2-hour private tours are 50 SF (by prior arrangement), tel. 036/51 11 23. There's a reasonable outdoor cafeteria inside the west entrance, and fresh baked bread, sausage, and mountain cheese, or other cooked goodies are on sale in several houses. Picnic tables and grills with free firewood are scattered throughout the park.

Before leaving, drive through the little wooden village of Brienzwiller (near the east entrance). It's a museum in itself with a lovely little church. (Trains go regularly from Interlaken to Brienz, where buses connect you with Ballenberg.)

▲**Interlaken**—When the nineteenth-century Romantics redefined mountains as something more than cold and troublesome obstacles, Interlaken became the original Alpine resort. Ever since then, tourists have flocked to the Alps "because they're there." Interlaken's glory days are long gone, its elegant old hotels eclipsed by the new, more jet-setty Alpine resorts. Today, its shops are filled with chocolate bars, Swiss Army knives, and sunburned backpackers.

But it's a good administrative and shopping center. You'll find a handy post office, a late-hours long-distance phone booth (7:30-12:00, 13:45-18:30 daily, next to the post office, easy 2 SF/minute calls to the U.S., even cheaper on Saturday, Sunday, and after 21:00), plenty of banks (the West train station exchange desk has fair rates and is open daily until 19:00, Sunday until 18:00), open-late Migros supermarket next to the West Station, and major trains to all corners of Europe.

Interlaken is a handy place to wash your filthy clothes. Helen Schmocker's Wascherei Laundry has a change machine, soap, English instructions, and a pleasant riverside place to hang out (from the post office follow Marktgasse over two bridges to Beatenbergstrasse, open 7:00-

22:00 daily for self-service, 8 SF to wash and dry 10 pounds; Monday-Friday 8:00-12:00 and 13:30-18:00 for full service: drop off 10 pounds and 12 SF in the morning and pick it up clean that afternoon; tel. 036/22 15 66).

Take care of business, give the town a quick look, and head for the hills. The tourist office (West Station, 7:30-12:00, 13:30-18:00 daily, until 19:00 in summer; tel. 036/22 21 21) has good information for the whole region and advice on Alpine lift discounts. Pick up a Bern map, a Jungfrau region map, and a Jungfrau region timetable. For mountain train information, tel. 036/26 42 33.

Luzern—Train travelers may pass through Luzern. Near the station is the tourist office and the pleasant old lakeside center with its charming covered bridges—worth a walk. The sightseeing highlight, apart from ogling the 50,000-SF watches in the shop windows near the lakefront (only the cheaper 10,000-SF ones are left out at night), is Luzern's huge Museum of Transportation (*Verkehrshaus der Schweiz*) outside town on the lake (boats and cable cars go there from the center). Europe's best transport museum, it's open daily from 9:00 to 18:00 (November-February, 10:00-16:00), 12 SF.

Sleeping and Eating in Gimmelwald (4,500 feet; 1.5 SF = about $1, zip code: 3826, tel. code: 036)

To inhale the Alps and really hold it in, sleep high in Gimmelwald. Poor, happily stuck in the past, avalanche-zone Gimmelwald has a happy youth hostel, a cranky pension, and a creaky hotel. The only bad news is that the lift costs 7 SF each way.

The **"Mountain Hostel"** (8 SF per bed in 2- to 15-bed rooms, 2 SF for sheets, closed mid-December through mid-January; 50 yards from the lift station, left at only intersection, tel. 551704, SE-B) is goat-simple, as clean as its guests, cheap, and very friendly. Its 45 beds are often taken in July and August, so call ahead to Lena, the elderly woman who runs the place. The hostel has low ceilings, a self-serve kitchen, co-ed washrooms, and enough hot water for ten (1 SF, 5 minutes) hot showers a day (or you can drop by the Mürren Sports Center with a towel and 3 SF).

This relaxed hostel is struggling to survive. Please read the signs, respect its rules, and leave it cleaner than you found it. Treat it and Lena with loving care. Without Lena, there's no hostel in Gimmelwald. The place, because of the spirit of its rugged but sensitive visitors and the help of Brian (a local Texan), almost runs itself.

The **Pension Gimmelwald** (20 SF dorm beds on its top floor without breakfast, D-90 SF, DB-110 SF with breakfast, two-night minimum, open mid-June through October, tel. 55 17 30), next door, serves meals.

Hotel Mittaghorn the treasure of Gimmelwald, is run by Walter Mittler, a perfect Swiss gentleman (D-60 SF, T-80 SF, Q-100 SF, Quint-120 SF, loft beds-25 SF, all with breakfast, family discounts; CH-3826 Gimmelwald/Bern, tel. 55 16 58, reserve by telephone only and then you must reconfirm by telephone the day before your arrival, at this time you can order dinner, a deal at 15 SF if Walter's cooking; don't show up without a reservation).

Hotel Mittaghorn is a classic, creaky, Alpine-style place with memorable beds, ancient (short) down comforters, and a million-dollar view of the Jungfrau Alps. The hotel has two rooms with a private shower and a single communal shower (1 SF for 5 minutes). Walter is careful not to get too hectic or big and enjoys sensitive, back-door travelers. He runs the hotel with the help of Don von Gimmelwald (actually Don Chmura, "von" Winnipeg), keeping it simple but with class. This is a good place to receive mail from home (mail barrel in dining room).

To some, Hotel Mittaghorn is a fire just waiting to happen, with a kitchen that would never pass code, lumpy beds, teeny towels, and nowhere near enough plumbing, run by an eccentric grouch. These people enjoy Interlaken, Wengen, or Mürren, and that's where they should sleep. Be warned, you'll meet maybe more of my readers than you hoped for, but it's a fun crowd, an extended family. (Walter closes his place for a week in early May and again in late November, when the local lift is closed for servicing.) He's also closed from mid-December through March.

Gimmelwald feeds its goats better than its people. The hostel has a decent members' kitchen but serves no food. There are no groceries in town. The wise and frugal buy food from the Co-ops in Mürren or Lauterbrunnen and pack it in. Walter, at Hotel Mittaghorn, is Gimmelwald's best cook (not saying much, but he is good). Dinners must be preordered and prepaid by 16:00 (15 SF). His salad is best eaten one leaf at a time with your fingers. There's no menu, and dinner's served at 19:30 sharp. When Walter's in the mood, his place is the best bar in town: good cheap beer and strong *kaffee fertigs* (coffee with schnapps). Otherwise, you can eat at the pension in the center of the village. For a rare bit of ruggedness and the best budget food in the center of Mürren, eat at the Stägerstübli.

Sleeping in Mürren (5,500 feet, zip code: 3825, tel. code: 036)

Mürren is as pleasant as an Alpine resort can be. It's traffic-free, filled with bakeries, cafés, souvenirs, old-timers

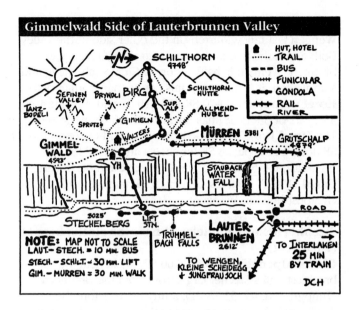

Gimmelwald Side of Lauterbrunnen Valley

with walking sticks, GE employees enjoying incentive trips, and Japanese making movies of each other with a Fujichrome backdrop. Its chalets are prefab-rustic. It sits on a ledge 2,000 feet above the Lauterbrunnen valley and is surrounded by a fortissimo chorus of mountains. It has all the comforts of home and then some, with Alp-high prices. Mürren's Tourist Office can find you a room and change money (in the Sporthaus, daily, 9:00-12:00, 14:00-18:00, less off-season, tel. 551616).

Hotel Belmont (D-100 SF, DB-130 SF, with breakfast, discounts for no view rooms, CC-VMA; across from the train station, tel. 553535, fax 553531, SE-A), run by Andreas and Anne Marie Goetschi, offers Mürren's best budget rooms. **Hotel Alpenblick** (tel. 551327, fax 551391, closed off-season), next door, also has affordable rooms.

Chalet Fontana (35 to 45 SF per person in doubles or triples with breakfast, view and kitchenette, tel. 55 26 86; behind the Stägerstübli in the town center, mid-June-September) is owned by Denise Fussel, who makes you feel right at home.

Sleeping in Wengen (4,200 feet, tel. code: 036)
Wengen is a fancy Mürren on the other side of the valley
Both are traffic-free and an easy lift ride above Lauter-
brunnen. Wengen is halfway up to Kleine-Scheidegg and
Männlichen. It has more tennis courts than budget beds.
Hotel Bernerhof (D-70 SF, DB-110 SF with breakfast, tel.
55 27 21 or 55 33 58) has dorm beds (16 SF, no sheets).
The **Hotel Jungfraublick**, open June-mid-October, has 20
SF dorm beds (plus 6 SF for sheets and 11 SF for
Breakfast, tel. 55 27 55). The **Chalet Schweizerheim
Garni** (100 SF doubles, tel. 55 15 81, summer only) is the
cheapest hotel in Wengen.

**Sleeping below Gimmelwald near the Stechelberg Lift
(2,800 feet)**
Chalet Alpenglühn (D or T-60 SF, kitchenette but no
breakfast, 3824 Stechelberg across from the Breithorn
Campground, tel. 55 18 21), a tiny drive before the
Schilthornbahn, is on the valley floor surrounded by the
meadow, waterfalls, and birds, and features low ceilings
and simple Alpine elegance. This is the home of Theo Van
Allmen, who makes art with leather and budget travelers
happy. **Klara von Allmen** (D-50 SF, minimum two
nights; just over the river from the Stechelberg post office
at big "Zimmer" sign, Pfang, 3824 Stechelberg, tel. 55 25
54, SE-F) rents out three rooms in a quiet, scenic, and
folky setting. Good luck communicating. There are several
other Zimmer in the neighborhood.

The local **Naturfreundehaus Alpenhof** (60 co-ed
beds, 4 to 8 per room, 14 SF per bed, 7 SF breakfast, 13
SF dinner, no sheets; Stechelberg, tel. 55 12 02, closed
November, near Stechelberg bus stop) is a rugged Alpine
lodge for local hikers at the far end of Lauterbrunnen
Valley. The neighboring **Hotel Stechelberg** (D-78 SF, DB-
98 SF and 118 SF, tel. 55 29 21) is clean, quiet and inexpensive.

Sleeping in Lauterbrunnen town (2,600 feet)
Masenlager Stocki (10 SF a night with sheets in an easy
going little 30 bed co-ed dorm, with a kitchen,

tel. 55 17 54, closed November-mid-December) is a great value; across the river, take the first left. **Gasthaus Bären** (D-64 SF, tel. 55 16 54) is at the far end near the waterfall Two campgrounds just south of town work very hard to provide 15- to 25-SF beds. They each have dorms, 2-, 4-, and 6-bed bungalows, no sheets, kitchen facilities, and big English-speaking tour groups. **Camping Jungfrau** (tel. 55 20 10), romantically situated just beyond the stones hurled by Staubbach Falls, also has fancier cabins and trailers for the classier camper. **Schützenbach Campground** (tel. 55 12 68), on the left just past Lauterbrunnen toward Stechelberg, is simpler.

Sleeping in Interlaken, Brienz, or halfway to the Jungfrau

Balmer's Herberge, an Interlaken institution (16-SF dorm beds, 26 SF per person in simple doubles, and 11 SF in overflow on-the-floor accommodations, all with breakfast; Haupstrasse 23, in Matten, a 15-minute walk from either Interlaken station, tel. 22 19 61) is run by a creative tornado of entrepreneurial energy, Eric Balmer. With movies, ping-pong, laundromat, a secondhand English book-swapping library, rafting excursions, plenty of tips on budget eating and hiking, and a friendly, hardworking, mostly American staff, this little Nebraska is home for those who miss their fraternity.

For 30-SF dorm beds with breakfast high in the mountains, you can sleep at Kleine Scheidegg's **Bahnhof Buffet** (tel. 55 11 51) or at **Restaurant Grindelwaldblick** (12-bed dorm rooms, 28 SF per bed with breakfast but no sheets, tel. 53 30 43, open June-October)

FREE DAY IN THE ALPS—HIKE!

Today is your vacation from this go-go vacation. And a great place to recharge your touristic batteries is up here high in the Alps where distant avalanches, cowbells, the fluff of a down comforter, and the crunchy footsteps of happy hikers are the dominant sounds. If the weather's good, ride the lift from Gimmelwald to a hearty breakfast at Schilthorn's 10,000-foot revolving Piz Gloria restaurant. Linger among Alpine whitecaps before riding, hiking, or hang gliding down (5,000 feet) to Mürren and home to Gimmelwald.

Suggested Schedule

8:00   Ride the Gimmelwald-Schilthorn lift.

8:30   Breakfast on the Schilthorn, ride or walk down to Mürren, browse, buy a picnic lunch. Hike to Gimmelwald via Gimmelen. Or, if the weather's great, consider doing the Männlichen-Kleine Scheidegg hike this afternoon.

Sightseeing Highlights

▲▲▲**Gimmelwald**—Saved from developers by its "avalanche zone" classification, Gimmelwald is one of the poorest places in Switzerland. Its economy is stuck in the hay, and many of the farmers, unable to make it in their disadvantaged trade, are subsidized by the Swiss government. For some, there's little to see in the village. Others enjoy a fascinating day sitting on a bench. Take a walk, noticing the traditional log-cabin architecture and blonde-braided children. The numbers on the buildings are not addresses but fire insurance numbers. The cute little hut near the station is for storing and aging cheese, not youth hostelers (the stone plates under it work to keep bugs out). Don't confuse obscure Gimmelwald with very touristy and commercialized Grindelwald just over the Kleine Scheidegg ridge.

Evening fun in Gimmelwald is found at the hostel (lots of young Alp-aholics and a good chance to share information on the surrounding mountains) and up at Walter's. Walter's bar is a local farmer's hangout. When they've made their hay, they come here to play. They look like what we'd call "hicks" but they speak some English and can be fun to get to know. Former city-slicker Walter still isn't fully accepted by the gang. He knows how many beers they've had according to whether they're talking, singing, fighting, or snoring. For less smoke and some powerful solitude, sit outside (benches just below the rails, 100 yards down the lane from Walter's) and watch the sun tuck the mountaintops into bed as the moon rises over the Jungfrau.

▲▲▲**Hike 1: The Schilthorn, Hikes, Lifts, and a 10,000-foot Breakfast**—If the weather's good, have breakfast atop the Schilthorn, in the slowly revolving, mountain-capping restaurant (of James Bond movie fame). The early-bird special gondola tickets (rides before 9:00) take you from Gimmelwald to the Schilthorn and back with a great continental breakfast on top for 55 SF— cheaper than the normal round-trip without breakfast. (Buy tickets from Walter or at the gondola station.) Bear with the slow service, and ask for more hot drinks if necessary. If you're not revolving, ask them to turn it on.

The Gimmelwald–Schilthorn hike is free. In fact, you'll gain 5,000 feet of altitude. I ride up and hike down or, for a less scary hike, go halfway down by cable car and walk down from the Birg station. Lifts go twice an hour, and the ride takes 30 minutes. Watch the altitude meter in the gondola. Buy the round-trip excursion early-bird fare (cheaper than the Gimmelwald-Schilthorn-Birg ticket) and decide at Birg if you want to hike or ride down.

Linger on top. Piz Gloria has been newly renovated. There's a souvenir shop, the rocks of the region on the restaurant wall, telescopes, and a "touristorama" film room showing explosive highlights from the James Bond thriller that featured the Schilthorn and a multi-screen slide show. (It's self-serve. Push the button for slides or 007.) Watch hang gliders set up, psych up, and take off, flying 30

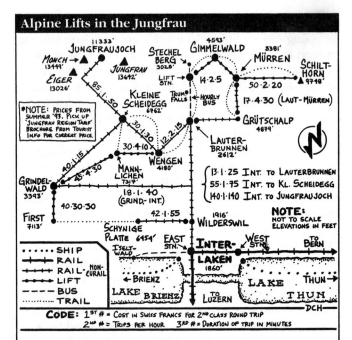

Alpine Lifts in the Jungfrau

Code: 1ST # = Cost in Swiss Francs for 2ND Class Round Trip
2ND # = Trips per Hour   3RD # = Duration of Trip in Minutes

Code: Round-trip price in Swiss francs—Departures per hour—Length of ride in minutes (e.g., 13-1-40 is 13 SF round-trip, 1 per hour, 40 minutes long).

Since round-trips are discounted only to stations above towns (e.g., to Kl. Scheidegg & Schilthorn), buy one-way between towns for flexibility. Maps, schedules, and price lists are available at any station. Lifts run from about 7:00 to 20:00. Groups of five or more receive about a 20 percent discount. Early and late Jungfraujoch trains (leaving Kl. Stechelberg to Gimmelwald lifts go at :25 and :55 past the hour, until 19:25; after that, hourly in summer. Any train or lift station can give you a free, complete, and up-to-date fare and time schedule.

minutes with the birds to distant Interlaken. Walk along the ridge out back to the "No High Heels" signpost. This is a great place for a photo of the "mountain climber you." For another cheap thrill, ask the gondola attendant to crank down the window, stick your head out, and pretend you're hang gliding (ideally, over the bump going down from Gimmelwald).

Think twice before hiking down from the Schilthorn (weather can change, have good shoes). Hiking down from Birg is easier but still very steep and gravelly. Just below Birg is the Schilthorn-Hutte. Drop in for soup, cocoa, or a coffee schnapps. You can spend the night in the hut's loft (40 mattresses, open July-September, tel. 55 11 67 or 55 25 12). Youth hostelers scream down the ice fields on plastic-bag sleds from the Schilthorn. (English-speaking doctor in Mürren.)

The most interesting trail from Birg (or Mürren) to Gimmelwald is the high one via Suppenalp, Schiltalp, Gimmeln, and the Sprütz waterfall. Mürren has plenty of shops, bakeries, tourist information, banks, and a modern sports complex for rainy days. Ask at the Schilthorn station in Mürren for a gondola souvenir pin or sticker.

▲▲▲**Hike 2: The Männlichen-Kleine Scheidegg Hike**—This is my favorite easy Alpine hike, entertaining you all the way with glorious Jungfrau, Eiger, and Mönch views. (That's the Young Maiden being protected from the Ogre by the Monk.)

If the weather's good, descend from Gimmelwald bright and early. Drive (or catch the post bus) to the Lauterbrunnen train station, parking at the large multi-storied pay lot behind the station. Buy a ticket to Männlichen and catch the train. Ride past great valley views to Wengen, where you'll walk across town (buy a picnic, but don't waste time here if it's sunny), and catch the Männlichen lift (departing every 15 minutes) to the top of the ridge high above you.

From the tip of the Männlichen lift, hike (20 minutes north) to the little peak for that king-of-the-mountain feeling. It's an easy hour's walk from there around to Kleine Scheidegg for a picnic or restaurant lunch. If you've got an extra 80 SF and the weather's perfect, ride the train through the Eiger to the towering Jungfraujoch and back. Check for discount trips up to Jungfraujoch; three trips a day (one early, two late, telephone information 26 41 11, weather 55 10 22). Jungfraujoch crowds can be frighten-

Berner Oberland

NOTE: THIS BIRD'S EYE VIEW LOOKS SOUTH...

EIGER 13026'   MONCH 13449'   JUNGFRAU 13642'   SCHILT-HORN 9748'

JUNG-FRAU-JOCH

GIMMEL-WALD 4593'

TUNNEL

KLEINE SCHEIDEGG 6762'

BIRG 8784'

HIKE #2

MÄNNLICHEN 7317'

W. ALP

HIKE #1

GRINDEL-WALD 3393'

MÜRREN 5381'

GRUND

STECHEL-BERG 3025'

← NICE WALK

GRÜTSCHALP 4879'

← TO FIRST

WENGEN 4180'

LAUTERBRUNNEN 2612'

HIKE #3

WILDERSWIL 1916'

ISELT-WALD

SCHYNIGE PLATTE 6454'

TO LUZERN

SPIEZ

E.   W.

LAKE   BRIENZ   INTER-LAKEN 1860   LAKE   THUN   TO BERN

BRIENZ ●

● BALLENBERG

━━ PRIVATE RAIL - EURAIL NOT VALID   --- BUS   NOT TO SCALE!
━━ OTHER RAIL - EURAIL VALID   ••••
○━○ MTN. LIFTS   ••••• TRAIL   DCH

ing. The price has been jacked up to reduce the mobs, but sunny days are still a mess.

From Kleine Scheidegg, enjoy the ever-changing Alpine panorama of the North Face of the Eiger, Jungfrau, and Mönch, probably accompanied by the valley-filling mellow sound of Alp horns and distant avalanches, as you ride the train or hike downhill (30 gorgeous minutes to Wengeralp, 90 more steep minutes from there into the town of Wengen). If the weather turns bad, or you run out of steam, catch the train early at the little Wengeralp station along the way. After Wengeralp the trail is steep and, while not dangerous, requires a good set of knees. Wengen is a fine shopping town. The boring final descent is knee-killer steep, so catch the train from Wengen to Lauterbrunnen. Trails may be snowbound into early summer. Ask about conditions at lift stations. If the Männlichen lift is closed, take the train straight from

Lauterbrunnen to Kleine Scheidegg. Many take the risk of slipping and enjoy the Kleine Scheidegg to Wengeralp hike even with a little snow.

▲▲**Hike 3: Schynige Platte to First**—The best day I've had hiking in the Berner Oberland is the demanding 6-hour ridge walk high above Lake Brienz on one side and all that Jungfrau beauty on the other. Start at Wilderswil where you catch the little train up to Schynige Platte (2,000 meters). Walk through the Alpine flower display garden and into the wild Alpine yonder. The high point is Faulhorn (2,680 meters, with its famous mountain-top hotel). Your destination is a chair lift called First (2,168 meters), where you descend to Grindelwald and catch a train back to your starting point, Wilderswil (or if you have no car, a regional train pass, or endless money, return to Lauterbrunnen from Grindelwald over Kleine Scheidegg).

▲**Other Hikes from Gimmelwald**—For a not-too-tough 3-hour walk (there's a scary 20-minute stretch that comes with ropes) with great Jungfrau views and some mountain farm action, ride the funicular from Mürren to Allmen-hübel (1,934 meters), walk to Marchegg, Saustal, and Grütschalp (1,500 meters), where you catch the panorama train back to Mürren. An easier version is the lower "Bergweg" from Allmenhübel to Grütschalp via Winteregg. Get specifics at the Mürren TI.

An easy, go-as-far-as-you-like trail from Gimmelwald is up the Sefinen Valley. Or, you can wind from Gimmelwald down to Stechelberg (1 hour). For the best rundown on the area (hikes, flora, fauna, culture, travel tips) get Don Chmura's fine 5-SF Gimmelwald guidebook (available at Hotel Mittaghorn).

Rainy Day Options
If clouds roll in, don't despair. They can roll out just as quickly and there are some good bad-weather options. There are easy trails and pleasant walks along the Lauterbrunnen valley floor. If all the waterfalls have you intrigued, sneak a behind-the-scenes look at the valley's most powerful one, Trümmelbach Falls (8 SF, on the

Lauterbrunnen-Stechelberg road, 9:00-18:00 daily, April-
October). You'll ride an elevator up through the mountain
and climb through several caves to see the melt of the
Eiger, Mönch, and Jungfrau grinding like God's bandsaw
through the mountain at the rate of up to 20,000 liters a
second. (That's double the beer consumption at
Oktoberfest.) The upper area, "chutes 6 to 10," are the
best, so if your legs ache you can skip the lower ones and
ride the lift down. Lauterbrunnen's Heimatmuseum (3 SF,
14:00-17:30, Tuesday, Thursday, Saturday, and Sunday,
mid-June through September, just over the bridge) shows
off the local folk culture.

Mürren's slick Sports Center (pool open only mid-June
through October) offers a world of indoor activities (7 SF
for use of the swimming pool and whirlpool).

From Interlaken there are regular boat trips on Lake
Thun and Lake Brienz. The super cute and quiet village of
Iseltwald is just a bus or boat ride from Interlaken. On
Lake Thun, both Spiez and Thun are visit-worthy towns.

WEST TO FRENCH SWITZERLAND

This morning, get your last fill of the Alps. Take a quick look at the Swiss capital of Bern, and set up in the medieval walled town of Murten, or should I call it Morat, since we're now in French Switzerland.

Suggested Schedule

7:30	Breakfast.
8:00	Lift to car, drive to Lauterbrunnen. Lift to Männlichen (via Wengen), hike down to Wengen.
13:00	Train to car, drive to Bern.
14:00	Explore downtown Bern.
18:00	Drive to Murten.

Transportation: Interlaken to Murten (50 miles)

From Lauterbrunnen, drive toward Interlaken and catch the autobahn (direction Spiez, Thun, Bern). After Spiez, the autobahn will take you right to Bern. Circle the city on the autobahn, taking the fourth Bern exit, Neufeld Bern, into the center. Signs to Zentrum will take you to the Bahnhof. Turn right just before the station into the Bahnhof Parkplatz (2-hour meter parking outside, all-day lot inside, 2 SF per hour). You're just an escalator ride away from a great tourist information center and Switzerland's compact, user-friendly capital. From the station, drive out of Bern following blue Lausanne signs, then green signs to Neuchatel and Murten. Notice the big gray Jacob Suchard Tobler chocolate factory overlooking the autobahn at the Bern-Brunnen autobahn exit. This is the home of Toblerone, recently purchased by Philip Morris and no longer giving tours. In about 20 minutes you'll be in Murten.

Parking within Murten's walls is medieval. If you have a dashboard clock (free at TIs and banks) you can try the blue spots near the Ringmauer Hotel, but it's best to settle for the large free lots just outside either gate and walk in. It's a tiny town.

Bern

The charming Swiss capital fills a peninsula bounded by
the Aare River, giving you the most (maybe even the only)
enjoyable look at urban Switzerland. Just an hour from
Interlaken, directly on your way to Murten, it's worth a
stop, especially if disappointing weather cuts your mountain time short.

Start your visit at the tourist office inside the train station
(8:00-20:30 daily, until 18:30 in winter, tel. 031/3116611).
Pick up maps for Bern and Murten, a list of city sights,
information on the Parliament tour, the clock, or whatever
you're interested in, and confirm your plans. Follow the
walking tour explained in the handy city map while
browsing your way downhill. Finish with a look at the
bear pits (*Bärengraben*) and a city view from the Rose
Garden across the river. Catch trolley #12 back up to the

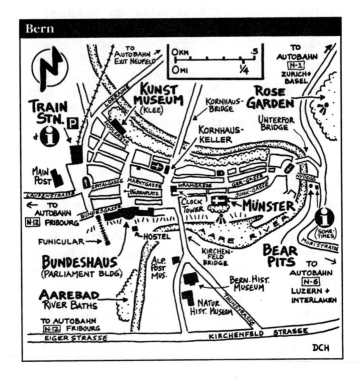

station (buy the cheapest, yellow-button ticket from the machine at the stop). Telephone code: 031.

Sightseeing Highlights—Bern

▲▲**The Old Town**—Window-shopping and people-watching through the lovely arcaded streets and busy market squares are Bern's top attractions. This is my favorite shopping town: prices are so high there's no danger of buying. Great browsing. (Shops open 8:00-18:30, Saturday 8:00-16:00, closed Sunday and Monday until 14:00.) The clock tower (*Zytglogge-turm*) performs at 4 minutes before each hour. Apparently this slowest-moving 5-minute non-event in Europe was considered entertaining in 1530. To pass the time during the performance, read the TI's brochure explaining what's so interesting about the fancy old clock. Enthusiasts can tour the medieval mechanics daily at 16:30 (May-October, tickets 5 SF at the TI or on the spot).

The 1421 Swiss late-Gothic Münster, or cathedral, is worth a look (closed 12:00-14:00). Climb the spiral staircase 100 yards above the town for the view, exercise, and a chance to meet a live church watchman. Peter Probst and his wife, Sigi, live way up there watching over the church, answering questions, and charging tourists for the view.

Nearby is the imposing Parliament building (*Bundeshaus*) of Switzerland (free 45-minute tours most days at 9:00, 10:00, 11:00, 14:00, 15:00, and 16:00, tel. 031/61 85 22 to confirm; closed about March, June, September, and December; minimum group size: five people). Don't miss the view from the Bundeshaus terrace. You may see some national legislators, but you wouldn't know it—everything looks very casual for a national capital.

Einstein did much of his most important thinking while living in a house on the old town's main drag. It was just another house to me, but I guess everything's relative (2 SF, Kramgasse 49, 10:00-17:00, Saturday until 16:00, closed Sunday, Monday, December, and January).

▲**Bear Pits and Rose Garden**—The symbol of Bern is the bear, and some lively ones frolic their days away (8:00-18:00) to the delight of locals and tourists alike in the big, barren, concrete pits, or *Graben* just over the river. Up the paved pathway is the Rosengarten. Worth the walk for the great city view. The Rosengarten restaurant's 16-SF lunch special comes with a great view (tel. 031/331 32 06).

▲▲**The Berner Swim**—For something to write home about, join the local merchants, legislators, publishers, students, and carp in a lunchtime float down the Aare River. The Bernese, proud of their very clean river and their basic ruddiness, have a tradition—sort of a wet, urban paseo. On hot summer days, they hike upstream 5 to 30 minutes and float playfully or relaxedly back down to the excellent (and free) riverside baths and pools (*Aarebad*) just below the Parliament building. If the river is a bit much, you're welcome to enjoy just the Aarebad. If the river is not enough, a popular day-trip is to raft all the way from Thun to Bern.

▲▲**Museum of Fine Arts (*Kunstmuseum*)**—While it features 1,000 years of local art and some impressionism, the real hit is its fabulous collection of Paul Klee's playful and colorful paintings. If you don't know Klee, I'd love to introduce you. (3 SF, four blocks from the station, #12 Holdergasse, 10:00-17:00, closed Monday.)

Other Bern Museums—Across the bridge from the Parliament building on Helvetiaplatz are several museums (Alpine, Berner History, Postal) that sound more interesting than they are. Nearly all are open 10:00-17:00 and closed on Monday.

Sleeping in Bern (1.5 SF = about $1, tel. code: 031)
These are in the old town about a 10-minute walk from the station. Get parking advice locally. You can park in the center free from 19:00-7:00 and on weekends. Garages cost about 1 SF per hour. Supposedly, non-Swiss cars aren't given parking tickets.

   Hotel Hospiz sur Heimat (S-62 SF, SB-85 SF, D-92 SF, DB-120 SF, T-123 SF, TB-147 SF, Q-164 SF, CC-VMA, elevator; Gerechtig-keitsgasse 50, on the main street near the bridge and bears, tram #12 from the station, tel. 311 04 36, fax 312 3386) is Bern's best budget hotel value.

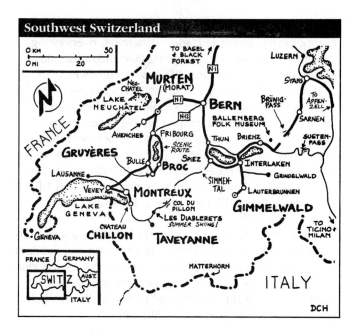

Hotel Goldener Schlüssel (S-60 SF, SB-82 SF, D-96 SF, DB-120 SF, prices will skyrocket with 1995 renovation, CC-VM, elevator, Rathausgasse 72, CH-3011 Bern, tel. 311 0216, fax 311 5688) is a basic, comfortable, crank-'em-out old hotel in the center.

Bern's big, newly renovated, sterile, well-run **IYHF hostel** (14 SF beds, nonmembers 21 SF, breakfast 5 SF; down the stairs from the Parliament building, by the river, at Weihergasse 4, 3005 Bern, tel. 311 6316 or 226316) has 8- to 26-bed rooms and provides an all-day lounge, laundry machines, and cheap meals (office open 7:00-9:30 and 15:00-24:00).

Murten

The finest medieval ramparts in Switzerland surround the 4,600 people of Murten, or Morat in French. We're on the lingua-cusp of Switzerland here: 25 percent of Murten speaks French; a few miles to the south nearly everyone does. Murten is a mini-Bern with three parallel streets, the middle one nicely arcaded with elegant shops and breezy outdoor cafés. Its castle is romantically set, overlooking the tiny Murtensee and the rolling vineyards of gentle Mount Vully in the distance. Try some Vully wine.

The town history museum in an old mill (closed Monday) is not quite worth a look. The only required sightseeing is to do the rampart ramble (free, always open, easy stairway access on east side of town). You can rent a bike just outside the wall or at the station for a lakeside ride. The lake-front offers a popular but pricey restaurant (Les Bain), a lavish swimming pool, and 1-hour lake cruises (free with train passes, departing daily in summer at 15:40).

The TI (tel. 037/715112, open April-October about 9:00-12:00, 14:00-17:30, closed Saturday afternoon and Sunday) tries to be helpful, but there's not much to say. Ask about their free town walks (10:30 in the summer). Murten is touristic but seems to be enjoyed mostly by its own people. Shoppers hate Mondays in Murten.

Sleeping and Eating in Murten (1.5 SF = about $1, tel. code: 037)

Hotel Ringmauer (that's German for "ramparts," S-50 SF, D-90 SF, CC-VM; 2 Deutsche Kirchgasse, near the wall on the side farthest from the lake, tel. 711101) is Murten's only good accommodations deal, and this place is great. Run by Frau Kramer (SE-A), the Ringmauer is friendly, very characteristic, a block from the town center, clean as a croissant, and has showers and toilets within a naked dash of each room. It's my nominee for the "best modern hallway art in an old hotel" and the "best bathroom hardware" awards. It's a bowl-of-apples and homemade-marmalade kind of place with a good restaurant (try the tasty 10-SF *Rösti*, restaurant closed on Saturday).

Hotel Murtenhof (DB-110-190 SF, CC-VMA, SE-A; next to the castle on Rathausgasse, tel. 715656, fax 715059), a full-fledged hotel, is a worthwhile splurge with all the comforts and a lake view.

I eat on **Hotel Murtenhof's terrace** every night for their salad bar (summer only, 7 SF small plate, 14 SF for the big one, the small one—carefully stacked—is plenty, comes with wonderful bread and a sunset over the lake). The small plate is meant as a side dish (no bread) but you can usually just come in, stack up the salad, eat it and get away with a 7-SF meal. The romantic terrace is a good place to try the Vully wine—just point to the vineyards across the lake. (Handy toddlers' play area next to restaurant.) For a cheap hot meal, the Migros and Co-op supermarkets (just outside three of the town gates) have cafeterias.

Avenches

Avenches, 4 miles south of Murten, was Aventicum, the Roman capital of the Confederation Helvetica. Back then its population was 50,000. Today it could barely fill the well-worn ruins of its 15,000-seat Roman amphitheater. You can tour the Roman museum but the best experience is some quiet time at sunset at the evocative Roman theater in the fields, a short walk out of town (always open). Avenches, with a pleasant small-French-town feel, is a quiet alternative to Murten for the night (TI tel. 037/751159).

Sleeping in Avenches

The Avenches **IYHF hostel** (21 SF for bed, sheets, and breakfast, more for nonmembers; Rue du Lavoir 5, three blocks from the center at the medieval lavoir, or laundry), the only hostel in the area, is a beauty. It's run by the Dhyaf family, with 4- to 8-bed rooms, a homey TV room, ping-pong, a big backyard, and a very quiet setting near the Roman theater (7:00-9:00 and 17:00-22:00, tel. 037/752666, fax 752717).

Hotel de L'Union (D-80 SF, DB-100 SF, TB-150 SF; rue Centrale 23, tel. 037/751384) is a simple old place, mostly a restaurant with a few 2- and 3-bed rooms upstairs, shower down the hall, right on the central square of Avenches, two blocks from the Roman amphitheater. It's nothing special except for its price and location. There are no Zimmer in this part of Switzerland.

FRENCH SWITZERLAND HIGHLIGHTS

A third of Switzerland is French and, as you'll see in today's circle south, that means more than language. The highest mountains in Europe are just over the border in France. But you've seen great Alps. Now it's time for Roman ruins, a folk museum, cheese making, a visit to one of Europe's most romantic castles and a taste of the Swiss Riviera along Lake Geneva (Lac Leman). This is an area so beautiful that Charlie Chaplin and Idi Amin both chose it as their second home.

Suggested Schedule

8:00	Breakfast.
8:45	Depart.
10:00	Château Chillon.
11:30	Quick visit/drive through Montreux, Vevey, and the Corniche de Laveau. Lunch on lakeside or in Gruyères/Moleson.
14:00	Cheese demonstration in Gruyères or Moleson.
15:30	Gruérien folk museum in Bulle.
18:00	Avenches Roman ruins
19:00	Home in Murten. Salad by the sea.

Transportation Tips—Murten to Lake Geneva (50 miles)

The autobahn corridor from Bern to Lausanne/Lake Geneva makes everything very speedy. Murten and Avenches are about 10 minutes from the autobahn. Broc, Bulle, and Gruyères are within sight of each other and the autobahn. It takes about an hour to drive from Murten to Montreux. The autobahn (direction Simplon) takes you high above Montreux (pull off at the great view point rest stop) and Chateau Chillon. Take the first exit east of the castle (Villeneuve). Signs will direct you along the lake back to the castle (easy parking). Continue along into Montreux.

By public transportation, you'll find plenty of cross-country trolleys and buses using Fribourg and Bulle as hubs. For example: Bulle-Gruyères (15 minutes, seven a day), Fribourg-Bulle (45 minutes, hourly), Avenches-Fribourg (30 minutes, seven a day), Murten-Fribourg (30 minutes, hourly). Buses connect towns along Lake Geneva every 15 minutes.

Sightseeing Highlights—Southwest Switzerland
▲**Caillers Chocolate Factory**—It's a sad time for choco-holics. The last Swiss chocolate factory tour is now dead . . . for hygienic reasons. While you can no longer drool in front of a molten river of your favorite chocolate, you can see a 40-minute movie and stuff yourself with free melt-in-your-hands samples at the Caillers Chocolate factory, the smell of which dominates the town of Broc (free, May-October, Monday afternoon through Friday, reservation required, tel. 029/65 151, follow signs to Nestle and Broc Fabrique). Broc town is just the sleepy sweet-smelling home of the chocolate-makers. It has a small, very typical hotel, the Auberge des Montagnards (D-60 SF, great Gruyères view, elegant dining room, tel. 029/61526).

▲▲**Musée Gruèrien**—Somehow the unassuming little town of Bulle built a refreshing, cheery folk museum that manages to teach you all about life in these parts and leave you feeling very good. It's small and easy (10:00-12:00, 14:00-17:00, closed Sunday morning and Monday, 4 SF plus 1 SF for the excellent English guide, tel. 029/27260). When it's over, the guide reminds you, "The Golden Book of Visitors awaits your signature and comments. Don't you think this museum deserves another visit? Thank you!"

▲**Gruyères**—This ultra-touristy town fills its fortified little hilltop like a bouquet. Its ramparts are a park, and the ancient buildings serve the tourist crowds. The castle is mediocre, and you don't need to stay long, but make a short stop for the setting. Minimize your walk by driving up to the second parking lot. Hotels in Gruyères are expensive.

▲▲**Gruyères Fromagerie**—There are two very different cheese-making exhibits to choose from. Five miles above Gruyères, a dark and smoky seventeenth-century farm-house in Moleson gives a fun look at the old and smelly craft (mid-May through mid-October, 9:30-18:30, tel. 029/62434. Closer, slicker and very modern, the cheese production center at the foot of Gruyères town (signs to Fromagerie) opens its doors to tourists with a good continuous English audiovisual presentation (free, 8:00-18:30 daily). Cheese is made at each place (usually 10:00-11:00 and 14:00-15:00). The cute cheese shop in the modern center has lunches and picnic stuff (closed from 12:00-13:30).

▲▲**Lake Geneva (Lac Leman)**—Separating France and Switzerland, surrounded by Alps, and lined with a collage of castles, museums, spas, resort towns, and vineyards, Lac Leman's crowds are understandable.

Boats carry its visitors comfortably to all sights of importance. The 15-SF ride from Lausanne to Chillon takes 2 hours with stops in Vevey and Montreux (six trips daily in each direction, Eurailers sail free, tel. 021/6170666). The 10-minute Montreux-Château Chillon cruise is fun even for those with a car.

Montreux is an expensive resort with a famous jazz festival each July (TI tel. 021/9631212). The casino is an entertainment center with a wimpy gaming room and the Bar du Festival, which plays great videos of the latest jazz festival. A beer here makes for an enjoyable evening. Vevey nearby is a smaller and more comfortable resort town.

The **Corniche de Lavaux**, the Swiss Wine Road, winds ruggedly through picturesque towns and the stingy vineyards that produce most of Switzerland's tasty but expensive wine, *Fendant*. Hikers can take the boat to Cully and explore on foot from there. A car tour is quick and frightening (from Montreux go west along the lake, through Vevey, following blue signs to Lausanne along the waterfront, taking the Moudon/Chexbres exit). Explore some of the smaller roads before you get to Chexbres where the green autobahn signs (to Bern) get you on the fast road home. It's 45 minutes from Chexbres to Murten.

Lausanne is the most interesting city on the lake. You can park near its impressive cathedral and walk through the colorful old town. The Collection de l'Art Brut (11 Avenue des Bergieres, 10:00-12:00, 14:00-18:00, closed Saturday and Sunday mornings and Monday, follow signs to Palais de Beaulieu) is a fascinating and thought-provoking collection of art by those who have been labeled criminal or crazy by society.

Geneva bores me. This big city is sterile, cosmopolitan, expensive, and full of executives, diplomats, and tourists looking for profits, peace, cheap rooms, and other worthy but elusive goals.

▲▲▲**Château Chillon**—Wonderfully preserved, this thirteenth-century castle, set wistfully at the edge of Lac Leman, is a joy. Follow the free English map brochure from one fascinating room to the next (or call to find out when an English group is scheduled)—tingly views, dank prison, battle-scarred weapons, interesting furniture, and even 700-year-old toilets. The long climb to the top of the keep (#25 in the brochure) isn't worth the time or sweat. Curl up on a window sill to enjoy the lake (9:00-18:30 daily, less off-season, 5.50 SF, 2 SF extra to join a tour, private tours for 30 SF, easy parking, tel. 021/963 3912).

Sleeping near Château Chillon and Montreux
Since Switzerland is so small with such fast roads, I'd sidetrip to Lac Leman from Murten. If you want to sleep on the lake, Montreux is expensive. But the town of Villeneuve, 3 miles (one autobahn exit) east, has the same palmy lakeside setting without the crowds or glitz. Its main drag runs parallel to the shore, 1 block in. It's a short walk from the waterfront promenade to the château and Montreux.

Le Romantica (D-60 SF, DB-80 SF; Grand-Rue 34, 1844 Villeneuve, tel. 021/960 1540, SE-F) is a rare value with frumpy, very French atmosphere. Even the stools are overstuffed. **Hotel du Soleil** (DB-150 SF; Grand-Rue 20, tel. 021/960 4206) is renovated with all the comforts, an expensive but likable place. The depressing **Hotel de l'Aigle** (D-76 SF; Grand-Rue 48, tel. 021/960 1004, SE-F) has only location and price going for it.

Haut Lac youth hostel (dorm bed, sheets and breakfast-21 SF, D-63 SF, non-members pay 7 SF extra, closed 9:00-17:00, cheap meals served; Passage de l'Auberge 8, 1820 Territet town, tel. 021/963 4934, train noise is a problem) at the edge of Montreux is on the lake, a 10-minute stroll north of the château and a long stroll from the fun of Montreux.

More Alp Sights between Interlaken and Lake Geneva
▲**Simmental**—The Simmen Valley (*tal* means valley) is famous in the United States for its great milk-cows. It's known locally for its fine medieval churches (the most in the Berner Oberland) and for the American farmers who come to see the cows. The Erlenbach Church (park at the market square) is worth a look. An English brochure explains that, as in most local churches, the beautiful paintings decorating the interior survived, ironically, because they were whitewashed over by baroque people.
▲**Glacier des Diablerets**—For another grand Alpine trip to the tip of a 10,000-foot peak, take the three-part lift from Reusch or Col du Pillon. A quick trip takes about 90 minutes and costs 40 SF. You can stay for lunch. From the top, on a clear day, you can see the Matterhorn and even a bit of Mont Blanc, Europe's highest mountain. This is your only good chance to do or watch some summer skiing. Normally expensive and a major headache, it isn't bad here. Lift ticket, rental skis, poles, boots, and a heavy coat cost about 65 SF. Since the slopes close at 14:00 and it's a 2-hour drive from Murten or Gimmelwald, you'll need to leave early.
▲▲**Taveyanne**—This enchanting and remote hamlet is a huddle of log cabins used by cowherds in the summer. These days the hamlet's old bar is a restaurant serving a tiny community of vacation-goers and hikers. Taveyanne is 2 miles off the main road between Col de la Croix and Villars. A small sign points down a tiny road to a jumble of huts and snoozing cows stranded at 5,000 feet. The inn is **Refuge de Taveyanne** (1882 Gryon), where the Seibenthal family serves hearty meals in a prize-winning rustic setting—no electricity, low ceilings, huge charred fireplace. This is French Switzerland, but these people speak some English. For a back-on-the-farm experience, consider sleeping in their primitive loft. It's never full (5 mattresses, access by a ladder outside, 7 SF, urinate with the cows, open May-October, closed Tuesdays except in July and August, tel. 025/681947). A fine opportunity to really know bell prize-winning cows.

FRENCH SWITZERLAND TO GERMANY'S BLACK FOREST

Take an easy morning, enjoy the bubbly streets of Murten, then drive or train 3 hours north to Freiburg. Tour the capital of Germany's Black Forest. Then set up in the town of Staufen.

Suggested Schedule

9:00	Free morning in Murten.
10:00	Drive or train north into Germany.
14:00	Tour Freiburg.
17:00	Drive or train 30 minutes to Staufen.

Transportation: Murten to the Black Forest (130 miles)

From Murten, follow signs to Bern, then Basel/Zürich. Before Basel you'll go through a tunnel and come to Raststätte Pratteln Nord, a strange orange shopping mall that looks like a swollen sea cucumber laying eggs on the freeway. Take a break here for a look around one of Europe's greatest freeway stops. You'll find a bakery and grocery store for picnickers, a restaurant, showers, and a change desk open daily until 21:00 with rates about 2 percent worse than banks.

At Basel, follow the signs to Karlsruhe and Deutschland. Once in Germany (reasonable bank at the border station, daily 7:00-20:00), the autobahn will take you along the French border, which, for now, is the Rhine River. Exit at Freiburg mitte. Park near TI and cathedral (single, tall, see-through spire). From Freiburg signs lead south to Lörrrach/road 3. In Bad Krozingen the yellow sign points to Staufen, on the left under the castle ruins. The dead-end road straight into town leaves you at a parking place near the pedestrian zone and your hotel.

Train travelers will catch the milk-run train from Murten into Bern, where an hourly train zips you to Basel in 75 minutes and then on into Germany. At least one train per

hour makes the 60-minute Basel-Freiburg trip. Regular
trains connect Freiburg and Staufen in 30 minutes (Staufen
station tel. 07633/5211).

Sightseeing Highlights

▲**Badenweiler**—If ever a town was a park, Badenweiler
is it; an idyllic, poodle-elegant, and finicky-clean spa town
known only to the wealthy Germans who soak there. Its
Markgrafen-*bad* (bath) is next to the ruins of a Roman
mineral bath in a park of imported and exotic trees
(including a California redwood). This prize-winning piece
of architecture perfectly mixes trees and peace with an
elegant indoor-outdoor swimming pool (8:00-18:00,
Monday, Wednesday, and Friday until 20:00). The locker
procedure combined with the language barrier makes getting to the pool more memorable than you'd expect (3
hours for 10 DM; towels, required caps, and suits are
rentable). Badenweiler is a 20-minute drive south of
Staufen, or get off at the Badenweiler autobahn exit on
your way north. (Bad Krozingen, just a couple of miles
from Staufen, has a fancy new spa pool if Badenweiler is
too much work.)

Badische Weinstrasse—The wine road of this part of
Germany staggers from Bedenweiler through the tiny
towns of Britzingen, Sulzburg, Dottingen, and Grunern
before sitting down in Staufen. If you're in the mood for
some tasting, look for the *Winzergnossenshaft* signs,
which invite visitors in to taste, buy, and often tour the
winery. There is a Winzergnossenshaft in Staufen at the
base of the castle hill.

▲▲**Freiburg im Breisgau**—The "sunniest town in
Germany" feels like the university town it is (30,000 students). It feels like it had a chance to start all over and do
it right (it was bombed almost flat in 1944). And it feels
cozy, almost Austrian (it was Habsburg territory for 500
years). It's the "capital" of the Schwarzwald, surrounded
by lush forests and filled with green (environmentally sensitive) people. Freiburg's worth a quick look.

Enjoy the pedestrian-only old center. Freiburg's trademark is its system of *Bächle*, tiny streams running down each street. A sunny day turns any kid into a puddle-stomper. Enjoy the ice cream and street-singing ambience of the cathedral square.

The church, or **Münster** and its towering tower (not worth the 116-meter ascent) are impressive. A local guide or guidebook will point out the symbolism that gave the church's fine windows and sculpture meaning to its parishioners 600 years ago. Find the "mooning" gargoyle and wait for rain.

Freiburg's **Augustiner Museum** offers a good look at the local culture and medieval art including a close-up look at at some of the Münster's medieval stained glass (downstairs, 4 DM, 9:30-17:00, closed Monday).

The TI (between old center and station, 9:00-20:00, Sunday 10:00-12:00, less off-season, tel. 0761/3689090) offers a good 5-DM city guidebook, room-finding service, almost daily 8-DM English-language guided walks, and information on the entire Black Forest region. Bounce your plan for the day off these people.

Schauinsland—Freiburg's own mountain is the handiest quick look at the Schwarzwald for those without wheels. A gondola system, one of Germany's oldest, was designed for Freiburgers relying on public transportation. At the 4,000-foot summit are a panorama restaurant, pleasant circular walks, a tower on a nearby peak offering a commanding Black Forest view, and the Schniederli Hof—a 1592 farmhouse museum. About 20 DM gets you up and back including the tram ride from the town center.

▲**Staufen in Breisgau**—This is a cute (the standard Black Forest adjective) town on the edge of the Black Forest. A mini-Freiburg, it's a perfect combination of smallness and off-the-beaten-path-ness with a quiet pedestrian zone of colorful old buildings bounded by a happy creek that actually babbles. There's nothing to do here but enjoy the marketplace atmosphere. Hike through the vineyards to the ruined castle overlooking the town and savor a good dinner with local wine.

Sleeping in Staufen (1.6 DM = about $1, zip code: 79219, tel. code: 07633)

Sleep in Staufen. The TI (on the main square in the Rathaus, Monday-Friday 8:00-16:30, closed Saturday afternoon and Sunday, tel. 07633/80536) has a list of private Zimmer (posted on the window after hours), but most don't like to take one-nighters. There's only one budget place in town, but for 30 more marks you'll get breakfasts and all the comforts.

Peewee Herman would enjoy **Gasthaus Bahnhof** (S-30 DM, D-70 DM, no breakfast; across from Shining Time Station, tel. 6190). This is the cheapest place in town, with a castle out back, self-cooking facilities, and one 12- to-14-SF dinner a day. It can seem a little depressing during the day, but at night, master of ceremonies Lotte makes it the squeezebox of Staufen. People come from miles around to party with Lotte. If you want to eat red meat in a wine barrel under a tree and still be low on the food chain, this is the place.

Gasthaus Hirschen (DB-100 DM; Haupstrasse 19 on the main pedestrian street, 7813 Staufen, tel. 5297), which has a storybook location in the old pedestrian center and a characteristic restaurant, is family-run with all the comforts. They also have a penthouse apartment for four.

Hotel Sonne (SB-70 DM, DB-100 DM; Albert-Hugard Strasse 1, tel. 7012, SE-B, family Stein), with 8 rooms, is at the edge of the pedestrian center and also very comfortable.

Hotel Krone (SB-80 DM, DB-120 DM, TB-150, CC-VMA, Hauptstrasse 30, on the main pedestrian street, tel. 5840, fax 82903, SE-B) gilds the lily. Its restaurant (closed Friday and Saturday) appreciates vegetables and offers good splurge meals.

Freiburg Youth Hostel (23 DM per bed with sheets and breakfast; Kartuserstr. 151, tram #1 to Römerhof, tel. 0761/67656) is the nearest hostel. This big, modern hostel is just outside of Freiburg on the recommended road into the Black Forest.

THE BLACK FOREST—GERMANY'S SCHWARZWALD

Spend the day exploring the best of this most romantic of German forests. By late afternoon you'll be set up in Germany's greatest nineteenth-century spa resort and ready for a stroll through its elegant streets and casino, finishing the day with a *kur*—sauna, massage, and utter restfulness.

Suggested Schedule

8:30	Drive into the Black Forest. Stop at Sankt Peter.
10:00	Furtwangen Clock Museum.
12:00	Picnic and tour open air museum at Gutach.
14:00	Drive north via Freudenstadt and the Schwarzwald-Hochstrasse to Baden-Baden.
15:30	Baden-Baden, set up, browse the elegant town center.
17:00	Take the kur (or go swimming).
19:30	Dine downtown.
21:00	Stroll Lichtentaler Allee.

Transportation: Staufen-Freiburg-Baden-Baden (70 miles)

From Staufen, drive to Freiburg, where signs to Donaueschingen will take you into the Black Forest. You'll need a decent map to do the recommended route In Baden-Baden, if you're going straight to the baths, look for "Thermen, parking" and follow that road around town and into the underground parking place at the baths (first 2 hours free if going to Caracalla Baths). Parking is tight in Baden-Baden. Use a garage (12 DM a day).

Train travelers need to simplify. There are two trains an hour from Freiburg through the scenic Höllental Valley to touristy Titisee. Your Eurailpass works on some Black Forest buses. Consider the Schauinsland excursion and the hourly 90-minute Freiburg to Baden-Baden train. The Baden-Oos station is 5 miles from the center. Bus 1 to

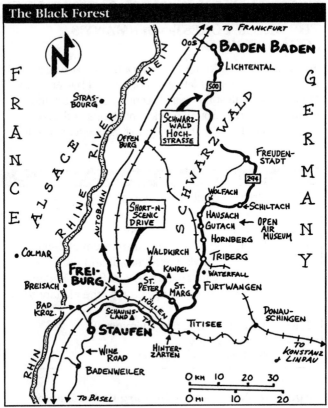

The Black Forest

Augustaplatz (hostelers get off long before the center at Grosse Dollen Strasse) connects the Oos station with the center and all my recommended hotels every 10 minutes.

The Black Forest

Called the *Schwarzwald* in German, this is a range of hills stretching 100 miles north-south along the French border from Karlsruhe to Switzerland. It's so thickly wooded, the people called it black. The poor farmland drove medieval locals to become foresters, glass-blowers, and great clock-makers. Today it's popular for its endless hiking possibilities, clean air, cuckoo clocks, cherry cakes, and cheery villages. The area is impressively Catholic and traditional. On any Sunday, you'll find volks marches and traditional costumes coloring the Black Forest.

Sightseeing Highlights—Black Forest
▲▲The Short and Scenic Black Forest Joyride—This pleasant loop from Freiburg takes you through the most representative chunk of the area, avoiding the touristy and overcrowded Titisee. Leave Freiburg on Schwarzwald-strasse, which becomes scenic road 31 down the dark and fertile-with-fairy tales Höllental (Hell's Valley) toward Titisee. Turn left at Hinterzarten onto road 500, follow signs to St. Margen, then to St. Peter—one of the healthy, go-take-a-walk-in-the-clean-air places that doctors actually prescribe for people from all over Germany. There is a fine 7-km walk between these two towns, with regular buses to bring you back. St. Peter's TI (Monday-Friday 8:00-12:00, 14:00-17:00, tel. 07660/274), just next to the Benedictine abbey (closed to the public), can recommend a walk. If you're feeling like an overnight, the traditional old **Gasthof Hirschen** (DB-100 to 130 DM; St. Peter/Hochschwarzwald, tel. 07660/204) is on the main square. **Pension Schwär** (D-56 DM; Schweighofweg 4, tel. 07660/219) is basic and friendly. Several morning and late-afternoon buses connect Freiburg and St. Peter.

From St. Peter, wind through idyllic Black Forest scenery up to Kandelhof. At the summit is the Berghotel Kandel. You can park here and take a short walk to the 4,000-foot peak for a commanding view. Then the road winds steeply through a dense forest to Waldkirch, where a fast road takes you to the Freiburg Nord autobahn entrance. With a good car and no long stops, this route gets you from Freiburg to Baden-Baden in 3 hours.

▲▲The Extended Black Forest Drive—Of course, you could spend much more time in the land of cuckoo clocks and healthy hikes. For a more thorough visit, still connecting Freiburg and Baden-Baden, try this drive. As described above, drive from Freiburg down Höllental. After a short stop in St. Peter, wind up in Furtwangen, which has the impressive **Deutsches Uhrenmuseum** (German clock museum, 4 DM, daily, April-October, 9:00-17:00, less off-season, tel. 07723-656-117). More than a chorus of cuckoo clocks, this museum traces the development of time-keeping devices from the dark age to the space age. It has an upbeat combo of mechanical musical instruments as well.

Triberg, deep in the Black Forest. is famous for its Gutach Waterfall (500-foot fall in several bounces, 3 DM to see it, drivers can drop passengers at top and meet them at the 1.50 DM putt-putt golf course in town, a 15-minute downhill walk) and more important, the Heimat Museum (4 DM, daily 8:00-18:00, fewer hours off-season), which gives a fine look at the costumes, carvings, and traditions of the local culture. Touristy as Triberg is, it offers an easy way for travelers without cars to enjoy the Black Forest.

The Schwarzwälder Freilichtermuseum (Black Forest open-air museum) offers the best look at this region's traditional folk life (north of Triberg, through Hornberg to Hausach/Gutach; 6 DM, April-October, 8:30-18:00, last entry 17:00, tel. 07831/230). Built around one grand old farmhouse, the museum is a collection of several old farms filled with exhibits on the local dress and lifestyles. The surrounding shops and restaurants are awfully touristy, but this is a place you're sure to find plenty of the famous Schwarzwald Kirchetorte (Black Forest Cherry Cake).

Continue north, through Freudenstadt, the capital of the northern Black Forest, and onto the Schwarzwald-Hochstrasse, which takes you along a ridge through 30 miles of pine forests before dumping you right on Baden-Baden's back porch.

Baden-Baden

Of all the high-class resort towns I've seen, Baden-Baden is the easiest to enjoy in blue jeans and with a picnic. One hundred and fifty years ago, this was the playground of Europe's high-rolling elite. Royalty and aristocracy would come from all corners to take the kur—soak in the curative (or at least they feel that way) mineral waters—and enjoy the world's top casino. Today this town of 55,000 attracts a more middle-class crowd, both tourists and Germans enjoying the fruits of their generous health care system. Baden-Baden's tourist office is in the center near the riverside park (Augustaplatz 8, 9:00-22:00, Sunday 10:00-22:00; tel. 07221/275200).

The best approach to Baden-Baden, given your tight schedule, is to get set up by 16:00, take a kur at 17:00,

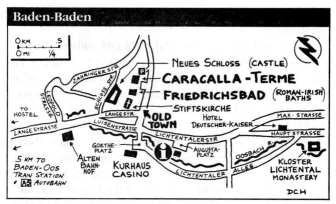

dine at 19:30 and finish the evening bestowing on yourself a royal title and promenading down the famous Lichtentaler Allee, a pleasant lane through a park along a stream and past old mansions (lit until 22:00). During the day consider taking city bus #1 to Klosterplatz and walking its entire length back into town.

The Germans who come to Baden-Baden generally stay put for two weeks, and the TI has enough recommended walks and organized excursions to keep even the most energetic vacationers happy. Telephone code: 07221.

▲▲**Casino**—Even if you don't gamble, tour the casino. It's open for gambling from 14:00 to 2:00 (5 DM entry, 5 DM minimum bet, tie and coat required—and rentable). A third of those who go in just observe; you don't need to gamble. The casino gives dicey 30-minute German-language tours of its Versailles-rivaling interior every morning from 9:30 to 12:00, 10:00 to 12:00 in winter (tours start on the half hour, last one at 11:30, 3 DM, and no ties, tel. 07221/275246, call to see if there's a free-loadable English tour scheduled). The nearby "Old Bahnhof" is a simpler gaming place for those in need of a room full of one-armed bandits.

▲▲▲**The Roman-Irish Bath, Friedrichsbad**—The highlight of most Baden-Baden visits is a sober 2-hour ritual called the Roman-Irish Bath. Friedrichsbad, on Römerplatz 1, pampered the rich and famous in its elegant surroundings when it opened 120 years ago. Today, this steamy world of marble, brass columns, tropical tiles, herons, lily pads, and graceful nudity welcomes gawky tourists as well as locals.

For 38 DM, you get the works (28 DM without the 8-minute massage, hotels give a guest card for 10 percent discounts). The complex routine is explained in the blue English brochure and on the walls in English as you go. Follow the numbered arrows: shower to clean; grab a towel and put on plastic slippers before hitting the warm air bath for 15 minutes; hot air bath for 5 minutes; shower; soap brush massage—rough, slippery, and finished with a spank; play Gumby in the shower; lounge under sunbeams and caryatids in one of several different thermal steam baths; glide like a swan under a divine dome in a royal pool; cold plunge; dry in warmed towels; wrapped like a cocoon, lay clean and thinking prenatal thoughts on a bed for 30 minutes in the silent room.

All you need is money. You'll get a key, locker, and towel (daily except Sunday from 9:00-22:00, men and women together all day Wednesday and Saturday and from 16:00-22:00 on Tuesday and Friday, last admissions at 19:00 if you'll get a massage, at 19:30 otherwise, tel. 02271/275920). The dress code is always nude. During separate times, men and women use parallel and nearly identical facilities. "Mixed" is still mostly separate with men and women sharing only the "royal pool." Couples will do most of the regimen separated. Being your average American, I'm not used to nude. But naked, bewildered, and surrounded by beautiful people with no tan lines is a feeling Woody Allen could write a movie about.

You don't appreciate how really clean you are after this experience until you put your dirty socks back on. (Bring clean ones.)

Afterward, browse through the special exhibits and Roman artifacts upstairs in the Renaissance Hall, sip just a little terrible but "magic" water from the elegant fountain with old ladies who don't seem to be getting much out of it, and stroll down the broad royal stairway feeling, as they say, five years younger—or at least no older.

▲▲**Caracalla Therme**—For more of a glorified swimming pool experience, spend a few hours at the Baths of

Caracalla (daily 8:00-22:00, last entry at 20:00), a huge palace of water, steam, and relaxed people next to the Friedrichsbad.

Bring a towel (5 DM rental) and swimsuit (any shorts are okay), pick up the blue English instruction sheet and buy a card (18 DM for the first 2 hours, 5 DM per half-hour after that), put the card in the locker to get a key, change, strap the key around your wrist, and go play. (Your key gets you into a pool-side locker if you want money for a tan or a drink. You can park under the *Thermen* for free for 2 hours if you validate your ticket at the Caracalla turnstile.)

It's an indoor/outdoor wonderland of steamy pools, waterfalls, neck showers, Jacuzzis, hot springs, cold pools, lounge chairs, exercise instructors, saunas, cafeteria, and bar. One area has a current simulating a river. Another area is for people who like water spankings. The steamy "inhalation" room seems like purgatory's waiting room, with six misty inches of visibility, filled with strange, silent bodies.

Climb the spiral staircase into a naked world of saunas, tanning lights, cold plunges, and sunbathing. There are three eucalyptus-smelling saunas: 80, 90, and 95 degrees. Read and follow the instructions on the wall. Towels are required, not for modesty but to separate your body from the wood that every other body sits on. The highlight for me was the arctic bucket in the shower room. Pull the chain. Only rarely will you feel so good.

As you leave, take a look at the old Roman bath that Emperor Caracalla himself soaked in to conquer his rheumatism nearly 2,000 years ago.

Sleeping in Baden-Baden (1.6 DM = about $1, zip code: 76530, tel. code: 07221)

Except for its hostel, rooms in Baden-Baden are expensive. The TI can always find you a room if you arrive by 17:00 (doubles in small hotels or private homes start at 80 DM). Rooms without private plumbing are a real deal. In Baden-Baden, of all places, you should be able to manage without a private bath. The only really tight times are dur-

ing the horse races (1994: May 28-June 5, August 26-
September 4. 1995: May 20-28, August 25-September 3)
The best budget strategy is to use the wonderful bus line
#1, connecting Baden-Baden's Oos train station (cheap
hotels, easy parking) with the center (Augustaplatz, TI,
baths, casino) and continuing to budget hotels on the east
end of town (runs every 8 minutes, buy 2 DM 2-hour tickets or the 5 DM 24-hour ticket on the bus).

There are five affordable hotels right in the nearly traffic
free old town, 2 minutes from the TI, baths, and casino.

Hotel am Markt (S-44 DM, SB-70 DM, D-80 DM, DB-
115, TB-150 DM, cheap kids beds available, CC-VMA;
Marktplatz 18, tel. 22747 or 22743, fax 391887, Herr und
Frau Bogner SE-A) is the best deal for a warm, small, family-run hotel with all the comforts a commoner could want
in a peaceful, central location, 2 cobbled blocks from the
baths. The church bells blast charmingly through each
room from 6:30 until 22:00. Otherwise, quiet rules. The
daily menu offers a good dinner deal (limited to guests
only).

Around the corner the **Hotel Bischoff** (DB-120,
Römerplatz 2, tel. 29999, fax 38308) and a strange place
called **Bratwurstglocrel** (DB-120, tel. 22968) embrace the
conformist values of private showers at all cost. But just
down the stairs, the funky **Gasthof Zum weissen Rössel**
(S-50 DM, SB-64 DM, D-83 DM, DB-93 DM, TB-122 DM;
Baldreitstrasse 5, tel. 25582, Herr Granz SE-F), with tidy
rooms above the closest thing to a real bar you'll find in
downtown Baden-Baden, has enough character for a
"Wanted" poster.

Gästehaus Löhr (one tiny S-40 DM, several S-55 DM,
SB-60 DM, one D-70 DM, DB-90 DM, CC-VMA, SE-B;
office at Café Löhr at 19 Lichtentaler Strasse, on the main
drag across from the TI, tel. 26204 or 31370) is basic,
clean enough, and a good deal if you don't mind the
Mickey-Mouse setup of the reception being in a café two
blocks from the hotel. I'd take their cheap shower-less
rooms over the hostel.

There are good budget beds, and easy parking, down
Lichtentaler Allee on the far side of town. **Deutscher**

Kaiser (S-47 DM, SB-70 DM, D-70 DM, DB-105 DM, communal showers cost 3 DM, CC-VMA; Hauptstr. 35, Baden-Baden-Lichtental, tel. 72152, fax 72154, Mrs. Peter speaks English) offers some of the best rooms in town for the money. This big, traditional guest house is in a down-to-earth suburb town right on bus #1 line (stop: Eckerle-strasse) about a 15-minute walk down polite Lichtentaler Allee. **Gasthof Cäcilienberg** (S-46 DM, SB-56 DM, D-76 DM, DB-86 DM; Geroldsauer Strasse 2, tel. 72297) is comfortable and beautifully situated even farther out in a quiet area at the end of Lichtentaler Allee (bus 1 first stop after the Kloster Lichtental).

Train travelers get only as close as the suburb of Oos Those driving in from the autobahn will hit Oos first. Connoisseurs of simplicity will check into one of the following three accommodations, save money, park easy, and ride bus #1. Each of these places is on Ooser Hauptstrasse, with easy parking, just a few minutes walk in front of the station. **Gasthof Adler** (S-50 DM, SB-55 DM, D-90 DM, DB-98 DM, CC-VMA; Ooser Hauptstrasse 1, 7570 Baden-Baden Oos, tel. 61858 or 61811, fax 17145) is plain, comfortable, and friendly. **Hotel Goldener Stern** (SB-55 DM, DB-100 DM, CC-VA; Ooser Hauptstrasse 16, 7570 Baden-Baden, tel. 61509) has big, bright rooms. **Gasthaus zum Engel** (S-25 DM, D-50 DM, with breakfast but absolutely no showers available; Ooser Hauptstrasse 20, tel. 61610) is not quite as depressing as it is cheap.

Baden-Baden's great new **Werner Dietz Youth Hostel** (beds in 6-bed rooms, sheets and breakfast for 24 DM, 28 DM if you're over 27, add 6 DM if you have no hostel card; Hardbergstr. 34, bus #1 to Grosse Dollenstr. from the station or downtown, tel. 52223, 7:00-23:30, but doesn't answer phone in midday, SE-A) is your budget ace in the hole. They always save 25 beds to be doled out to "travelers" at 17:00, have an overflow hall when all beds are taken, give 4-DM discount coupons for both city baths, and serve cheap meals. (Those driving, turn left at the first light after the freeway into Baden-Baden ends, and follow the signs winding uphill to the big modern hostel next to a public swimming pool.)

BADEN-BADEN TO THE RHINELAND

After touring one of the world's most lavish casinos and enjoying a leisurely midday in the spas of Baden-Baden, scurry north into the fairy-tale world of Rhine legends and castles.

Suggested Schedule

9:30	Tour Baden-Baden casino.
10:30	Midday free to browse or bathe in Baden-Baden.
15:00	Travel to the Rhine Valley.
17:00	Find a room in Bacharach or St. Goar.

Transportation: Baden-Baden to the Rhine
From Baden-Baden it's a straight 90-minute shot on the autobahn north; follow signs to Frankfurt/Mannheim, then Koblenz. At Bingen, road 9 (direction St. Goar) takes you along the Rhine.

Eurailers take the express to Mainz or Koblenz (Baden-Baden to Koblenz, changing in Mannheim, 2 per hour, 2-hour ride). Hourly milk-runs down the Rhine hit every town.

Sightseeing Lowlights
Heidelberg—This famous old university town attracts hordes of Americans, and any former charm is stained almost beyond recognition by commercialism. Skip it—you've seen better on this trip.
Speyer—You'll be driving right by Germany's most impressive Romanesque cathedral. You'll see Speyer's spires in the distance from the autobahn.
Mainz, Wiesbaden, Rüdesheim, and Frankfurt—These towns are all too big or too famous. They're not worth your time. Mainz's Gutenberg Museum is also a disappointment.
Rhine Valley sights—Follow my narrated Rhine Castle tour from the moment you hit the Rhine at Bingen. (See Day 20.)

Sleeping and Eating on the Rhine in Bacharach (1.6 DM = about $1, zip code: 55422, tel. code: 06743)
The Rhine is the easiest place for cheap sleeps on this tour. Zimmer and Gasthäuser abound, offering beds for 25 to 30 DM per person. Several exceptional Rhine-area youth hostels offer even cheaper beds. Each town's helpful TI is eager to set you up. Finding a room should be easy any time of year. St. Goar and Bacharach, the best towns for an overnight stop, are about 10 minutes apart, connected by the same milk-run trains, river boats and riverside bike path. Bacharach is less touristic; St. Goar has the famous castle. The only other Rhine town worth a look is Boppard.

Bacharach's youth hostel, Jugendherberge Stahleck, is a twelfth-century castle on the hilltop high above Bacharach with a royal Rhine view (IYHF members of all ages welcome, 20 DM dorm beds, 5 DM for sheets, normally places available but call and leave your name, they'll hold a bed until 18:00, tel. 1266, SE-A). This is a gem but very much a youth hostel—dorms crowded with metal bunk beds, showers in the basement, and often filled with school groups. A major renovation is planned for 1994. It's a 15-minute climb on the trail from the town church, or you can drive up. It's warmly and energetically run by Evelyn and Bernhard Falke (pronounced fall-kay) who serve hearty, cheap meals.

Hotel Kranenturm gives you the feeling of a castle without the hostel-ity or the climb. This is my choice for the best combination of comfort and hotel privacy with Zimmer warmth, central location, and medieval atmosphere (DB-80 DM with this book, discounts for staying several nights, kid-friendly, family rooms available, request Rhine view with train noise or the quieter back side, CC-VMA, easy reservations by phone, SE-A; Langstr. 30, tel. 1308, fax 1021). Run by hardworking Kurt Engel and his intense but friendly wife Fatima, this is actually part of the medieval fortification. Its former *Kranen* (crane) towers are now round rooms. When the riverbank was higher, cranes on this tower loaded barrels of wine onto Rhine boats. Hotel Kranenturm is 18 inches from the train tracks (just under the medieval gate at the Frankfurt end of town), but a combination of medieval sturdiness and triple-pane windows make the riverside rooms sleepable. The Kranenturm really stretches it to get toilets and showers in each room. Kurt is a great cook, and his big-enough-for-three Kranenturm ice cream special may ruin you (9 DM). For a quick trip to Fiji in a medieval German cellar, check out Kurt's tropical bar.

Hotel zur Krone is a lame-duck place, a bit musty but with good beds, bright rooms, and little train noise (D-60 DM, S-35 DM, 10 percent cheaper for two-night stays; Langstr. 7, tel. 1573, SE-F).

Frau Amann (D-50 DM; Oberstr. 13, in the old center on a side lane a few yards off the main street, tel. 1271) rents two rooms in her quiet, homey, traditional place. Guests get a cushy living room, a self-serve kitchen, and the free use of bikes. You'll laugh right through the language barrier with this lovely woman. Zimmer normally discount their prices if you're staying longer.

Annelie and Hans Dettmar (DB-50 DM; Oberstr. 8, on the main drag in the center, tel. 2661 or 2979, SE-A, kid-friendly) are a young entrepreneurial couple who rent six smoke-free rooms (one is a huge family-of-four room, several have kitchenettes) in a modern house above their craft shop. You'll eat breakfast surrounded by things for sale. They rent three-speeds for 10 DM per day.

Frau Erna Leischied (D-50 DM, Blucherstr. 39, tel. 1510, speaks German fluently) shares with travelers her ancient, higgledy-piggledy, half-timbered house, 3 blocks uphill from the church, next to the medieval town gate. The rooms are very comfortable.

For inexpensive and atmospheric dining in Bacharach, try the **Hotel Kranenturm** or **Altes Haus** (the oldest building in town).

Sleeping on the Rhine in St. Goar (1.6 DM = about $1, zip code: 56329, tel. code 06741)

Hotel Montag (DB-130, price can drop if you arrive late or it's a slow time, CC-VMA; Heerstr. 128, just across the street from the world's largest free-hanging cuckoo clock, tel

1629, fax 2086). Mannfred Montag, his wife Maria and son Mike speak New Yorkish and run an adjacent good crafts shop (especially for steins). Even though Montag gets a lot of bus tours, it's friendly, laid back, and comfortable.

Hotel Hauser (DB-98 DM, DB with Rhine view balconies-130 DM, S-42 DM, plead poverty and you may get a view room at the low price, CC-VMA, SE-B; Heerstr. 77, tel. 333, fax 1464), newly redone and very central, is run by Frau Velich.

Hotel Traube (DB-85 DM, all with great Rhine views; Heerstr. 75, tel. 7511) is well-antlered and well-located, but not very friendly. The dining room flutters with stuffed birds of prey. The carpets are depressing and the rooms are plain and a bit musty but nicely furnished.

If you don't mind a splash of Greece, St. Goar's most sleepable cheap and central hotel is the **Hotel Pallas Athens** (S-35 DM, D-60 DM, DB-70 DM; near the station at Pumpengasse 5, tel. 1646).

St. Goar's best Zimmer deals are the homes of **Frau Kurz** (S-34 DM, D-60 DM, showers-5 DM, minimum two nights with rare exceptions; Ulmenhof 11, 5401 St. Goar/Rhein, tel. 459, 2-minute walk above the station) and similarly priced **Frau Wolters** (Schlossberg 24, tel. 1695; on the road to the castle, also two-night minimum, D-60 DM or S-34 DM). Both are cozier and more comfortable than hotels, with homey TV rooms and great river and castle views.

The Germanly run **St. Goar hostel** (15 DM beds, Bismarckweg 17, tel. 388 morning and after 17:00), the big beige building under the castle, is a good value with cheap dorm beds, a few smaller rooms, a 22:00 curfew, and hearty 8-DM dinners

THE RHINE AND ITS CASTLES

Spend today on the romantic Rhine. Cruise the most excit-ing stretch, past the famous Pfalz castle on an island in mid-stream and around the treacherous Loreley. For some hands-on castle thrills, climb through the Rhineland's great-est castle, Rheinfels. Spend the afternoon exploring more of the Rhine or in the neighboring Mosel Valley.

Suggested Schedule

9:55   Boat from Bacharach to St. Goar.
11:00   Explore Rheinfels Castle. Picnic on ramparts?
13:35   Boat further up Rhine to Koblenz where you
           can return home by train.

Itinerary note: Look ahead to see how your travel plans can best do the Mosel, Köln, and Berlin. You could reasonably spend the afternoon and evening on the Mosel today and bed down in Zell (see accommo-dations tomorrow). You could even do the Rhine and Köln today and take the night train to Berlin.

Transportation on the Rhine

While the Rhine flows from Switzerland to Holland, the one-hour drive from Mainz to Koblenz is by far the most interesting. This stretch, studded with the crenelated cream of Germany's castles, is busy with boats, trains, and high-way traffic. Have fun exploring with a mix of big steamers, tiny ferries, bikes, and trains. While many do the whole trip by boat, the most scenic hour is from St. Goar to Bacharach. Sit on the top deck with your handy Rhine map-guide and enjoy the parade of castles, towns, boats, and vineyards. Rhine boats only cruise from Easter through October. Off-season is so quiet that many hotels close down.

There are several boat companies, but most travelers sail on the bigger, more expensive and romantic Köln–Düsseldorf line (free with Eurail, tel. 0221/2088). Boats run daily in both directions (no express boat on Monday) from May through September with fewer boats off-season.

Complete, up-to-date, and more complicated schedules are posted at any station, Rhineland hotel, TI, or current Thomas Cook Timetable.

Rhine Steamer Schedule (Köln-Düsseldorf Line)					
Daily/dates	Koblenz	Boppard	St. Goar	Bacharach	Bingen
May-Sept	—	9:00	10:15	11:20	12:55
Apr-Oct	9:00	10:40	11:55	12:55	14:20
May-Sept	11:00	12:40	13:55	14:55	16:20
Apr-Oct	14:00	15:40	16:55	17:55	19:20
fast, May-Oct	11:05	11:30	11:50	12:08	12:28
July-Aug	12:30	14:10	15:25	16:25	17:50
		⟶			
		⟵			
May-Oct	12:20	11:20	10:35	9:55	9:10
July-Aug	15:50	14:40	13:35	12:45	12:00
fast, May-Oct	16:17	15:55	—	—	15:05
Apr-Sept	20:00	18:50	18:00	17:20	16:35

Koblenz–Bingen tickets cost 55 DM, St. Goar–Bacharach 15 DM, free with Eurail; groups of 20 get a 20 percent discount. The fast boat is not free with Eurail.

Purchase tickets at the dock 5 minutes before departure. The boat is never full. (Confirm times at your hotel the night before.)

The smaller Bingen–Rüdesheimer line (tel. 06721/ 14140, Eurail not valid, tickets at St. Goar TI) is 25 percent cheaper than K-D with three 2-hour St. Goar–Bacharach round-trips daily in summer (departing St. Goar at 11:00, 14:10, and 16:10; departing Bacharach at 10:10, 12:30, 15:00; 10 DM one way, 13 DM round-trip).

Drivers have these options: (1) skip the boat; (2) take a round-trip Bingen–Rüdesheimer ride from St. Goar or Bacharach; (3) draw pretzels and let the loser drive, prepare the picnic, and meet the boat; (4) rent a bike, bring it on the boat (free) and bike back; or (5) take the boat one way and return by train (milk-run Rhine Valley trains go every hour or so, St. Goar–Bacharach 12 min., Bacharach–Mainz 30 min., Mainz–Frankfurt 30 min.).

There's a lovely riverside bike path from St. Goar to
Bacharach, and you can rent bikes at the St. Goar TI or at
several Bacharach Zimmer. Those with more time and
energy can sail to Bingen and bike back, visiting Rheinstein Castle and Reichenstein Castle and maybe even tak
ing a ferry across the river to Kaub (where a tiny boat
shuttles sightseers to the castle on the island). While there
are no bridges between Koblenz and Mainz, several small
ferries do their job constantly and cheaply.

**Sightseeing Highlights—The Romantic Rhine
(working north from Bingen to Koblenz)**
▲▲▲**Der Romantische Rhine Blitz Zug Fahrt** (fast
train tour, south to north, from Mainz to Koblenz)—One
of Europe's great train thrills is zipping along the Rhine
Here's a quick and easy, from-the-train-window tour
(works for car, boat, or bike also) that skips the syrupy
myths and the life story of Dieter V von Katzenelnbogen
that fill normal Rhine guides.
     The stretch from Bacharach to St. Goar is best by boat,
but you could argue it's the same river by 50-mph train.
For more information than necessary, buy the handy
Rhine Guide from Mainz to Cologne (5 DM book with
foldout map, at most shops). Sit on the right (river) side of
the train going north from Bingen. While nearly all the
castles listed are viewed from this side, clear a path to the
left window for the times I yell, "Crossover."

Rhine Overview
You'll notice large black-and-white kilometer markers
along the riverbank. I put those up years ago to make this
tour easier to follow. They tell the distance from the
Rhinefalls where the Rhine leaves Switzerland and
becomes navigable. Now the river-barge pilots have
accepted these as navigational aids as well.
     We're tackling just 36 miles of the 820-mile-long Rhine
Ever since Roman times, when this was the Empire's
northern boundary, the Rhine has been one of the world's
busiest shipping rivers. You'll see a steady flow of barges
with 1,000- to 2,000-ton loads. Along both banks are

Best of the Rhine

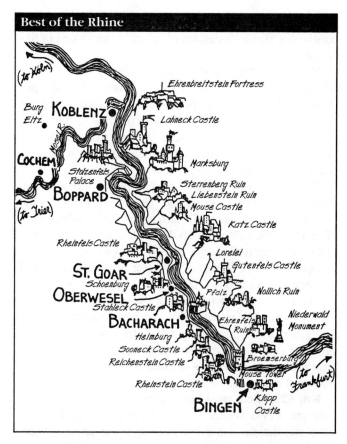

buses packed with tourists, hot train tracks, and highways. Many of the castles you see today were "robber baron" castles, put there by petty rulers (there were 300 independent little countries in medieval Germany) to levy tolls on all the passing river traffic. There were ten customs stops between Mainz and Koblenz alone (no wonder merchants were early proponents of the creation of larger nation-states).

A robber baron would put his castle on, or even in, the river. Then, often with the help of chains and a tower on the opposite side of the river, he'd stop each ship and get his toll. Other castles were built to control and protect settlements. Some were the residences of kings. As times changed, so did the life-styles of the rich and feudal. Many castles were abandoned for comfortable mansions in the towns.

Most of the Rhine castles were originally built in the eleventh, twelfth, and thirteenth centuries. When the pope successfully asserted his power over the German emperor in 1076, local princes ran wild over the rule of their emperor. The castles saw military action in the 1300s and 1400s as emperors began reasserting their control over Germany's many silly kingdoms.

The castles were also involved in the Reformation wars that saw Europe's Catholic and "protesting" dynasties fight it out using a fragmented Germany as their battleground. The Thirty Years War (1618–1648) devastated Germany. The outcome: each ruler got the freedom to decide if his people would be Catholic or Protestant, and one-third of Germany was dead.

The French destroyed most of the castles prophylactically (Louis XIV in the 1680s, the Revolutionary army in the 1790s, and Napoleon in 1806). They were often rebuilt in neo-Gothic style in the romantic age—the late 1800s—and today are enjoyed as restaurants, hotels, youth hostels, and museums.

Km 528: Niederwald monument—Your Blitz Rhine tour starts near Mainz, Rüdesheim, and Bingen. Across from the Bingen station on a hilltop is the 120-foot-high Niederwald monument, a memorial built with 32 tons of bronze in 1877 to commemorate "the reestablishment of the German Empire." A lift takes tourists to this statue from the famous and extremely touristic wine town of Rüdesheim.

Km 530: Ehrenfels Castle—Opposite the Bingerbrück station, you'll see the ghostly Ehrenfels Castle (clobbered by the Swedes in 1636 and by the French in 1689). Since it had no view of the river traffic to the north, it built the cute little *Mäuseturm* (Mouse Tower) on an island (the yellow tower you'll see near the station today). Rebuilt in the 1800s in neo-Gothic style, today it's used as a Rhine navigation signal station.

Lower Rhine

Km 538 (cross to other side of train): Castle Sooneck, built in the eleventh century, was twice destroyed by people sick and tired of robber barons. On the same side (at km 534), you'll see Burg Reichenstein and (at km 533) Burg Rheinstein, which was one of the first to be rebuilt in the Romantic era (both are tourable and are connected by a pleasant trail, info at TI).

Km 540: Lorch—is a pathetic stub of a castle (barely visible by car). Notice the small car ferry, one of several between Mainz and Koblenz, where there are no bridges.

Km 543 (cross to other side of train): Bacharach is a great stop (see below) with fourteenth-century fortifications preserved throughout the town. One of the old towers is my favorite Rhine hotel. The train screams within 10 yards of Hotel Kranenturm. Bacharach prospered from its wood and wine trade. The thirteenth-century Berg Stahleck above the town is now a youth hostel.

Km 546: Burg Gutenfels (white painted "Hotel" sign) and the ship-shape **Pfalz Castle** (built in the river in the 1300s, notice the overhanging his and hers "outhouses") worked very effectively to tax medieval river traffic. The town of Kaub grew rich as Pfalz raised its chains when boats came and lowered them only when the merchants had paid their duty. Those who didn't pay spent time touring its fascinating prison, on a raft at the bottom of its well. In 1504, a pope called for the destruction of Pfalz, but a six-week siege failed. Pfalz is tourable but pretty empty, accessible by 3-DM ferry from Kaub on the other side (4 DM, 9:00-13:00, 14:00-18:00, tel. 06774/570).

Km 550 (cross to other side of train): Oberwesel— A Celtic town in 400 B.C., then a Roman military station, it has some of the best Roman wall-and-tower remains on the Rhine. Notice how many of the train tunnels have entrances designed like medieval turrets, built in the Romantic nineteenth century. Okay, back to the river side.

Km 554: The Loreley—Steep a big slate rock in centuries of legend and it becomes a tourist attraction, the ultimate Rhinestone. The Loreley (two flags on top, name painted near shoreline) rises 450 feet over the narrowest and deepest point of the Rhine. (The fine echoes were thought to be ghostly voices in the old days, fertilizing the legendary soil.)

Because of the killer reefs just upstream (Km 552, called the "Seven Maidens"), many ships never made it to St. Goar. Sailors (after days on the river) blamed their misfortune on a wunderbar Fräulein whose long blond hair almost covered her body. (You can see her statue at about km 555.) Heinrich Heine's *Song of Loreley* (the *Cliff Notes* version is on local postcards) tells the story of how a count sent his men to kill or capture this siren after his son was killed because of her. When the soldiers cornered the nymph in her cave, she called her father (Father Rhine) for help. Huge waves, the likes of which you'll never see today, rose out of the river and carried her to safety. And she has never been seen since.

But alas, when the moon shines brightly and the tour buses are parked, a soft, playful Rhine whine can still be heard from the Loreley. As you pass, listen carefully ("Sailors . . . sailors . . . over my bounding mane   ").

Km 556: Burg Katz—From the town of St. Goar, you'll

see Burg Katz (Katzenelnbogen) across the river. Look back on your side of the river to see the mighty Rheinfels castle over St. Goar.

Together, Burg Katz (b. 1371) and Rheinfels had a clear view up and down the river and effectively controlled traffic. There was absolutely no duty-free shopping on the medieval Rhine. Katz got Napoleoned in 1806 and rebuilt around 1900; today it's a convalescent home.

St. Goar (a recommended stop, see below) was named for a sixth-century hometown monk. It originated in Celtic times (really old) as a place where sailors would stop, catch their breath, send home a postcard, and give thanks after surviving the seductive and treacherous Loreley crossing.

Burg Rheinfels (b. 1245) withstood a siege of 28,000 French troops in 1692, but was creamed by the same team in 1797. It was huge, biggest on the Rhine, then used as a quarry. Today it's a hollow but interesting museum (your best single hands-on castle experience on the river; see below).

Km 557: Rheinfels and St. Goar—See below.

Km 559: Burg Maus got its name because the next castle was owned by the Katzenelnbogen family. In the 1300s, it was considered a state-of-the-art fortification . . . until Napoleon had it blown up in 1806 with state-of-the-art explosives. It was rebuilt true to its original plans around 1900.

Km 567: The "Hostile Brothers" castles (with the white square tower)—Take the wall between Burg Sterrenberg and Burg Liebenstein (actually designed to improve the defenses of both castles), add two greedy and jealous brothers and a fair maiden, and create your own legend. They are restaurants today.

Km 570: Boppard—Boppard was a Roman town with some impressive remains of fourth-century walls. Notice the Roman tower just after the Boppard station and the substantial chunk of Roman wall just before (stop-worthy, see below).

Km 580: Marksburg (with the three modern chimneys behind it) is the best looking of all the Rhine castles and the only surviving medieval castle on the Rhine. Because of its commanding position, it was never attacked. It's now open as a museum with a medieval interior second only to Burg Eltz (9:30-17:00, by 7-DM tour only, tours generally in German, worth a visit only if you can tag along with a rare English tour, call ahead, tel. 02627/206).

Km 585: Burg Lahneck (above the modern autobahn bridge over the Lahn river) was built in 1240 to defend local silver mines, ruined by the French in 1688, and rebuilt in the 1850s in neo-Gothic style. Burg Lahneck faces the yellow Schloss Stolzenfels (out of view above the train, open for touring, a 10-minute climb from the tiny car park, closed Monday).

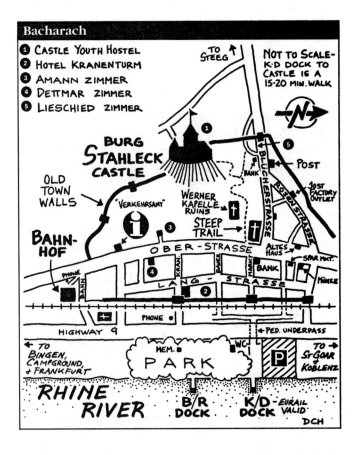

Bacharach

❶ Castle Youth Hostel
❷ Hotel Kranenturm
❸ Amann Zimmer
❹ Dettmar Zimmer
❺ Lieschied Zimmer

To Steeg

Not to Scale- K·D Dock to Castle is a 15-20 min. Walk

N

Burg Stahleck Castle

Post

Bank

Blücherstrasse

Rosenstrasse

Jost Factory Outlet

Old Town Walls

Verkehrsamt

Werner Kapelle Ruins

Steep Trail

Bahn-Hof

Ober-Strasse

Altes Haus

Spar Mkt.

Bahn

Kran.

Bauer

Markt

Bank

Münze

Lang-Strasse

Phone

Phone

Highway 9

Ped. Underpass

To Bingen, Campground, & Frankfurt

Mem.

P

A R K

WC

P

To St Goar & Koblenz

Rhine River

B/R Dock

K/D Dock

Eurail Valid

DCH

Km 590: Koblenz—The Romantic Rhine thrills and the Blitz Rhine tour ends at Koblenz city with Ehrenbreitstein Castle fortress across the river (described below).

Recommended Stops along the Rhine Gorge

▲**Bacharach**—Bacharach is just a pleasant medieval town that misses most of the tourist glitz. Next to the K-D dock is a great park for a picnic (TI, Monday-Friday 9:00-12:30 and 13:30-17:00, tel. 06743/1297; look for "i" on the main street, follow signs to "Verkehrsamt" up the stairs, and down the squeaky hall). Some of the Rhine's best wine is from this town, whose name means "altar to Bacchus." The huge Jost beer stein "factory outlet" is a block north of the church (8:30-18:00, till 16:00 on Saturday, 11:00-15:00 on Sunday).

▲**St. Goar**—A pleasant town, established as a place where sailors who survived the Loreley could stop and thank the gods, St. Goar has good shops (steins and cuckoo clocks, of course), a waterfront park, and a helpful TI. It's worth a stop for its Rheinfels castle. The small supermarket (EDEKA) on Main Street is fine for picnic fixings. The friendly and helpful Montag family in the shop under the Hotel Montag has

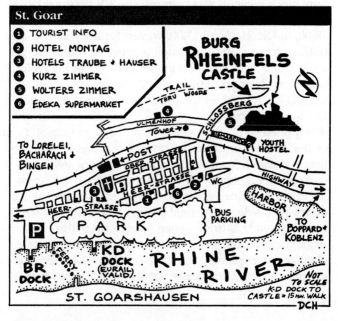

St. Goar

❶ TOURIST INFO
❷ HOTEL MONTAG
❸ HOTELS TRAUBE + HAUSER
❹ KURZ ZIMMER
❺ WOLTERS ZIMMER
❻ EDEKA SUPERMARKET

BURG RHEINFELS CASTLE

TRAIL THRU WOODS

SCHLOSSBERG

ULMENHOF TOWER

HEMLICH

YOUTH HOSTEL

TO LORELEI, BACHARACH + BINGEN

POST STRASSE

OBER STRASSE

HEER-STRASSE

WC

HIGHWAY 9

HARBOR

HEER-STRASSE

P PARK

BUS PARKING

TO BOPPARD + KOBLENZ

P

FERRY

KD DOCK (EURAIL VALID)

RHINE RIVER

BR DOCK

ST. GOARSHAUSEN

NOT TO SCALE
KD DOCK TO CASTLE = 15 MIN. WALK

—DCH

Koblenz-to-Mainz Rhine guidebooks, fine steins, and copies of this guidebook. And across the street, you'll see what must be the biggest cuckoo clock in the world

The St. Goar TI (8:00-12:30, 14:00-17:00, Saturday 9:30-12:00, closed Sunday and earlier in winter, tel. 06741/383) now functions as the town's train station with free left-luggage service and 10-DM per day bike rentals (50 DM or a passport deposit). They have information on which local wineries do English-language tours and tastings for individuals.

▲▲**Rheinfels Castle**—Sitting like a dead pit-bull above St. Goar, this mightiest of Rhine castles rumbles with ghosts from its hard-fought past. Follow the castle map with English instructions (.50 DM from the ticket window) If you follow the castle's perimeter, circling counterclockwise, and downward, you'll find an easy-to-explore chunk of the several miles of spooky tunnels. Bring your flashlight (and bayonet). These tunnels were used to lure in and entomb enemy troops. You'll be walking over the remains (from 1626) of 300 unfortunate Spanish soldiers The reconstruction of the castle in the museum shows how much bigger it was before Louis XIV destroyed it Climb to the top for the Rhine view (4 DM, daily 9:00-18:00, in October until 17:00; winter, Saturday and Sunday only; form a group of ten English-speaking tourists to get a cheaper ticket and a free English tour tel. 383; 15 minutes' steep hike up from St. Goar, you can call a taxi at tel. 430 for a 7-DM lift from the boat dock to the castle, 15 DM for a mini-bus).

▲**Boppard**—This is a more substantial town than St. Goar or Bacharach. Park near the center (or at the DB train station and walk). Just above the market square are the remains of a Roman wall. Below the square is a fascinating church. Notice the carved Romanesque crazies at the doorway. Inside, to the right of the entrance, you'll see Christian symbols from Roman times. Also notice the painted arches and vaults. Originally, most Romanesque churches were painted this way. Down by the river, notice the high water (*Hochwasser*) marks on the arches from various flood years. (Throughout the Rhine and Mosel valleys you'll see these flood marks.)

Koblenz—Not a nice city, it was really hit hard in World War II, but its place as the historic *Deutsches-Eck* (German corner)—the tip of land where the Mosel joins the Rhine—gives it a certain magnetism. "Koblenz," Latin for "confluence," has Roman origins. Walk through the park, noticing the blackened base of what was once a huge memorial to the kaiser. Across the river, the yellow Ehrenbreitstein fortress is now a youth hostel. It's a long hike from the station to the Koblenz boat dock.

MOSEL VALLEY, KÖLN, BONN, NIGHT TRAIN TO BERLIN

Spend the morning on the Mosel and touring my favorite German castle. Then, head for Köln with Germany's greatest Gothic cathedral, best collection of Roman artifacts, a world-class art museum, and a good dose of German urban playfulness. After an evening in people-friendly Bonn, the city of Beethoven, catch the night train to Berlin.

Suggested Schedule

9:00	Mosel morning. Tour Burg Eltz.
14:00	Turn in rental car. Train to Köln.
15:00	Tour Köln's cathedral and museums.
18:00	Train to Bonn for people-watching and dinner.
22:00	Night train to Berlin (or fly home tomorrow).

Transportation: Rhine-Mosel-Köln

Drivers can easily tour the Mosel. Take the small-road short-cut up and over, from the Rhine into the Mosel valley. Drive the Mosel valley from Zell to Koblenz with a stop at Burg Eltz. Turn your car in at Koblenz if possible and catch the train from there to Köln. All the important sights in Köln and Bonn are near the train stations. If you drive to Köln, follow signs to Zentrum and then to the huge Dom/Rhein pay lot under the cathedral.

Trains cover this area quickly and easily: Cochem-Köln, 80 minutes direct every two hours. Bacharach or St. Goar-Köln, 90 minutes with one change, hourly. Koblenz-Köln, 60 minutes, twice an hour. Köln-Bonn, 30 minutes, twice an hour.

Tonight you'll catch the 8-hour train to Berlin. You should reserve your bed for the ride as early in this trip as you are comfortable committing yourself to a date. Any train station or travel agency can book you a bed in a 6-bed cabin (26 DM) or a 4-bed cabin (40 DM) plus your first- or second-class ticket.

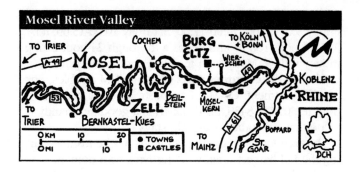

Sightseeing Highlights on the Mosel Valley

The Mosel is what many visitors hoped the Rhine would be—peaceful, sleepy, romantic villages slipped between the steep vineyards and the river, fine wine, plenty of castles, and lots of friendly Zimmer. Boat, train, and car traffic here is a trickle compared to the roaring Rhine. While the Mosel moseys from France to Koblenz, where it dumps into the Rhine, the most scenic piece of the valley lies between the towns of Bernkastel-Kues and Cochem. I'd savor only this section.

For sightseeing along the Mosel, Eurailers have some interesting transportation options. While the train can take you along much of the river, consider riding the K-D (Köln–Düsseldorf) line, which sails once a day in each direction (May through mid-October, Koblenz to Cochem 10:00-14:30, or Cochem to Koblenz 15:50-20:10, free with Eurail). You can also rent bikes at some stations and leave them at others, or rent a bike from Zenz at Enderstrasse 3 in Cochem. If you find yourself stranded in some town, hitching isn't bad.

Cochem, with a majestic castle and picturesque medieval streets, is the touristic hub of this part of the river. The Cochem TI has a free town history and a walking tour brochure. The Cochem castle is the work of over-imaginative nineteenth-century restorers (March-October, 9:00-17:00, German language—with written English explanation—tours on the hour, 4 DM). Consider a boat ride from Cochem to Zell (3 hours) or Beilstein (1 hour, four per day, 16-DM round-trip). The Beilstein-Cochem bus takes only 15 minutes (4 DM). The Cochem TI (Monday-Friday 9:00-13:00, 14:00-17:00, Saturday 10:00-15:00, tel. 3971) books rooms and keeps a thorough 24-hour listing in its window. Many train travelers end up sleeping in Cochem. **Gästezimmer Götz** (7 big 60 DM doubles, one family apartment, CC-MA, Ravenestr. 34, next to the station, tel. 02671/8438, SE-B, EZ-B) is a good and handy value that welcomes one-night stays.

Throughout the region on summer weekends and during the fall harvest time, wine festivals with oompah bands, dancing, and colorful costumes are powered by good food and wine.

▲▲▲**Burg Eltz**—My favorite castle in all of Europe lurks in a mysterious forest, left intact for 700 years, and furnished throughout as it was 500 years ago. Burg Eltz is still owned by the aristocratic family Eltz. The countess arranges for new flowers in each room weekly. The only way to tour the castle is by hour-long German-only tours (depart every 15 minutes, English fact sheets provided). It's worth a phone call to see if there's an English-language tour scheduled you can tag along with (8 DM, April-October, Monday-Saturday, 9:30-17:30, tel. 02672/1300, constant 1.50-DM shuttle bus service from car park).

Driving to Burg Eltz, leave the river at Hatzenport following the white "Berg Eltz P&R" sign. More signs will direct you past Wiersheim to the castle car park, a 10-minute walk from the castle. (It seems like a long detour, but I promise it's worth it.) By train, walk 1 steep hour from Moselkern station (midway between Cochem and Koblenz) through a pine forest where sparrows carry crossbows, and maidens, disguised as falling leaves, whisper "watch out."

▲**Beilstein**, farther downstream, is the quaintest of all Mosel towns. Check out its narrow lanes, ancient wine cellar, resident (and very territorial) swans, and ruined castle. (For accommodations, see below.)

▲**Zell** is the best Mosel town for an overnight stop—peaceful, with a fine riverside promenade, a pedestrian bridge over the river, plenty of Zimmer, a long pedestrian zone filled with colorful shops, restaurants, and wines-tubes. (For accommodations, see below.)

▲▲**Trier**—Germany's oldest city lies at the head of the scenic Mosel Valley, near the border with Luxembourg. Founded by Augustus in 15 B.C., it was 80,000 strong when Emperor Constantine used the town as the capital of the fading western Roman Empire. A short stop here offers you a look at Germany's oldest Christian church, the Dom, or cathedral, which houses the "Holy Robe" of Christ (found by Constantine's mother, St. Helena, and only very rarely on display, next showing in 1996). Connected to the Dom is the Liebfrau church from 1235, which claims to be the oldest Gothic church in Germany (7:00-18:00). Communists can lick their wounds at Karl Marx's house (15-minute film at 20 past each hour, 10:00-13:00, 15:00-18:00, Monday 15:00-18:00).

Trier has some epic Roman ruins. The basilica is the largest intact Roman building outside of Rome. It's now a church but you can still imagine Constantine giving audiences from his altar-like throne. From the basilica a fragrant garden leads to the remains of a Roman bath and a 25,000-seat amphitheater. On the other side of town, next to the TI, is the famous and huge Porta Nigra (best Roman fortifications in Germany, climb-able). You can skip the city museum in the adjacent courtyard.

The Hauptmarkt square is a people-filled swirl of fruit stands, flowers, painted facades, and fountains—with a handy public W.C. Trier's tourist office, next to the Porta Nigra (9:00-18:30, Sunday 9:00-15:30, tel. 0651/978080) organizes 2-hour, 8-DM town walks in English daily at 14:00. (For accommodations, see below.)

Sightseeing Highlights on the Unromantic Rhine

▲▲▲**Köln (Cologne)**—A big, no-nonsense city, Germany's fourth largest, Köln has a compact and lively center. The Rhine was the northern boundary of the Roman Empire and 1700 years ago Emperor Constantine (the first Christian emperor) made "Colonia" the seat of a bishop. Five hundred years later, under Charlemagne, it became the seat of an archbishop. With 40,000 people living within its walls, it was an important cultural and religious center throughout the Middle Ages. To many, the city is most famous for its toilet water. "Eau de Cologne" was first made here by an Italian chemist in 1709. Even after World War II bombs destroyed 95 percent of it, Köln has remained, after a remarkable recovery, a cultural and commercial center as well as a fun, colorful, and pleasant-smelling city. And it couldn't be easier to visit: Köln's three important sights gather within two blocks of its train station and TI. This super pedestrian zone is a constant carnival of people.

The Gothic **Dom**, or cathedral, is far and away Germany's most exciting church (100 yards from the station, open 7:00-19:00). Inside, under its 500-foot-tall spires, you'll find the amazingly realistic and way-ahead-of-its-time "Gero Crucifix," sculpted in 976. The "Shrine of the Magi" is a lavish gold altarpiece containing the "bones of the three kings," which, by some stretch of medieval Christian logic, justified the secular power of the local king. These important relics, acquired in the twelfth century, made Köln a big enough stop on the pilgrimage trail to merit the construction of this magnificent cathedral.

Next to the Dom is the outstanding **Römisch-Germanisches Museum**, Germany's best Roman museum (5 DM, Tuesday-Sunday 10:00-17:00). Cheapskates can view its prize piece, a fine mosaic floor, free from the front window. Proudly, the museum offers not a word of English among its elegant and fascinating display of Roman artifacts (fine glassware, jewelry, and mosaics). Next door, the **Wallraf-Richartz and Ludwig Museum** offers a world class collection of medieval, northern Baroque, impressionist, and twentieth-century painting, thoughtfully described in English. (8 DM, Friday-Sunday 10:00-18:00, Tuesday-Thursday 10:00-20:00, closed Monday, buy the .50 DM guide/map, great cafeteria with a salad bar, tel. 0221/221 2379.) The TI is near the station, opposite the Dom's main entry (daily 8:00-22:30, closes early in winter, has a list of reasonable private guides, tel. 0221/221 3345).

▲**Bonn**—Bonn was chosen for its sleepy, cultured, and

peaceful nature as a good place to plant Germany's first post-Hitler government. Now that Germany is one again, Berlin will retake its position as capital. Apart from the tremendous cost of switching the seat of government, more than 100,000 jobs are involved, and lots of Bonn families will have some difficult decisions to make.

Today Bonn is sleek, modern, and, by big-city standards, remarkably pleasant and easygoing. Stop here not to see Beethoven's house (10:00-17:00, Sunday 10:00-13:00, 5 DM, tel. 0228/635188) but to come up for a smoggy breath of the real world after the misty, romantic Rhine. The excellent TI is directly in front of the station (open 8:00-21:00, Sunday 9:30-12:30, tel. 0228/773466, free room-finding service).

The pedestrian-only old town stretches out from the station and makes you wonder why the United States can't trade in its malls on real, people-friendly cities. The market square and Münsterplatz are a street-musician-filled joy. People-watching doesn't get much better.

Hotels are expensive in Bonn. **Hotel Eschweiler Taco** (S-69 DM, SB-79 DM, D-105 DM, DB-115; Bonngasse 7, tel. 0228/631760 or 631769, fax 694904) is plain but well-located, just off the market square on a pedestrian street next to Beethoven's place above a taco joint (7-minute walk from the station).

▲**Remagen**—Little remains of the Bridge at Remagen, of World War II fame. But the memorial and the bridge stubs are enough to stir the emotions of Americans who remember when it was the only bridge that remained, allowing the Allies to cross the Rhine and race to Berlin in 1945. The small museum tells the bridge's fascinating story in English (March-October daily 10:00-17:00, 2.50 DM). Located on the west bank of the Rhine, just north of Koblenz. Follow the "Brücke von Remagen" signs through the small town.

▲**Charlemagne's Capital at Aachen**—Aachen was the capital of Europe in AD 800, when Charles the Great (Charlemagne) called it Aix-la-Chapelle. The remains of his rule are there, including an impressive Byzantine/Ravenna-inspired church with his sarcophagus and throne.

The city also has a headliner newspaper museum and
great fountains including a clever arrange-'em-yourself
version.

Flying home from Frankfurt?
Be sure to telephone your airline (phone numbers undei
Frankfurt, Day 1) three days in advance to confirm your
seat. Also, call the morning of your departure to check the
departure time.

To get to the airport by autobahn, head toward
Frankfurt. After you cross the Rhine, follow the little air-
plane signs to the airport (*Flughafen*), which is right on
the autobahn.

By train, it's even easier. The airport has its own train
station, and many of the trains from the Rhine stop there
on their way into Frankfurt (e.g., hourly 90-minute rides
direct from Bonn). A 12-minute shuttle train connects
Frankfurt's central station and its airport six times an hour

Sleeping on the Mosel
**Zell (1.6 DM = about $1, zip code: 56856, tel. code:
06542)**
If the Mosel charms you into spending the night, do it in
Zell. By car, this is a natural. By train, you'll need to go to
Bullay (hourly from Cochem and Trier) where the hourly
10-minute bus ride takes you to little Zell (TI, 8:00-12:30,
13:30-17:00, tel. 06542/4031 or 70122). Zell's hotels are a
disappointment, but its private homes are great. The owners speak almost no English and discount their rates if you
stay more than one night. My favorites are on the south
end of town, a 2-minute walk from the town hall square
and the bus stop.

The comfortable and modern home of **Fritz and
Susanne Mesenich** is quiet, friendly, clean, central, and
across from a good winestube (D-60 DM, 50 DM if you
stay two nights, Oberstr. 3, tel. 4753). Frau Mesenich can
find you a room if she's full. Herr Mesenich can take you
into his cellar for a look at the haus wine. Notice tl.e flood
marks on the wall across the street and flood photos in
her breakfast room and hope it doesn't rain.

Gästhaus Gertrud Thiesen (S-35 DM, D-60 DM for one night, 50 DM for two nights; Balduinstr. 1, tel. 4453) is across the street, just as much fun but classier, with a TV-living-breakfast room and a river view. The Thiesen house has big, bright rooms and is on the town's first corner overlooking the Mosel from a great terrace.

The cheapest beds in town are in the simple but comfortable home of **Natalie Huhn** (D-40 DM for one night, 35 DM for two; near the pedestrian bridge behind the church at Jakobstrasse 32, tel. 41048 or 4793).

If you're looking for room service, a sauna, pool, and elevator, sleep at **Hotel Grüner Kranz** (DB-140 DM with Mosel views, CC-VMA, elevator, tel. 4549 or 4276, fax 4311)

Weinhaus Mayer, next door, is a better hotel value. This classy old pension is perfectly central with Mosel view rooms (13 rooms, DB-90 to 100 DM depending on the view, Balduinstr. 15, tel. 4530).

Sleeping in Cinderella Land, Beilstein on the Mosel

Cozier and farther north, Beilstein is very small and quiet, with no train nearby and almost no cars but plenty of Cochem bus connections. (TI, daily in summer 7:00-19:00, tel. 02673/1417, or 7912 in the winter, zip code: 56814.)

Hotel Haus Lipmann (5 rooms, DB-120 DM to 150 DM, tel. 02673/1573) is your chance to live in a medieval mansion with hot showers and TVs. A prize-winner for atmosphere, it's been in the Lipmann family for 200 years The creaky wooden staircase and the elegant dining hall with long wooden tables surrounded by antlers, chandeliers, and feudal weapons will get you in the mood for your castle sightseeing but the riverside terrace may mace your momentum.

The half-timbered, river-front **Altes Zollhaus Gästzimmer** (DB-95, tel. 02673/1574 or 1850, open March-October) has crammed all the comforts into tight, bright and modern rooms.

Gasthaus Winzerschenke an der Klostertreppe (DB-60, tel. 02673/1354) is comfortable and a great value, right in the tiny heart of town. There are cheaper rooms in Beilstein's gaggle of private ꞌomes.

Sleeping in Trier

For reasonable beds near the train station try **Hotel Monopol** (S-60 DM to 90 DM, D-110 DM, DB-120 DM to 150 DM, CC-VM, buffet breakfast; Bahnhofsplatz 7, tel. 0651/714090) or **Hotel Kurfürst Balduin** (S-50 DM, D-90 DM, DB-105 DM, CC-VMA; Theodor Heuss Allee 22, tel. 0651/25610). To sleep in a near-palace that tries too hard to be cute and antique, check into **Fassbender's Central Hotel** (DB-140 DM, CC-VMA; Sichelstrasse 32, tel. 0651/978780, fax 9787878). The best value in town is the Catholic Church-run **Kolpinghaus Warsberger Hof** (23 DM per bed with sheets and breakfast in 2- to 6-bed dorm rooms or 33 DM per person in the S, D, or T hotel rooms, no private showers; 1 block off the market square, Dietrichstrasse 42, tel. 0651/75131, fax 74696). This place is super-clean, well-run, and serves inexpensive meals in its open-to-anyone restaurant. On the same street, **Hotel Frankenturm** (S-60 DM, D-80 DM, DB-130 DM, CC-V, Dietrichstrasse 3, tel. 0651/45712, fax 9782449) is plain, comfortable and simple, above a classy saloon.

FLY HOME OR VISIT BERLIN

You've completed the 22-day Germany, Austria and Switzerland circle and the Frankfurt airport is just an hour from your last stop on the Rhine. But no tour of Germany is complete without a look at its historic and newly united capital, Berlin. If you have the time and money, plug it in. It's connected by easy overnight trains from Bonn, Köln, Frankfurt, Munich, Vienna, and Copenhagen. From Bonn it's 8 hours and $100 (about 23:00-7:00, second-class ticket with a bunk bed on the train).

Berlin is wrapping up a tumultuous 50-year chapter in its 750 years of history. After being flattened in World War II,

Suggested Schedule

7:00	Arrive (overnight trains arrive early), at Berlin's Bahnhof Zoo. Walk to Europa Center for breakfast (open 7:00) visit the TI (open 8:00), leave bags at your hotel.
9:00	Visit Memorial church, tour KaDeWe Department Store.
10:30	Catch bus 100 (Hotel Palace at Europa Center). Ride to Siegessaule (climb-able), visit history museum in the Reichstag building, walk through Brandenburg Gate. Or stroll down Unter den Linden, ride to top of TV tower (*Fernsehturm*), and munch lunch on Alexanderplatz or in the old fashioned-restored Nikolai Quarter.
14:30	Tour Pergamon Museum.
16:00	Walk down Friedrichstrasse to what was Checkpoint Charlie, walk to the right, down Zimmerstrasse a few blocks to see remains of the wall, tour the "Topography of Terror" exhibit, then tour the Museum of the Wall. Subway home or venture into Kreuzberg.

Suggested Schedule Day 23 (We're cheating.)

8:00	Breakfast, check out of hotel (pick up bag later or store it at the station).
9:00	Tour Charlottenburg Palace, cross the street for Egyptian Museum, see Nefertiti.
13:00	U-Bahn to Adenauerplatz, stroll Ku'damm to Wittenbergplatz, finding lunch along the way.
15:00	Tour Gemäldegalerie (picture gallery) at Dahlem.
22:00	Catch night train west.

Note: With only one day for Berlin, I'd do Day 1 as recommended but splice in a walk down Ku'damm at 10:00 and choose either the Dahlem picture gallery or the Pergamon museum. The Wall museum is open late.

it was divided by the Allied powers. The American, British, and French sectors became what we knew as West Berlin. The Russian sector was East Berlin. The division was set in stone when the East built the infamous Berlin Wall in 1961. On November 9, 1989, the wall fell, and on October 3, 1990, Germany was formally reunited. Today the city is like a man who had a terrible accident and half the body was given the best of care and the other was denied therapy. The West, benefiting from a generation of government schemes to keep the city vital (tax breaks, draft deferments, transportation subsidies, business incentives), provides a striking contrast to the East, which remains dreary with ersatz jeans, new Fiats made from antiquated factory molds, war-scarred buildings, and people still gawky in their new capitalist lives.

Crossing "into the East" is now like stepping on a dead dragon, no longer mysterious and foreboding—just ugly. The thrill is gone, but the grey remains . . . and many districts of newly freed eastern Berlin continue to vote PDS (the political ghost of the now outlawed Communist party). But even with the scars of the Cold War, the city holds the soul of the German nation. Within a few years the German government will have moved in. And in the year 2000 a well-mended Berlin hopes to host the Olympics.

Transportation—Bonn, Köln, or Frankfurt to Berlin (about 350 miles)

By train, it's a direct, 8-hour overnight trip from Bonn or Köln (22:30-7:00, 125 DM), Frankfurt or Munich. A *Liegeplatz*, or bunk bed, on the train is money well spent (26 DM for a place in a 6-bed cabin, 40 DM in the same cabin with two beds left empty). The beds are the same for first- and second-class tickets. Trains are rarely full, but get your bed reserved a few days in advance from any travel agency or train station.

Orientation

Berlin's central station, called Bahnhof Zoo because it's near Berlin's famous zoo, has a little TI (8:00-23:00, closed Sunday). The main TI office (tel. 030/262-6031) is 5 minutes from the station, in the Europa Center (the skyscraper with the Mercedes-Benz symbol on top, enter outside to the left, on Budapesterstr., 8:00-22:30, 9:00-21:00 on Sunday). Their free "Berlin Berlin" magazine has good reading on Berlin and lists all sights and hours. The "Berlin Program" is a 3-DM German language monthly listing upcoming events. Consider buying the 3-DM transit map.

The tourist's Berlin can be broken into chunks: (1) The area around the Bahnhof Zoo and the grand Kurfürstendamm boulevard (transportation, information, hotel, shopping, and nightlife hub), (2) former downtown East Berlin (Brandenburg Gate, Unter den Linden boulevard, Pergamon museum, Wall-related sights), (3) the museums and palace at Charlottenburg, and (4) the museums at Dahlem. Chunks 1 and 2 can be done on foot or with bus 100. Catch the U-Bahn to chunks 3 and 4. Of course, Berlin is a much bigger place. But for a 2-day visit, pretend this is all there is. I've described Berlin's sightsee-

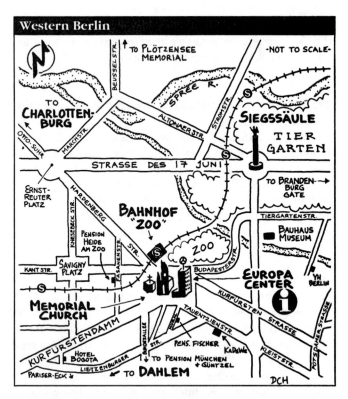

ing highlights in a logical geographical order. Train info:
tel. 297 47580. Telephone code: 030.

Transportation within Berlin
Use Berlin's fine public transit system. The U-Bahn, S-
Bahn, and buses of east and west are now one "BVG" sys-
tem operating conveniently on the same tickets. (The S-
Bahn is free with a Eurailpass.) Ask at the TI for specifics.
A basic buy-as-you-board or buy-from-machines
(Erwachsene Normaltarif) 3.20-DM ticket gives you 2
hours of travel on buses or subways. For a single short
ride (six bus stops or three subway stations, one transfer)
get the "Einzelfahrschein" ticket (2.10 DM each or four, a
"Sammelkarte," for 6.70 DM). The 12-DM "Berlin Ticket"
gives you the works for 24 hours. It's an honor system sitting on a foundation of frequent checks and steep fines.

Eastern Berlin

The 3-DM transit (*Liniennetz*) map shows all. The double-decker buses are a joy to ride, and the subway is a snap. Bus 100, the tourist's favorite, goes every few minutes from Bahnhof Zoo, Europa Center/Hotel Palace, Siegessaüle, Reichstag, Brandenburg Gate, Unter den Linden, Pergamon museum, to Alexanderplatz. Taxis are easy to catch but not cheap.

Sightseeing Highlights—Berlin
Sights Near the Bahnhof Zoo
▲**Kurfürstendamm**—Throughout the Cold War, economic subsidies from the West made sure that the full flashy vibrancy of capitalism thrived on Ku'damm, as western Berlin's main drag is popularly called. The old charm has been drowned in commercial neon, but this hamburgerized Champs-Elysées of Berlin is still the place to feel the pulse of the city and enjoy its most elegant

shops. Ku'damm, starting near the main train station, Europa Center, and Kaiser Wilhelm memorial church, does its commercial can-can for over 2 miles.

Europa Center—A shiny high-rise shopping center where you'll find the city tourist information, lots of shops and restaurants. If your overnight train arrives before the TI opens, the French café (ground floor, open at 7:00, 8:00 Sunday) is a more pleasant place to brush your teeth and start your day than the seedy Bahnhof Zoo.

▲**Kaiser-Wilhelm Gedachtniskirche (Memorial Church)**—This important World War II memorial, the charred and gutted ruins of a bombed-out church (built 1895, bombed 1943, open Tuesday-Saturday 10:00-18:00), has great ceiling mosaics and an interesting photo exhibit about the bombing. Next to it is a new church (1961) offering a world of blue glass. You'll see why they call this complex the broken tooth, the lipstick, and the powder compact.

▲**Kaufhaus des Westens (KaDeWe)**—The "department store of the West" is the biggest department store in Europe. It takes a staff of more than 3,000 to help you find and purchase what you need from the vast selection of more than 200,000 items. You can get everything from a haircut and train ticket to souvenirs (fourth floor). The sixth floor is a world of taste treats. This biggest selection of deli and exotic food you'll ever see offers plenty of reasonable opportunities to sit down and eat some of it (9:00-18:30, Saturday until 14:00, Thursday until 20:30, closed Sunday, tel. 21210, U-Bahn: Wittenbergplatz).

The Berlin Zoo—1,500 different kinds of animals call Berlin's famous zoo home (or so the zookeepers like to think). It stretches out from Berlin's central station (8 DM, 9:00-17:00, feeding times posted at entry, morning is the best visiting time, enter on Budapesterstr., tel. 254010). Next to the zoo sprawls Berlin's biggest and most pleasant city park, the Tiergarten.

Tiergarten/Siegessaüle—Berlin's "Central Park" stretches about 2 miles from the Zoo train station to the Brandenburg Gate. Its centerpiece, the Siegessaüle Tower, was built to commemorate the Prussian defeat of France in 1870. You can climb its 285 steps for a fine Berlin-wide view (1.50 DM, 9:00-18:00, Monday 15:00-18:00, bus 100) or you might not. From the tower the grand Strasse des 17 Juni leads to the Brandenburg Gate (via a thriving flea market each Saturday and Sunday).

Sights in Eastern Berlin

▲**The Reichstag**—The old parliament building, burned by Hitler to frame the communists, now houses a modern German history exhibit, "Questions on German History" (10:00-17:00 Tuesday-Sunday, free, enter from side opposite the bus 100 stop, cheap cafeteria, lots of free literature on the German government). Nothing is explained in English but you can follow a good, socio-economico-meaty and exhausting 45-minute tape recorded tour for 2 DM. In 1995 this collection will move to the Deutscher/Französischer Dom as the Reichstag resumes its real function as Germany's parliament building. On the Brandenburg Gate side of the building, there's a memorial to those killed trying to cross The Wall.

▲▲**Brandenburg Gate**—The historic Brandenburg Gate was the symbol of Berlin and then the symbol of divided Berlin. It sat, sad and quiet, in a no-man's-land part of the wall, for over 25 years. Now a free little photo exhibit in the gate and postcards all over town show the ecstatic day, December 23, 1989, when the world enjoyed the sight of happy Berliners jamming the gate like flowers on a parade float. A carnival atmosphere continues as tourists stroll, past hawkers with "authentic" pieces of the wall and DDR flags and military paraphernalia, to the traditional rhythm of an organ grinder. In Berlin, freedom hasn't come cheap. As you walk through Brandenburg Gate, look down the vacant swath of formerly fortified land, breathe in the freedom . . and remember those who fought and still fight for it. Ebertstrassa leads from Brandenburg Gate to Potsdamer Platz, formerly the busiest square in all of Europe. Since East and West grew facing away from each other, Potsdamer Platz today is strangely vacant.

▲▲**A Walk through Eastern Berlin**—In Berlin's good old days, Unter den Linden was one of Europe's grand

boulevards. Walk or catch bus 100 from Brandenburg
Gate to Alexanderplatz. Along the way, you'll pass sights
that used to be important: the now-closed Memorial to the
Victims of Fascism and Militarism, the former East Berlin's
German History Museum, and what was the proud show-
piece of East Berlin, the boxy glass Palace of the Republic
(now closed and slated for the wrecking ball). The huge,
domed church is the 100-year-old Berlin Cathedral or
"Dom" (peek inside at the great reformers who stand
around the dome like stern saints guarding their theol-
ogy). Don't miss the famous Pergamon museum, behind
the cathedral (described below). Continue east over the
Spree River and linger among the happy-to-be-free but
yet-to-be-rich people, fountains, and flowers to the 1,200-
foot-tall Fernsehturm TV tower (built 1969, fine view from
600 feet at the deck and café, 9:00-24:00, 5 DM). Farther
east, pass under the S-Bahn station into the best-the-east-
could-do Alexanderplatz with fast-food stalls and the
huge, formerly-proud Centrum Warenhaus department
store on the left. This was the East Berlin consumer's par-
adise. Alexanderplatz still is the heart of eastern Berlin.

From Alexanderplatz, Rathaus Strasse leads to the black-
spired, red brick City Hall (*Rathaus*), decorated with a
sculpted history of Berlin. From here, Spandauer Strasse
leads into the cute, restored ye olde Berlin neighborhood
called the Nikolai Quarter (*Nikolaiviertel*) with Berlin's
"oldest" church (the rebuilt double-spired *Nikolaikirche*),
more than enough shops, restaurants, and cafés, and the
Berlin Crafts Museum (*Mühlendamm* 5, closed Monday).
The Mühlendamm bridge leads to "Checkpoint Charlie."

▲▲▲**The Museum of the Wall (*Haus am Checkpoint
Charlie*) and a surviving chunk of The Wall**—The 100-
mile "Anti-Fascist Protective Rampart," as it was called by
the DDR, was erected almost overnight by East Germany
(and friends) in 1961. The opposite of a medieval rampart,
this wall kept people in. It was 13 feet high with a 16-foot
tank ditch, 160 feet of no-man's-land, and 300 sentry towers. In its 28 years there were 1,693 cases when border
guards fired, 3,221 arrests, 5,043 documented successful
escapes (565 of these were DDR guards), and 80 deaths.

The commercial but fascinating **Haus am Checkpoint Charlie** museum tells the gripping history of The Wall and the many ingenious escape attempts. Since 1989, it's become a happier place, and a visit includes plenty of video and film coverage of those heady days when people power tore it down. An American can only imagine what the Germans watching these clips are feeling (U-Bahn to Kochstr., daily 9:00-22:00, 7.50 DM).

Checkpoint Charlie was the famous American military border crossing which, until 1989, was the place from which nervous tour groups, cowering in the shade of the American flag as mirrors were slid under their buses, crossed into the "Communist Block." Today the gate stands permanently raised as a memorial and a tiny vacant lot is filled with an interesting collection of Wall defenses and paraphernalia.

When it fell, The Wall was literally carried away by the euphoria. Little remains. From Checkpoint Charlie, Zimmerstrasse leads to a small surviving stretch. Walk the length of this bit. Then look left to see the "Topography of Terror" exhibit.

The **Topography of Terror**, built on the recently excavated basement of the former Gestapo headquarters, shows the story of Nazism in Germany (English translation 1 DM, free, 10:00-18:00, closed Monday). Between this building and "Checkpoint Charlie" is a park with English descriptions of this once-formidable center of tyranny.

▲▲**Pergamon Museum**—Many of Berlin's top museums cluster on the Museuminsel (Museum Island), just off Unter den Linden, in Berlin's eastern section. Only the Pergamon Museum, with the fantastic Pergamon Altar, the Babylonian Ishtar Gate, and many ancient Greek and Mesopotamian treasures, is of interest to the normal tourist. (Walk along the canal, passing the first bulky neo-Classical building on your right, to a bridge that leads to a second bulky neo-Classical building, 4 DM, daily 9:00-17:00, but only the Pergamon Altar and Ishtar Gate sections are open on Monday and Tuesday). Take advantage of the free 30-minute tape-recorder tours of the museum's highlights.

Sights around Charlottenburg Palace
Schloss Charlottenburg—This only surviving
Hohenzollern Palace is Berlin's top baroque palace (8 DM,
Tuesday-Friday 9:00-17:00, Saturday and Sunday 10:00-
17:00, U-1 to Sophie-Charlotte Platz and a 10-minute walk,
or bus 121, bus 145, or bus 204 direct from Bahnhof Zoo).
If you've seen the great palaces of Europe, this is
mediocre, especially since its center is tourable only with
a German guide. For a quick look, the Knöbelsdorff Wing
(3 DM) is set up to let you wander on your own, a substantial hike through restored-since-the-war, gold-crusted
white rooms filled with no-name baroque paintings.
▲▲**The Egyptian Museum**—Across the street from the
palace is a fine little museum filled with Egyptian treasures. It offers one of the great thrills in the world of art
appreciation—gazing into the still-young and beautiful
face of 3,000-year-old Queen Nefertiti, the wife of King
Akhenaton (4 DM, Monday-Thursday 9:00-17:00, Saturday
and Sunday 10:00-17:00).
▲**The Bröhan Museum** is like walking through a dozen
beautifully furnished Art Nouveau (Jugendstil) and Art
Deco living rooms. The final rooms are not worth the six
flights of stairs (4 DM, next to the Egyptian Museum,
across the street from the Charlottenburg Palace, 10:00-
18:00, Thursday until 20:00, closed Monday).

Other Berlin Sights
▲▲**Dahlem Gemälde-galerie**—Dahlem is actually a
cluster of important museums that, one by one over the
next decade, will be moved to the new museum complex
in the Tiergarten. The *Gem lde-galerie* (picture gallery) is
Dahlem's essential stop. It has more than 600 canvases by
the likes of Dürer, Titian, Botticelli, Rubens, Vermeer, and
Bruegel, and one of the world's greatest collection of
Rembrandts. The *Man with the Golden Helmet*, recently
determined not to have been painted by Rembrandt, still
shines (4 DM, free on Sunday, Tuesday-Sunday 9:00-17:00,
U-Bahn to Dahlem-Dorf).
Gedenkstätte Plötzensee Memorial—This is a powerful
memorial to Nazi victims in Hitler's former execution

chambers (free, 8:30-16:00, bus 105, 123, 126 to Charlotten-burg, Hüttigpfad).

Kreuzberg—This poorer district along The Wall, with old restored and unrestored buildings and plenty of student and Turkish street life, offers the best look at melting-pot Berlin in a city where original Berliners are as rare as old buildings. Berlin is the fourth-largest Turkish city. This is its "downtown." But to call it a little Istanbul insults the big one. For a dose of Kreuzberg, wander the area between the Kottbusser Tor and Schlesisches Tor subway stops, ideally on Tuesday and Friday afternoons when a Turkish Market sprawls along the bank of the Maybach-ufer River (subway: Kottbusser Tor, 12:00-18:00).

East Side Gallery—The biggest remaining stretch of The Wall is now "the world's longest art gallery" stretching for about a mile and completely covered with murals painted by artists from around the world, mostly in celebration of The Wall's demise. While not overly impressive, and in dire need of restoration, it does make for a thought-pro-voking walk. From Schlesisches Tor (end of Kreuzberg) walk across the river on the pedestrian bridge, turn left, follow the wall to the Berlin Hauptbahnhof (a train station two stops from Alexanderplatz).

Käthe-Kollwitz Museum—This local artist (1867-1945), who experienced much of Berlin's most tumultuous centu-ry, conveys some powerful and mostly sad feelings through the black-and-white faces of her art (6 DM, off Ku'damm at Fasanenstr. 24, 11:00-18:00, closed Tuesday).

Museum of Natural History (*Museum für Naturkunde*)—Worth a visit just to see the largest dinosaur skeleton ever assembled. While you're there meet "Bobby," the stuffed ape. (3 DM, open 9:30-17:00, closed Monday; U-6 to Zinnowitzer Str., at Invalidenstr. 43).

City Bus Tours—Several companies do quick, 30-DM ori-entation tours by city bus. Severin & Kühn buses leave from Ku'damm 216 (near Bahnhof Zoo at the Ku'damm U-Bahn stop). Dial English on the earphones and look out the window at the top two hours of downtown Berlin (30 DM, departures daily at 11:00, 13:30, and 16:00, tel. 883 1015)

Late-Night Berlin

Zitty and *Tip* (sold at kiosks) are the top guides to youth
and alternative culture. The TI's *Berlin Program* lists the
non-stop parade of concerts, plays, exhibits, and cultural
events. Berlin's top night spots are near Ku'damm. If you
just wander around Savignyplatz, Olivaerplatz, Leniner-
platz, and Ludwigskirchplatz, you'll find plenty of action.
Contributing to Berlin's wild late-night scene is the fact
that while the rest of Germany must close down at midnight or 1:00, Berlin night spots must close only one hour
a day.

Sleeping in Berlin (1.6 DM = about $1, tel. code: 030)

Arriving early, on the overnight train, room-finding in
Berlin is easy. But things are expensive, the best deals fill
up first, and my listings all speak English and will hold a
room for a phone call, so call ahead. For a 5-DM fee, the
TI can nearly always find you a room (best between 9:00
and 10:00, 32 DM in a hostel with breakfast, for any age,
or 90 DM per double in a small nearby hotel).

These listings are a 5- to 15-minute walk from the Zoo
Bahnhof, near the Ku'damm, in decent and comfortable
neighborhoods. Landlords and taxes have made running a
budget hotel tough since German reunification. There simply aren't any cheaper rooms and these are an endangered species. Nearly all are a couple flights up in big
run-down buildings. But inside they are clean, quiet, and
big enough so that their well-worn character is actually
charming. Most rooms are big with high ceilings on relatively quiet streets. Rooms in the back are on quiet courtyards. Unless otherwise noted, hallway showers are free,
breakfast is included, and they take no credit cards. Notice
that many of the cheapest prices don't include breakfast.

Pension Heide am Zoo (S-80 DM, SB-105 DM, D-120
DM, DB-140 DM; Fasanenstr. 12, near corner of Kant and
Fasanenstr., 10623 Berlin, tel. 310496), run by friendly
Frau Bäumer, is stylish but homey on a quiet street a 5-
minute walk from the station. Call first; no rooms are
given to drop-ins. Farther down the same street, **Hotel-
Pension Funk** (S-70, SB-75, D-100, DB-120; Fasanenstr.

69, tel. 8827193) offers elegant, richly furnished old rooms for less.

Pension Fischer (S-50 DM, D-70 DM, DB-80 to 90 DM, 35 DM for third or fourth person, breakfast 7 DM, elevator; right at the Augsburgerstr. U-Bahn stop, Nürnberger Strasse 24a, tel. 218 6808, fax 2134225) is basic but cheap with simple, quiet rooms. Just downstairs, **Hotel-Pension Nürnberger Eck** (SB-62 DM, DB-110 DM, extra bed 35 DM, breakfast 8 DM, tel. 2185371, fax 2141540) is well-run by friendly Herr Böhm.

Hotel Pension München (S-50 to 60 DM, D-75 to 95 DM, DB-115 to 130 DM, 5 DM extra for one-night stays, breakfast 9 DM, elevator; at the Güntzelstr. U-Bahn stop, Güntzelstr. 62, 10717 Berlin, tel. 854 2226, fax 853 2744) is bright, cheery, and filled with modern art. At the same address, **Pension Güntzel** (D-110 to 130 DM, DB-130 to 150 DM, tel. 857 9020, fax 853 1108) is also good.

Hotel-Pension Pariser-Eck (D-98 DM, DB-128 DM, 3, 4 or 5 people at 48 DM each, Pariser Str. 19, tel. 881 2145, fax 883 6335) has narrow halls but giant rooms on a street that feels a bit Parisian.

Hotel Bogota (S-68 DM, SB-95 DM, D-110 DM, DB-140 DM, DBWC-180 DM, CC-VMA, elevator, Schlüterstr. 45, 10707 Berlin, tel. 881 5001, fax 883 5887) has big, bright, modern rooms in a spacious old building half a block off Ku'damm. The service is brisk and hotelesque. This is the best no-nonsense hotel-type listing.

Hotel-Pension Bialas (S-65 DM, SB-95 DM, D-95 DM, DB-150 DM, T-135 DM, TB-200 DM, metered 1 DM/two minutes showers down the hall; just off colorful Savignyplatz on quiet street, Carmerstr. 16, tel. 312 5025, fax 312 4396) feels a bit like a hostel with thirty big, bright, airy rooms.

Hostels feature small rooms, are open to all, and save you about 33 percent. While many are often packed with West German school groups field-tripping to Berlin, the TI has a long list of places renting cheap beds. **Jugendgastehaus Berlin** (33 DM beds with sheets and breakfast in 4- to 8-bed rooms; Kluckstr. 3, take bus 129 from the Europa Center or the Ku'damm U-Bahn stop, tel. 261 1097

or 261 1098; over 400 beds, but often filled with groups
so call up to two weeks in advance and leave your name,
non-members pay 6 DM extra, 9 DM lunches and dinners)
is most central. The **Studenten Hotel Berlin** (34-38 DM
per bed in doubles and quads with sheets and breakfast;
Meiningerstr. 10, tel. 784 6720, near the City Hall on JFK
Platz or U-Bahn to Rathaus Schoneberg) is also decent.

Eating in Berlin
Berlin has plenty of fun food places, both German and
imported. If kraut is getting wurst, try one of the many
Turkish, Italian, or Balkan restaurants. Those counting
pennies fill up on a hearty stew at a funky pub called
Dicke Wirtin (5 DM per bowl with a roll, 9 Carmer-
strasse, just off Savignyplatz). **Wertheim** department store
(at Ku'damm U-Bahn) has cheap basement food counters
and a fine self-service cafeteria up six banks of escalators
with a view. **KaDeWe's** sixth-floor deli food department is
a picnicker's nirvana. Drool your way through over 1,000
kinds of sausage and 1,500 types of cheese. You can even
get peanut butter here! Put together a picnic and grab a
sunny bench. For cheap and substantial kebabs, eat
Turkish in Kreuzberg.
   The local pubs, called *Kneipe*, are colorful places to get
a light meal and to try out the local beer, Berliner Weiss
Ask for it *mit Schuss* and you'll get a shot of syrup in
your suds.

PRACTICAL EXTRAS

TRANSPORTATION

The chart below lists the major train segments you may use with average duration of journey, cost in U.S. dollars for a one-way second-class ticket (for first class, just add 50 percent, and spit out your gum), and about how many trips are made per day. Any journey of six or more hours can be done overnight. To figure fares yourself, remember second-class ticket prices are based on 20 DM for 100 km (about $12 for 60 miles).

Train Almanac for Germany, Austria, and Switzerland

From-To	Length of Trip	Approx 1994 cost in $, o/w, 2nd class	Trips/Day
Frankfurt-Würzburg	1 hr. 20 min.	20	20
Frankfurt-Berlin	8 hrs.	66	7
Frankfurt-Munich (train)	4 hrs.	55	17
Frankfurt-Munich (bus tour)	11 hrs.	55	1
Frankfurt-Köln	2 hrs. 10 min.	30	20
Frankfurt-Amsterdam	5 hrs. 30 min	60	11
Würzburg-Rothenburg, via Steinach	1 hr.	8	20
Rothenburg-Munich (bus)	5 hrs	30	1
Rothenburg-Füssen	6 hrs.	35	1
Füssen-Reutte in Tirol (bus)	45 min	3	11
Reutte-Munich, via Garmisch	3 hrs.	20	8
Munich-Füssen	1 hr.	16	12
Munich-Salzburg	2 hrs	20	15
Munich-Vienna	5 hrs. 30 min.	54	7
Munich-Venice	9 hrs.	52	2
Vienna-Venice	10 hrs.	58	5
Salzburg-Vienna	3 hrs. 20 min.	34	16
Vienna-Mauthausen	2 hrs.	17	20
Vienna-Innsbruck	5 hrs. 30 min	60	8
Vienna-Zürich	9 hrs. 30 min.	90	5
Vienna-Budapest	3 hrs. 30 min	25	4
Vienna-Prague	6 hrs.	31	4
Innsbruck-Zürich	4 hrs.	42	7
Zürich-Munich	4 hrs. 30 min	51	5
Zürich-Paris	6 hrs. 30 min.	70	5
Zürich-Luzern	50 min.	13	20
Luzern-Interlaken	2 hrs.	13	20

Train Almanac (cont.)

From-To	Length of Trip	Approx 1994 cost in $, o/w, 2nd class	Trips/Day
Interlaken Ost-Gimmelwald	1 hr. 30 min	7	20
Interlaken-Montreux	3 hrs.	30	16
Interlaken-Bern	1 hr.	13	20
Montreux-Lausanne	20 min.	5	30
Lausanne-Murten	1 hr.	13	12
Murten-Bern	1 hr.	13	12
Bern-Freiburg (Germany)	3 hrs.	30	4
Freiburg-Baden-Baden	1 hr. 20 min.	13	30
Baden-Baden-Koblenz	2 hrs. 30 min.	35	20
Koblenz-Cochem	40 min.	7	17
Cochem-Trier	45 min.	8	17
Koblenz-Mainz, train	50 min.	13	40
Koblenz-Mainz, boat	6 hrs.	30	5
Koblenz-Bonn	30 min.	7	40
Bonn-Köln	30 min.	5	40
Koblenz-Frankfurt	1 hr. 30 min.	17	20
Frankfurt-Frankfurt Airport	15 min.	3	50
Berlin-Munich	10 hrs.	85	3
Berlin-Vienna	12 hrs.	68	1
Berlin-Amsterdam	10 hrs.	85	5
Berlin-Copenhagen	10 hrs.	54	2

Train Itinerary

Day		Overnight in
1	Arrive Frankfurt, train to Rothenburg	Rothenburg
2	Sightsee Rothenburg	Rothenburg
3	Morning in Rothenburg, afternoon Romantic Road bus tour	Füssen
4	Castle Day, Bavarian highlights	Füssen
5	Munich	Munich
6	All day in Munich	Night train
7	All day in Budapest	evening to Vienna
8	Sightsee in Vienna	Vienna
9	Sightsee in Vienna, Danube side-trip	Vienna
10	Salzkammergut Lakes	Hallstatt
11	Sightsee Salzburg	Night train
12	Bern, Interlaken, Grindelwald, hike to...	Gimmelwald
13	Free to frolic in the heart of the Alps	Gimmelwald
14	Château Chillon, Montreux, Lake Geneva	Montreux

Train Itinerary (cont.)

Day		Overnight in
15	French Switzerland, Murten, Bern	Murten or Bern
16	Explore Germany's Black Forest, Freiburg	Baden-Baden
17	Free day in old spa town, soak, massage . . .	Baden-Baden
18	Train up Rhine to castle country	St. Goar
19	Rhine and Mosel River, Cochem,	St. Goar
20	Bonn, Köln	Night train
21	Berlin	Berlin
22	Berlin, tour over, fly home	

Train Lines: Germany, Austria, Switzerland

TELEPHONING

Country Codes
U.S.A.—1
Canada—1
France—33
Belgium—32
Germany—49
Italy—39
Netherlands—31
Switzerland—41
Austria—43
Great Britain—44

International Code to Call Out of:
Germany—00; Switzerland—00; Austria—050; USA—011

USA Direct toll-free access numbers for calling home from Europe (your credit card will be billed about $2.50 plus the cheaper USA-to-Europe long-distance rate.)

	ATT	MCI	SPRINT
Germany	0130-0010	0130-0012	0130-0013
Austria	022-903-011	022-903-012	022-903-014
Switzerland	155-00-11	155-02-22	155-97-77

Climate Chart

1st line: average daily low; 2nd: average daily high; 3rd: days of no rain

	J	F	M	A	M	J	J	A	S	O	N	D
GERMANY	29	31	35	41	48	53	56	55	51	43	36	31
Frankfurt	37	42	49	58	67	72	75	74	67	56	45	39
	22	19	22	21	22	21	21	21	21	22	21	20
AUSTRIA	26	28	34	41	50	56	59	58	52	44	36	30
Vienna	34	38	47	57	66	71	75	73	66	55	44	37
	23	21	24	21	22	21	22	21	23	23	22	22
SWITZER-	29	30	35	41	48	55	58	57	52	44	37	31
LAND	39	43	51	58	66	73	77	76	69	58	47	40
Geneva	20	19	21	19	19	19	22	21	20	20	19	21

Metric Conversions (approximate)

1 inch = 25 millimeters

1 foot =0.3 meter

36-24-36 = 90-60-90

1 yard = 0.9 meter

1 mile = 1.6 kilometers

1 square yard = 0.8 square meter

1 acre = 0.4 hectare

1 quart = 0.95 liter

1 ounce = 28 grams

32 degrees F = 0 degrees C

82 degrees F = about 28 degrees C

1 kilogram = 2.2 pounds

1 kilometer = .62 mile

1 centimeter = 0.4 inch

1 meter = 39.4 inches

National Tourist Information Offices in the USA

Austrian National Tourist Office, PO Box 491938, Los Angeles, CA 90049, (310)477-3332. 500 Fifth Ave., #2009-2022, New York, NY 10110, (212)944-6880.

German National Tourist Office, 122 East 42nd St., 52nd floor, New York, NY 10168, (212)661-7200. 11766 Wilshire Blvd., Suite 750, Los Angeles, CA 90025, (310)575-9799.

Swiss National Tourist Office, 665 Fifth Ave., New York, NY 10020, (212)757-5944. 260 Stockton St., San Francisco, CA 94108, (415)362-2260

INDEX

Rick Steves' ████████████████████

EUROPE THROUGH THE BACK DOOR CATALOG

*All items are field tested, discount priced (prices include tax and shipping),
completely guaranteed, and highly recommended for European travel.*

CONVERTIBLE BACK DOOR BAG $75

At 9"x21"x13" our specially designed, sturdy bag is maximum carry-on-the-plane size (fits under the seat) and your key to footloose and fancy-free travel. Made of rugged water resistant cordura nylon, it converts easily from a smart looking suitcase to a handy rucksack. It has padded hideaway shoulder straps, top and side handles, and a detachable shoulder strap (for use as a suitcase). Lockable perimeter zippers allow easy access to the roomy 2,500 cubic inch central compartment. Two large outside compartments are perfect for frequently used items. A nylon stuff bag is also included. Rick Steves and over 40,000 other Back Door travelers have lived out of these bags all around the world. Available in black, grey, navy blue and teal green.

MONEYBELT $8

Absolutely required for European travel, our sturdy
nylon, ultra-light, under-the-pants pouch is just big enough
to carry your essentials (passport, airline tickets, travelers checks, and so on) comfortably. Rick won't travel without one, and neither should you. Comes in neutral beige, with a nylon zipper. One size fits all.

EUROPEAN RAILPASSES

We sell the full range of European railpasses, and with every Eurailpass we give you these important extras — *free:* Rick Steves' 90-minute 'How to get the most out of your railpass' video; your choice of one of Rick's seven "2 to 22 Days in..." guidebooks; and our comments on your 1-page proposed itinerary. Call us for a free copy of our 48-page *1994 Back Door Guide to European Railpasses.*

BACK DOOR 'BEST OF EUROPE' TOURS

We offer a variety of European tours for those who want to travel in the Back Door style, but without the transportation and hotel hassles. These tours feature small groups, our own guides, Back Door accomodations, and lots of physical exercise. Our tours aren't for everyone, but they may be just the ticket for you. Call us for details.

FREE TRAVEL NEWSLETTER/CATALOG

Give us a call at (206) 771-8303, and we'll send you our free newsletter/catalog packed full of info on budget travel, books, maps, videos railpasses and tours. We'll help you travel better *because* you're on a budget -- not in spite of it.

*Prices are good through 1994 (maybe longer), and include tax and shipping (allow
2 to 3 weeks). Sorry, no credit cards or phone orders. Send checks in US $ to:*

**Europe Through the Back Door ❖ 109 Fourth Avenue North
PO Box 2009, Edmonds, WA 98020 ❖ Phone: (206)771-8303**

Other Books from John Muir Publications

Asia Through the Back Door, 4th ed., 400 pp. $16.95 (available 7/93)

Belize: A Natural Destination, 336 pp. $16.95

Costa Rica: A Natural Destination, 2nd ed., 310 pp. $16.95

Elderhostels: The Students' Choice, 2nd ed., 304 pp. $15.95

Environmental Vacations: Volunteer Projects to Save the Planet, 2nd ed., 248 pp. $16.95

Europe 101: History & Art for the Traveler, 4th ed., 350 pp. $15.95

Europe Through the Back Door, 11th ed., 432 pp. $17.95

Europe Through the Back Door Phrase Book: French, 160 pp. $4.95

Europe Through the Back Door Phrase Book: German, 160 pp. $4.95

Europe Through the Back Door Phrase Book: Italian, 168 pp. $4.95

Europe Through the Back Door Phrase Book: Spanish & Portuguese, 288 pp. $4.95

A Foreign Visitor's Guide to America, 224 pp. $12.95

Great Cities of Eastern Europe, 256 pp. $16.95

Guatemala: A Natural Destination, 336 pp. $16.95

Indian America: A Traveler's Companion, 4th ed., 448 pp. $17.95 (available 7/93)

Interior Furnishings Southwest, 256 pp. $19.95

Mona Winks: Self-Guided Tours of Europe's Top Museums, 2nd ed., 448 pp. $16.95

Opera! The Guide to Western Europe's Great Houses, 296 pp. $18.95

Paintbrushes and Pistols: How the Taos Artists Sold the West, 288 pp. $17.95

The People's Guide to Mexico, 9th ed., 608 pp. $18.95

Ranch Vacations: The Complete Guide to Guest and Resort, Fly-Fishing, and Cross-Country Skiing Ranches, 2nd ed., 396 pp. $18.95

The Shopper's Guide to Art and Crafts in the Hawaiian Islands, 272 pp. $13.95

The Shopper's Guide to Mexico, 224 pp. $9.95

Understanding Europeans, 272 pp. $14.95

Undiscovered Islands of the Caribbean, 3rd ed., 288 pp. $14.95

Undiscovered Islands of the Mediterranean, 2nd ed., 224 pp. $13.95

Undiscovered Islands of the U.S. and Canadian West Coast, 288 pp. $12.95

Unique Colorado, 112 pp. $10.95 (available 6/93)

Unique Florida, 112 pp. $10.95 (available 7/93)

Unique New Mexico, 112 pp. $10.95 (available 6/93)

A Viewer's Guide to Art: A Glossary of Gods, People, and Creatures, 144 pp. $10.95

The Visitor's Guide to the Birds of the Eastern National Parks: United States and Canada, 410 pp. $15.95

2 to 22 Days Series

Each title offers 22 flexible daily itineraries useful for planning vacations of any length. Aside from valuable general information, included are "must see" attractions *and* hidden "jewels."

2 to 22 Days in the American Southwest, 1993 ed., 176 pp. $10.95

2 to 22 Days in Asia, 1993 ed., 176 pp. $9.95

2 to 22 Days in Australia, 1993 ed., 192 pp. $9.95

2 to 22 Days in California, 1993 ed., 192 pp. $9.95

2 to 22 Days in Europe, 1993 ed., 288 pp. $13.95

2 to 22 Days in Florida, 1993 ed., 192 pp. $10.95

2 to 22 Days in France, 1993 ed., 192 pp. $10.95

2 to 22 Days in Germany, Austria, & Switzerland, 1993 ed., 224 pp. $10.95

2 to 22 Days in Great Britain, 1993 ed., 192 pp. $10.95

2 to 22 Days Around the Great Lakes, 1993 ed., 192 pp. $10.95

2 to 22 Days in Hawaii, 1993 ed., 192 pp. $9.95

2 to 22 Days in Italy, 208 pp. $10.95

2 to 22 Days in New England, 1993 ed., 192 pp. $10.95

2 to 22 Days in New Zealand, 1993 ed., 192 pp. $9.95

2 to 22 Days in Norway, Sweden, & Denmark, 1993 ed., 192 pp. $10.95

2 to 22 Days in the Pacific Northwest, 1993 ed., 192 pp. $10.95

2 to 22 Days in the Rockies, 1993 ed., 192 pp. $10.95

2 to 22 Days in Spain & Portugal, 192 pp. $10.95

2 to 22 Days in Texas, 1993 ed., 192 pp. $9.95

2 to 22 Days in Thailand, 1993 ed., 180 pp. $9.95

22 Days (or More) Around the World, 1993 ed., 264 pp. $12.95

Automotive Titles

How to Keep Your VW Alive, 15th ed., 464 pp. $21.95

How to Keep Your Subaru Alive 480 pp. $21.95

How to Keep Your Toyota Pickup Alive 392 pp. $21.95

How to Keep Your Datsun/Nissan Alive 544 pp. $21.95

The Greaseless Guide to Car Care Confidence, 224 pp $14.95

Off-Road Emergency Repair & Survival, 160 pp. $9.95

TITLES FOR YOUNG READERS AGES 8 AND UP

"Kidding Around" Travel Guides for Young Readers

All the "Kidding Around" Travel guides are 64 pages and $9.95 paper, except for **Kidding Around Spain** and **Kidding Around the National Parks of the Southwest**, which are 108 pages and $12.95 paper.

Kidding Around Atlanta
Kidding Around Boston, 2nd ed.
Kidding Around Chicago, 2nd ed.
Kidding Around the Hawaiian Islands
Kidding Around London
Kidding Around Los Angeles
Kidding Around the National Parks of the Southwest
Kidding Around New York City, 2nd ed.
Kidding Around Paris
Kidding Around Philadelphia
Kidding Around San Diego
Kidding Around San Francisco
Kidding Around Santa Fe
Kidding Around Seattle
Kidding Around Spain
Kidding Around Washington, D.C., 2nd ed.

"Extremely Weird" Series for Young Readers. Written by Sarah Lovett, each is 48 pages and $9.95 paper.

Extremely Weird Bats
Extremely Weird Birds
Extremely Weird Endangered Species
Extremely Weird Fishes
Extremely Weird Frogs
Extremely Weird Insects
Extremely Weird Mammals (available 8/93)
Extremely Weird Micro Monsters (available 8/93)
Extremely Weird Primates
Extremely Weird Reptiles
Extremely Weird Sea Creatures
Extremely Weird Snakes (available 8/93)
Extremely Weird Spiders

"Masters of Motion" Series for Young Readers. Each title is 48 pages and $9.95 paper.

How to Drive an Indy Race Car
How to Fly a 747
How to Fly the Space Shuttle

"X-ray Vision" Series for Young Readers. Each title is 48 pages and $9.95 paper.

Looking Inside Cartoon Animation
Looking Inside Sports Aerodynamics

Looking Inside the Brain
Looking Inside Sunken Treasure
Looking Inside Telescopes and the Night Sky

Multicultural Titles for Young Readers
Native Artists of North America, 48 pp. $14.95 hardcover
The Indian Way: Learning to Communicate with Mother Earth, 114 pp. $9.95
The Kids' Environment Book: What's Awry and Why, 192 pp. $13.95
Kids Explore America's African-American Heritage, 112 pp. $8.95
Kids Explore America's Hispanic Heritage, 112 pp. $7.95

Environmental Titles for Young Readers
Rads, Ergs, and Cheeseburgers: The Kids' Guide to Energy and the Environment, 108 pp. $12.95
Habitats: Where the Wild Things Live, 48 pp. $9.95
The Kids' Environment Book: What's Awry and Why, 192 pp. $13.95

Ordering Information
Please check your local bookstore for our books, or call 1-800-888-7504 to order direct from us. All orders are shipped via UPS; see chart below to calculate your shipping charge to U.S. destinations. **No P.O. Boxes please; we must have a street address to ensure delivery.** If the book you request is not available, we will hold your check until we can ship it. Foreign orders will be shipped surface rate unless otherwise requested; please enclose $3.00 for the first item and $1.00 for each additional item.

For U.S. Orders Totaling	**Add**
Up to $15.00	$4.25
$15.01 to $45.00	$5.25
$45.01 to $75.00	$6.25
$75.01 or more	$7.25

Methods of Payment
Check, money order, American Express, MasterCard, or Visa. We cannot be responsible for cash sent through the mail. For credit card orders, include your card number, expiration date, and your signature, or call (800) 888-7504. American Express card orders can be shipped only to billing address of cardholder. Sorry, no C.O.D.'s. Residents of sunny New Mexico, add 6.125% tax to total.

Address all orders and inquiries to:
John Muir Publications
P.O. Box 613
Santa Fe, NM 87504
(505) 982-4078
(800) 888-7504